The Dance of Opposites

4ʳᵈ Edition

Dr. Rudy Scarfalloto

Other Books by Rudy Scarfalloto

Cultivating Inner Harmony
What Should I Eat? Book 1, Finding your Ideal Diet
What Should I Eat? Book 2, Food as Medicine
Nutrition for Massage Therapists
The Edge of Time

Acknowledgments

I would like to thank the following individuals whose teachings and insights helped me in writing this book:

- Dr. Camden Clay, for putting into application the idea, "The only way out is way in."
- Joseph Collins and Dr Jerry Epps, for those spontaneous and enlightening discussions.
- Lee and Suzanne Harris, for teaching me the key idea that opposites are two sides of the same coin.
- Robert Stephens, for his excellent work in Mastery of Words.
- Justin Sterling, for his insights into the interaction of men and women.
- Special thanks to my beloved former wife, Angelea Wicker, whose magical presence was instrumental in bringing this book to life.

Readers' Comments

"Dr. Scarfalloto's work breaks free from the restrictions and assumptions of other models. His work has exceeded my expectations."
— Joel Rachelson, Ph.D., Psychotherapist

"This book gives us profound insight into one of the most fundamental features of life — the interaction of opposites."
— William Richards, Author of *Pearls of Wisdom*

"In this book, the author tells a compelling story of how the world actually works. Dr. Scarfalloto combines mysticism and science in a way that transcends our mental pictures."
— Michael Craig, Author of *The Logical Soul™*

"When I'm stuck — in writing, in work, or in life — *The Dance of Opposites* helps me find my way forward. Dr. Scarfalloto offers clarity without oversimplifying, and depth without overwhelm. Each reflection is a gentle reminder that what feels like contradictions are often just two parts of the same whole, expressions of a deeper harmony. This book is a quiet, steady companion, one I return to again and again."
— Suneel Gupta, Author of *Backable* and *Everyday Dharma*

"*The Dance of Opposites* is amazing! It is an insightful read, blending practical guidance with a spiritual perspective. If you're looking for a book that supports personal growth and inner peace, this one's worth the time!"
— L. Sandler. National Sales Leader

"*The Dance Of Opposites*, 4th edition is food for the soul. It is one of those rare gems that will have a transformational impact on me. Rich with fun parables from the authors life, this book is a delightful adventure weaving through opposites in all facet of our lives, including politics and religion. It is a deeply insightful teaching book, changing how we think and live."
— Laura Starace, corporate sales.

5

"I found *The Dance of Opposites* to be both grounding and elevating. Dr Scarfalloto shares his understanding of health and inner peace, as he gently guides the reader in cultivating 'the capacity to appreciate everyday life.' This book transcends your typical personal transformation book. There are no 'shoulds' or 'musts', only practical insights into what is possible for any one of us. I learned a lot from this book and find myself going back to it for certain quotes, such as:

- 'Question your thoughts. Accept your emotions.'
- 'Pride is about flesh. Humility is about spirit.'
- 'Retreat to the purity and simplicity of the essential self.'

~Heidi E. Dickens, PhD. Retired Educator

Contents

Forward 9

Introduction 11

The Steps of the Dance

Not Just Apples and Oranges 19

Opposites and Energy.. 23

Duality & Singularity 27

The Inner Dance

The Brain.. 33

Pleasure & Pain 39

Fear & Desire 45

The Two Sides of Self-Worth 51

Pride & Humility... 57

Purity & Fullness... 61

Conscious & Unconscious 69

Will and Feeling 73

Thoughts & Emotions 85

Intellect & Intuition 93

Sanity.. 97

Austerity & Wild Abandonment 105

The Outer Dance

The Two Sides of Relationship 117

Holding On & Letting Go 125

Truth 129

Giving & Receiving 137

Love.. 141

Sexuality.. 149

Creativity... 159

Mother & Father 169

Child & Adult... 175

Responsibility & Freedom 179

Separateness & Unity 183

The Yin & Yang of Politics................................... 189

Equality 195
Rebellion & Conformity 199
Hero & Villain 201
The Martyr 205
Judgement 211
Forgiveness 219
War & Peace 225

Finding Your Way Home

Time 231
Birth & Death..235
Order & Chaos 239
Known & Unknown..241
Motion & Stillness 245
Darkness & Light...249
Choice & Destiny...255
Flesh & Spirit..265
God..281
Religion...289
Remembering Who I Am..299

Forward

By Robert Anton Wilson

Every month I receive a pile of books the publishers want me to read and to comment upon. Very, very rarely do I receive one that arouses my enthusiasm as much as the present work, which manages to bring some of the most advanced concepts of Oriental and Occidental mysticism into a framework so down-to-earth that even the allegedly esoteric "unity underlying all opposites", seems so obvious that you wonder how anyone could ever have overlooked it.

Indeed, the singular achievement of this book consists in making you understand why the human mind must overlook unity once we begin thinking at all, and why we must rediscover it if we continue thinking clearly enough and long enough. Only one other book explains so clearly why we always begin by positing polar opposites and why we must end by reconciling the opposites: G. Spencer Brown's Laws of Form does this, but alas, you need some background in mathematical logic and cybernetics to understand Spencer Brown. You just need common sense and an open mind to understand Dr. Scarfalloto.

Dr. Scarfalloto begins with an enlarged Y to illustrate the bifurcation of the nervous system when the brain stem splits into the right and left-brain hemispheres. This hauntingly resembles Dr. Wilhelm Reich's famous diagram for the bioenergetic unity under-lying biology and psychology. And that, in turn, suggests the bottom, or root, of the well-known emblem of medicine, the staff with two intertwined serpents (which appeared in the dream that inspired this book), as Dr. Scarfalloto explains.

In China, the same symbolism appears in the philosophy of the *Tao,* the cosmic energy that always manifests as the opposing forces of *yin* and *yang.*

A symbolism that appears in so many places and times does not belong in the category of "beliefs" or "concepts." It pre-exists such front-brain abstractions. It comes, rather, from that timeless abyss which Carl Jung called the "collective unconscious," or from Sheldrake's "morphic field," or the "akashic records" of Theosophy—*i.e.,* from a level so deep that we cannot profitably consider its symbols as ideas but only as the preconditioning forms (or archetypes) out of which all of our fewer primitive images, and eventually abstract ideas, can grow.

Dr. Scarfalloto's method of reducing all opposites to their underlying unities uses only everyday examples from ordinary human life so that anybody can understand this book. (Few can understand Jung, Sheldrake, Leary, etc.) Consider by contrast the shock tactics of Aleister Crowley: "Nothing is. Nothing becomes. Nothing is not."

The mind whirls. If one has the taste for this kind of meta-logic, one struggles with Crowley for a long time before understanding what these Strange Loops communicate. Most people lack that taste and give up quickly. Nobody will give up on *The Dance of Opposites,* I suspect. It deals immediately and urgently with our most intimate and painful conflicts and shows us with great clarity how we got into them and how we can work our way out of them again.

A last word: this book seems too good for simple "reading." Rather, you should keep it handy and re-read a chapter a day for a few years, until you begin to feel deeply the simple path that Dr. Scarfalloto presents.

Introduction

This book was born early one morning when I awoke from a startling dream. The main feature of the dream was a snake. Snakes in dreams are not that unusual. However, this creature was thousands of feet long and proportionately wide. And, it had *two* extremely ferocious looking heads.

In the dream, I was flying close to the snake's heads, high in the air among the clouds. The beast undulated in a most menacing manner. Its tail was far below on the ground. The two heads had intense, ravenous eyes. Each mouth was wide open, revealing dagger-like teeth and a sharply forked tongue.

In the dream, I also knew that the serpent was extremely venomous. It was obviously capable of annihilating me with no effort at all. In addition, I saw that its power was so great that it could easily swoop down and destroy all of humanity.

Even though I was afraid, I prepared myself to fight. I did so by climbing into a two-headed snake costume, which was going to act as my "battleship." And so, we squared off, ready to do battle, high in the air among the clouds. At that point, I awoke.

For a while, I remained motionless in bed with my eyes closed. Behind my closed eyelids, I still saw the gigantic snake, and I continued sensing its horrific power. Even after I opened my eyes, I continued feeling its deadly presence. I stared at the sky through the open window, watching the clouds drift by.

For me, the dream was, to say the least, unprecedented. Still seeing the snake clearly in my mind, I said to myself, "This probably means something."

As the emotional impact of the dream gradually wore off, I took note of my initial impressions as to the meaning of the dream. Later that day, I consulted books and experts to get additional information as to the possible meaning of the symbols of my dream. However, I found no reference to extremely ferocious two-headed snakes of monstrous proportions. So, I went back to my strong initial impressions, which were as follows:

- The two-headed snake symbolized duality - the dance of opposites. This idea was reinforced by the appearance of the second snake (me in the costume).
- The humongous size of the snake suggested that the duality in question was not merely one particular pair of opposites. It was the granddaddy of dualities, containing within it all other pairs of opposites.
- The foreboding feeling that the snake was extremely powerful and dangerous suggested that I would either master it or be devoured by it – devoured by the conflicting opposing forces within me.
- The dreaded fear that the snake could destroy me and all people on Earth suggested that the snake not only symbolized duality within me personally, but also touched into the collective consciousness of humanity. This impression was reinforced by the snake's tremendous size and extremely high altitude above the earth - its two heads ready to swoop down on the population below.
- The final impression was that if I tried to overpower and destroy the snake, I would surely lose. The message was, *do not kill it, just understand it.* If this had been an actual snake in the outer world, I would have laughed at such an idea. However, since the snake seemed to symbolize the opposing forces within my own mind, the idea that I could master it through understanding was reasonable.

Duality is Fun, Except When It Isn't

In the days that followed the dream, my mind was flooded with a variety of opposites. I had the notion that duality is beautiful and that it does not have to be synonymous with conflict. I saw a man and woman dancing, rejoicing in their differences; the strength of him delighting in the grace of her, and the grace of her embracing the strength of him. I then had the frightening and exciting notion that *all opposites* can be experienced in this manner.

When inner duality is *not* fun, it shows up as neurosis, which I perceived as the result of opposites at war within the mind. We set them at war with each other by judging one as good and the other as bad. We then identify ourselves with the one that is judged as good and pretend the other does not exist – except maybe in someone else.

The Big Joke

With regard to dancing opposites, the big joke is this: *With any pair of opposites, the side we have judged as inferior is the one that rules us.* This is a commonly known principle, even for individuals who are not familiar with how opposites dance. It is the basis for the cliché, "What you resist persists."

Likewise, when we recognize both sides of any duality as partners in the dance of Creation, the inner conflict ends. However, it does not die as a soldier on a battlefield. It dies as a seed dies when it breaks its shell and germinates. The sprout is the vision of life wherein opposites make love instead of war. Such a vision leads us naturally to the primordial unity beyond opposites.

Introduction to Forth Edition

As a way of introducing the current edition to *The Dance of Opposites*, I wish to point out that the first edition was called *The Alchemy of Opposites.* I initially wrote the book in response to the dream described above. The dream turned out to be a life changer. After publication of the original book, the torrent of information continued. Furthermore, some of my original ideas would not hold still. They insisted on evolving.

One facet of the evolution was the realization that my work was closely related to the Taoist concepts of Yin and Yang. That relationship should have been obvious to me from the start, but it was not. In fact, during the months that I was furiously writing down all the cool ideas that came to me after my dream, I never once considered the relation of my work to Yin and Yang. Even after Robert Anton Wilson briefly commented on this in his Forward to my book, it went right over my head.

Yes, I was peripherally aware of Taoism and Yin and Yang. However, I never once focused on their connection to my work. I never said, "Hummm, opposites, Yin and Yang, Taoism, that's what I'm writing about."

Finally, after the original book was in print, during a conversation with one of my readers, he casually commented that my ideas were very much akin to Taoism. For a moment, I just stood there, sort of stunned and embarrassed, as if he had just informed me that my fly was open.

"Uh…yeah," I nodded stupidly.

In retrospect, my oversight is understandable because the ideas I was exploring during the writing of my original book were based, not so much on my academic study of other works, but rather upon personal experience. When the realization finally sank in, I started an intense and prolonged study of Taoism, Traditional Chinese Medicine, Acupuncture, and the Martial Arts. I was astounded. "Those crooks," I said, "They stole my stuff – four thousand years ago!"

My initial blindness to the Tao connection turned out to be a blessing. It was a blessing because I was able to contemplate the ideas emerging from my mind, from a perspective that was free of the language and mental constructs of Taoism. I was able to freely explore the dance of opposites outside the box of traditional Taoist thinking.

None-the less, when I finally took the time to study Taoism and its practical applications, it was like coming home. Consequently, I absolutely had to update my book. I also felt compelled to change the title from *The Alchemy of Opposites* to *The Dance of Opposites.* This reflects the understanding that we do not *make* the opposing qualities within us and around us interact harmoniously through an act of will, no more than we can order two individuals to love one another. We simply cultivate the ability to recognize how they naturally dance harmoniously. When we do so, we tend to cooperate with that dance — which invites health and happiness, as the ancient Taoists well understood.

So, what is this current edition all about? As with the previous editions, it incorporates the fruits of my deepening understanding of the subject, while retaining the core principles and flavor of the original book. For example, in the years since the publication of the original book, political discourse has become increasingly polarized and divisive. Therefore, for the first time in my life, I started paying attention to it. However, rather than getting emotionally pulled into partisan politics, I found myself looking at current events through the lens of dancing opposites. The result was chapter 29 of the current edition, which is called, *The Yin & Yang of Politics.* In addition, I have rearranged, reworked, condensed , and updated the existing material, with the intent of promoting clarity and readability, and to facilitate practical application.

Practical Application

Essentially, there are two ways that you may benefit from this book. One is immediate, and the other is long-term.

Immediate Benefit: Since Creation is a dance of opposites, any aspect of your inner or outer world can be understood more deeply when seen as part of the dance. In that sense, this book is essentially a handbook for understanding various common issues that impact our health and happiness.

Long-Term Benefit: The more deeply we understand the dance of opposites within us, the more we tend to spontaneously cooperate with it. Therefore, the long-term benefit of applying the information in this book is that the reader gradually becomes free from the habit of consciously or unconsciously placing opposites at war with one another. By thus setting the mind free of inner conflict, we deepen our potential for healing and renewal of body and mind. We also tend to be more at peace with the world around us.

Stated differently, the short-term benefit has to do with the way you think, while the long-term benefit has to do with the way you feel. For example, one specific short-term benefit is that you might see the usually hidden contradictions and inconsistencies in the behavior of people around you. A specific long-term benefit is the awareness that any such contradictions that you perceive (and emotionally react to) in the outer world are probably reflections of your own inner contradictions. That awareness is usually experienced as a feeling. That feeling is commonly called "compassion."

In other words, you can simply use this book as a handbook for getting perspective on specific subjects or issues that are of interest to you in the moment. In addition, if you make it a habit of looking at life in this manner, your efforts will, more than likely, compel a gradual evolution or transformation in the feeling areas of your mind. The more deeply we see and appreciate the dance of opposites within us and around us, the more we invite the vision of Unity beyond opposites. That vision isn't necessarily overwhelming or other-worldly. It usually shows up quietly as gentleness and grace.

We will begin our journey by asking a question: What is it about the dance of opposites that makes it so fundamentally important to life? This question is answered in Chapter One.

Part I
The Steps of the Dance

"The keystone to the entire structure of the spiritual and physical universe is the Rhythmic Balanced Interchange between all opposites."
– Walter Russell

Chapter 1
Not Just Apples and Oranges

"What about apples and oranges" asked a young lady sitting in the first row. I was teaching my anatomy and physiology class to a lively group of budding massage therapists. When the student asked her question, I stopped in my tracks, at first, not knowing what to say. You see, up to that moment, the class was not actually focused on anatomy and physiology. We had gone off on a tangent and somehow found ourselves talking about the interaction of opposites and its relevance to just about everything.

"When the dance is harmonious," I declared, "life renews itself."

The class had been happily rambling on about the dance of opposites when the student asked about apples and oranges. In her mind, apples and oranges were opposites. They are not, but she didn't know that because I had not defined the word, "opposites."

So, the class went off on another tangent as we endeavored to give a clear definition of opposites. We were neglecting our regular class work; but that was okay because they were a bright group and we were ahead of schedule anyway.

If Two Things Are Opposites...

If two things are opposites, they define each other. Each side has meaning only in the presence of the other. If we eliminate one, the other loses its identity. For example, night defines day, up defines down, hot defines cold, young defines old. On the other hand, apple and orange do not define each other. We can certainly recognize an apple without comparing it to an orange.

In other words, opposites are relative terms. Life is about relationship, and the dance of opposites is the most fundamental way of relating things. When we take the time to understand the simple dance of opposites in the created universe, the complex relationships that follow make more sense. For example, once we understand that opposites are simply two things that define each other, we would not say that two people are opposites.

The term opposite specifically refers to a pair of qualities, ideas, or choices that define each other. You cannot completely know yourself by just comparing yourself to others. The wholeness of being is ultimately beyond comparison, therefore, you can't be someone's "opposite."

Granted, you can understand some things about yourself by comparing some of your qualities with the opposing qualities exhibited by others. For example, one person defines himself as a male by comparing himself to a female. There is nothing wrong with this, provided we recognize that such knowledge is limited; each individual has qualities that go beyond gender and beyond duality, qualities that cannot be completely understood or appreciated through comparison.

True Opposites define each other. Neither side can exist without the other.

Each Carries the Seed of the Other

We can easily understand that opposites are two things that define each other. Opposites, however, have another calling card: *If two things are opposites, each side bears the seed of the other*. When each side expresses itself in fullness, it brings forth the seed or essence of the other. In one sense, each side *becomes* the other. And so, the dance of opposites is, among other things, a dance of transformation. This is the dance of transformation that makes life possible.

In other words, true polar opposites are not static. They may be likened to the roots and the fruit of a single plant. The root gives rise to the fruit whose seed brings forth new roots. Simplicity swells into complexity which then returns to simplicity. All motion comes from stillness, and then returns to stillness. Spirit condenses into flesh, and then returns to spirit. The child becomes an adult, and the adult must once again become a child.

When this dance of transformation is allowed to unfold naturally, life goes on with ease and grace. To the extent that we resist or disrupt the flow of this dance, we suffer.

20

The life within the body may be seen as consisting of many pairs of opposing functions and qualities interacting harmoniously in a dance of transformation: hot and cold, rigidity and flexibility, contraction and expansion, acid and alkaline, positive and negative ions, emptiness and fullness, motion and stability, building up and tearing down, breathing in and breathing out, etc.

The mind also consists of many opposites in a dance of transformation. The dance occurs whether we are aware of it or not. However, as conscious beings, we have the choice of cooperating or not cooperating with it.

Cooperation does not mean that we have to identify the many pairs of opposites in the body and mind so we can figure out how to make them fit together. They tend to integrate automatically. The more deeply we understand this dance, the more we tend to flow with it. The more we flow with it, the more we invite vibrant health, mental clarity, and emotional serenity. Likewise, as we cultivate inner harmony, we tend to create outer harmony.

In summary, if two things are opposites, they define one another. In addition, if we examine any pair of opposites closely enough, we see that each side bears the seed of the other; this is the dance of transformation which makes life possible. The next chapter describes more specifically how opposites dance with each other to create life.

When we become aware that life is a dance of opposites, we
tend to cooperate with it.

Chapter 2
Opposites and Energy

What makes something alive? What makes a puppy different from a rock? The answer is energy. In the none-living world, energy dissipates, while living organisms have the miraculous ability to gather energy and then use in a purposeful manner. This is why a rock can only role down the hill, while a puppy can run up the hill.

What is happening within the puppy's body which causes energy to gather and then flow in a purposeful manner? If we try to answer this question in the language of Western physiology, we would fill a thick book and still not have an answer. We just throw our hands in the air and call it a miracle. It *is* a miracle. However, in the language of the ancient Taoists, we can describe this miracle in a way that is both simple and practical. Life gathers energy and then causes it to flow purposefully through the harmonious dance of opposites.

Understanding the Dance

Gathering of energy translates into the separation of polar opposites. Flowing of energy translates into the rejoining of opposites. An obvious example of this is a battery. A battery is charged by separating positive ions from negative ions. The flowing of electrical energy from the battery translates into positive and negative ions rejoining.

Each of the cells in the puppy's body functions as a battery. It is a battery with the capacity to recharge itself! And that is the miraculous part.

In order for the separation and rejoining of opposites to create life, it must proceed in a harmonious manner. Another miracle! However, such harmony may be simplistically described as a balance of *competing* and *complementing*.

In other words, through the harmonious blend of competition and complementing among polar opposites, livings system can gather energy and then allow it flow in purposeful ways.

Competing Opposites

When the many opposing qualities and functions of the body "compete," each side restrains or subdues the other, so as to avoid harmful excess. This why the body does not get too hot or too cold, too wet or too dry, too acidic or too alkaline, too relaxed or too tense, etc.

An example of the competing elements of the dance of opposites may be seen in the relationship of the sympathetic and parasympathetic nervous systems. The sympathetic system makes us alert, brings us to attention, and causes the body to expend energy. The parasympathetic system allows us to relax and gather energy. The natural harmony between the two includes each side subduing the other so the body doesn't get to agitated or too relaxed.

Without the restraining presence of the parasympathetic system, the sympathetic system would be overactive; we would not be able to relax, recharge, and regenerate. Likewise, without the retraining presence of the sympathetic system, the parasympathetic system would be over active, and we would not be able to wake up. Either way, the body would degenerate and die.

The same holds true for the workings of the mind. Sanity may be viewed as a product of harmony among the many polar opposites in the mind. Mental clarity and emotional serenity are made possible by the many opposing thoughts, beliefs, choices, emotions, fears, and desires that push against each other. They test and temper each other, as described in later chapters.

In everyday language, when we refer to two things as "opposites", we typically use the term in a loose sort of way which alludes to the competing qualities of the pair of opposites, but not their complementing qualities. We assume that opposites are contradictory, antagonistic, or mutually destructive. However, if we wish to understand how the dance of opposites creates life and maintains optimum health, we must also consider their complementing qualities. If we wish to promote health, happiness, and prosperity, we must consider both the competing and complementing aspects of the dance of opposites.

24

Complementing Opposites

When opposites complement one another, they enhance and exalt each other. One side "fits" into the other. Each derives its identity from the other. Each side supports the other and ultimately gives birth to the other. Each reaches the fullness of its expression in the presence of the other, thus creating a wholeness that otherwise would not be possible.

For example, the normal posture and alignment of the body is the result of *rigid* bones connected to *flexible* muscles, tendons, and ligaments. We can move because of *active* muscles pulling on *passive* bones. We would not say the rigidness of bones is more important than the flexibility of muscles. Neither would we consider the active nature of muscles as greater than the passive nature of bones.

With regard to the workings of the mind, *mental* clarity is supported by *emotional* serenity, and vice versa. *Intellect* and *intuition* reach the fullness of their potential when they are allowed to complement one another. Our capacity to *give* is enhanced by our capacity to *receive*, and vice versa. *Work* supports *play*, and play supports work. *Freedom* is made possible by personal *responsibility*, and vice versa. The willingness to *change* and our capacity to *let it be*, are mutually supportive. All these will be described in later chapters.

In summary, we are alive and healthy because of the many opposing functions and qualities interacting harmoniously within the body and mind. Harmony specifically means that they compete and complement in ways that allows energy to gather and then flow in ways that translates into vibrant health of the body and mind.

The Foundation of Health

In Traditional Asian Medicine, the harmony of opposites (called Yin and Yang) is central to the diagnosis and treatment of diseases and the realization of optimum health. Yin qualities include cool, contractive, soft, rounded, and dark. Yang qualities include hot, expansive, hard, angular, linear, and bright.

When Yin and Yang interact harmoniously, they simultaneously challenge and support one another. In a healthy living system, when the various Yin and Yang functions "complement" one another, they enhance and exalt each other. When they "compete" in a healthy living system, each side restrains and subdues the other, so as to avoid harmful excess.

The ecological harmony of the natural world includes a balance of competition and complementing among plants and animals. The competitive part shows up as survival of the fittest which drives living organisms to evolve and improve themselves. However, living organisms also cooperate and support each other in countless ways which are also important to the advancement and evolution of life.

Understanding Disease

In Traditional Asian Medicine, disease is understood as the result of opposing functions in a state of disharmony. "Diagnosis" of any disease translates into identifying the pattern of disharmony, and treating it accordingly.

The doctor of Traditional Asian Medicine might speak of conditions of *deficiency* and conditions of *excess.* If there is too much competition and not enough complementing among opposing functions, the body can become depleted; too much competition translates into conflict, which results in a depletion of energy. Likewise, if there is not enough competition and too much complementing, the body and mind might gather too much energy too fast. There might be an accumulation of so-called "stagnant" energy which can cause the mind to become unstable and the body to become congested, feverish, inflamed, or "burned out."

Opposites and Beyond

One of the natural consequences of viewing life through the lens of dancing opposites is that we are eventually compelled to contemplate (or even experience) the hypothetical unity beyond opposites. Likewise, contemplation of the primordial unity beyond opposites has the effect of bringing our inner opposites into harmony, as described in the chapter that follows.

Chapter 3
Duality & Singularity

To be in duality consciousness is to perceive opposites. To be in singularity[1] consciousness is to experience unity. The perception of duality occurs through thinking. The experience of singularity or unity is more of a feeling.

Duality: It is a Thought

Whether we are aware of it or not, we mentally understand something by comparing it to its opposite. The perception of duality allows us to think, speak, compete, cooperate, analyze, and set goals. Singularity consciousness cannot do any of these, because it does not recognize anything outside of self. There is nowhere to go because all is here. There is nothing to do because everything simply is. Singularity does not say, "There is duality and here am I, singularity." It does not say, "I am in a sublime state of unity, and that poor slob out there is stuck in duality." One must be in a state of duality to reject duality. One must be in duality to even speak of it.

Singularity: It is a Feeling

The awareness of unity does not have be a non-ordinary transcendental experience. In everyday life, the awareness of unity flavors our perception of duality. We feel warmly connected to the life around us. Singularity consciousness gives us a feeling of kinship with those around us. Awareness of unity may show up as conscience, motivating us to treat others as we would want to be treated.

These echoes of unity reverberate through the mind, allowing us to relate to our fellow humans with a sense of the sacred. Such awareness of unity is silent, but if it could speak, it might say something like, "I love being alive, and I love experiencing life in its diversity!"

(1) The term *singularity* is borrowed from astronomy. It is the mathematical expression for a point in space where there is no space in the usual sense. A singularity is not here or there, now or then. It is a point where time and space have merged into something beyond time and space, as we know them.

From Duality to Singularity

The notion that we are moving along a continuum from duality into singularity has meaning only for the mind operating in duality. However, once we "shift" into the full-blown awareness of singularity, we perceive that we really have not gone anywhere. There was no race, and no one came in first.

In other words, when our experience of unity is strong enough, the numbered scale used to measure our progress no longer has meaning. Neither would we entertain the idea that one person is farther along than another.

Nonetheless, as long as duality is real to us, the notion of progress is a useful one. The mind in duality wants to know, "How do I increase my awareness of primordial unity?"

As suggested on the previous page, the awareness unity can show up as appreciation for life in its diversity. Therefore, we can invite a deeper awareness of unity by just cultivating the capacity to appreciate everyday life. When singularity is experienced in the world of duality, the bus driver has as much intrinsic value as the king; the prostitute is as holy as the priest. The sinner is as sacred as the saint. If the silent awareness of singularity could speak it would look upon the wholeness of Creation and declare, "Behold, it is all very good."

One reason most of us cannot sustain the timeless bliss of "the unity Beyond Opposites" is the lingering perception that it is better or more important than doing laundry, driving to work, or telling your friend that you feel sad. In other words, one of the ways that we are pulled into the mundane drama of duality is through our tendency to reject or otherwise devalue it. On the other hand, when our perception of duality and experience of unity are balanced, they support each other and work together to promote clear thinking, emotional serenity, and the joy of living.

There are many reports of near-death experiences in which the almost-departed soul feels the overwhelming presence of cosmic love and peace beyond duality. When they were compelled to go back to Earth, they became disappointed or even angry. Why did they have to return? They were told they have work to do. The nature of the work, stripped down to its essence, is to move beyond the judgment that the grandness of there is better than the smallness of here. Stated differently, the nature of our work is to allow the formless awareness of unity to take form as appreciation of our physical experience.

Neutrality

Experiencing unity does not mean we become neutral. Neutrality is just another way of being in duality. Neutrality is literally in the middle of opposing forces, with no preference for either side.

Neutrality is zero; singularity is infinity. Neutrality is neither; singularity is both and beyond both. Neutrality sees two opposing forces as mutually exclusive; singularity sees them as inseparable. Neutrality sees incompatibility; singularity sees that the two side fit together very nicely. Neutrality perceives that one side can defeat the other; singularity recognizes that whatever is done to one is done to both. Neutrality is the impartial and judge; singularity does not judge, for it sees no separation. Neutrality says, "I don't care who wins," Singularity says, "I care about both, for I am both." Neutrality might show up as the earnest attempt to forgive sins; singularity is the awareness that there is no sin. Neutrality can show up as indecision; singularity is a quiet certainty that needs no validation. Neutrality is emotionless; singularity is the deep and silent tranquility which embraces all emotions.

In everyday life, neutrality is reached by being disengaged, propped squarely between two polarities. Singularity is experienced by being fully engaged, going all the way to one side with deep sincerity, which allows us to spontaneously and organically bring forth the seed of the other. In fact, the inner call to go beyond duality might compel us to move beyond neutrality. As long as we remain detached and neutral on any two opposing views, we cannot discover that one is contained within the other; we do not experience the birth of one within the other. Perhaps this explains the wisdom of the biblical passage which advises us to be hot or cold, but not lukewarm.

The Value of Neutrality

At the risk of being at odds with the Bible, there is value in neutrality. In fact, if we wish to move beyond neutrality, we must first appreciate its value.

As long as we honestly perceive duality, neutrality is a useful discipline. It is an exercise in objectivity. If we sincerely do not know the solution to a given issue, the honest thing to do is to gather data so we can be fair to both sides, as any honest judge or true scientist would do. This is the act of being *consciously* neutral

To be consciously neutral is different from being unconsciously neutral. To be unconsciously neutral is to be stuck in neutral. We do it, not by choice, but by fear and self-doubt. We do it because we are internally conflicted. This condition of immobility is a far cry from the deep stillness that occurs when we feel internally unified. Such deep stillness is energizing because it is associated with the harmony of inner opposites. In contrast, the immobility of being stuck in neutral is debilitating because, like any conflict, it depletes energy.

On the other hand, conscious neutrality is a skill that requires self-awareness, intellectual honesty, and sometimes humility. For example, while I was in my office, I happened to overhear a phone conversation in the adjacent room. My friend and colleague was acting as the mediator in a fight between a husband and wife. Let us call them "Jane" and "Bob." My friend was speaking to one of the warring parties and declared that he was perfectly neutral and was not interested in taking sides. He spoke for quite a while on this, making a strong point of his neutral stance. Later that day he spoke with another friend to whom he passingly said, "Bob is having a problem with Jane."

Interesting choice of words: "Bob is having a problem with Jane," instead of, "Bob and Jane are having a problem." I brought this to my friend's attention. He looked inside and discovered that he did indeed have an emotional leaning toward Bob. After a moment of self-reflection, he laughed about it.

Part II
The Inner Dance

"God turns you from one feeling to another and teaches by means
of opposites so that you will have two wings to fly, not one."
-Rumi

Chapter 4
The Brain

As described in the previous chapter, we perceive duality by thinking, and we experience unity by feeling. Thinking allows us to separate things. Feeling allows us to bring things together. Our normal waking consciousness is a blend of thinking and feeling.

The correlation of duality with thinking and of unity with feeling is crudely reflected in the anatomy and physiology of the brain. The cerebrum, or new-brain, houses the capacity to think, discern, dissect, analyze, and compare. The brainstem, or old-brain, contains centers for our animal desires and instincts.

The cerebrum consists of two well-defined hemispheres that seem to grow out of the brainstem. The two-pronged cerebrum and the singular brainstem may be visualized as the letter Y.

The "Y" Model of the Brain

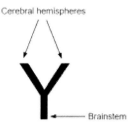

The cerebral hemispheres are like the upper branches of the letter Y, and the brainstem is like the base. The lower end of the brainstem, called the old reptilian brain, integrates and unifies our vital body functions. The upper end of the brainstem, also called the diencephalon, interfaces with the cerebrum to generate the full spectrum of our everyday human emotions.

By virtue of the intimate connection between the cerebrum and brain stem, the two are functionally united. Our logical thoughts are influenced by the primal impulses emerging from the brainstem. Likewise, our animal urges are influenced by the thoughts emerging from the cerebrum.

The smooth operation of the cerebrum depends on the smooth operation of the brainstem, and vice versa. The two interact in a seemingly infinite variety of ways to create the unique tapestry of physical and psychological qualities of the individual.

Cut Off

As with other dualities, if we value the thinking of the new brain over the feelings and instincts of the old brain, or vice versa, the one that is regarded as inferior becomes the secret ruler. In this case, the separation my be described as a "cutting off" of our rational thinking from our feelings. In reality, this is impossible without seriously endangering physical survival. However, the two can become somewhat dissociated and conflicted. This can happen when the thinking of the new brain represses or censors the instincts and urges of the old brain. As a result, the discerning power of the cerebrum becomes cold, calculating, intellectual tyranny and harsh judgment, while the instincts and urges of the brain stem translate into hysteria and chaos. These two "opposing" states can exist only in the presence of each other. Each is the result of lack of harmony between the animal (feeling) consciousness of the brainstem and the human (thinking) consciousness of the cerebrum.

In Western cultural and religious traditions, this inner split is personified as Satan, often shown as a two-horned beast. The two horns represent conflicted duality. The ferocious animal/human face represents the primordial impulses that have become monstrous because they were rejected, subjugated and exploited by the human intellect.

Reunited

The two parts of the brain are reintegrated when the cerebrum recognizes the feelings rising out of the brainstem. The cerebrum uses its power of discernment to simply report the truth of those feelings, as well as providing respectful boundaries for those feelings to flow and find their rightful place in the individuals life.

The harmonious blending of human discernment of the new brain with the primordial impulses of the old brain, results in the everyday experiences of kindness and respect. The integration deepens as the new brain cultivates the ability to be still, so that it can listen more deeply to the echoes of singularity rising up as feelings from the old brain. Such deeper integration of the new and old brain may translate into religious ecstasy, transpersonal bliss, timeless peace, More commonly, it shows up as a sense of warm connection with the life around us.

The Three Healers

In everyday life, there are three ways of promoting inner integration: *truthfulness, stillness, and loving touch*. These three activities support the brain in integrating itself. This is how we create wholeness of the body and mind. Wholeness shows up tangibly as vibrant health, mental clarity, and emotional serenity.

In other words, the inner integration of opposites in the mind, and the eventual transcending of opposites, do not require mystical knowledge. We quietly promote inner integration through the daily practice of truthfulness, stillness, and loving touch. These three activities are instinctual. We are drawn to them whenever we feel a need for healing of the body or mind.

Staying in Touch

Most of us can recognize the importance of truthfulness and stillness for health and well-being. However, loving touch is often neglected. The importance of loving touch reflects the fact that we are mammals, like dogs, cats, and horses. The mammalian brain needs sensory input in the form of frequent touch. Without such sensory input, the brain's integrative ability declines.

For infants, touching is critically important. Inner integration, especially integration of the new and old brain activities, depends on physical touch. This is especially true in the first precious hours following birth. The quality of those first stimuli to the uninitiated nervous system of the infant is of prime importance.

Animal studies have shown that, with many mammals, if the mother does not lick the infant, it dies. Likewise, if human babies are not touched sufficiently, they experience physical and psychological disturbance.

Loving touch remains important throughout life, not only in interpersonal relationships but also in the relationship of the thinking self to the feeling self. Depression, sexual abuse, self-destructive behavior, addiction, and brutality can be linked to touch deprivation.

The Oral Instinct

Though the human mamma relies on her hands to touch the baby, the older instinct to use her mouth is apparently still intact. This was dramatically illustrated by a woman who gave birth while she did not have full use of her arms and hands. The attendant in the delivery room was going to take the baby away, since the mother obviously could not hold it. However, the mother still wanted her baby, and she screamed bloody murder until the attendant complied.

As per the mother's demand, the attendant placed the baby — still covered with birth slime — upon the mother's chest. The woman then proceeded to lick the infant all over.

With our civilized sensibilities, we might conclude that the woman was being abhorrent. However, my own conversations with women patients over the years suggest that if the new mom is being spontaneous, she is likely to taste, lick and bite her baby. She is likely to place her mouth on the baby's bare tummy and play motorboat. She might even stick the baby's entire hand or foot in her mouth and give it a thorough massage with her teeth and tongue. And, the baby loves it. I suspect that for every mother who yields to this old oral instinct, there are many others who have a notion to do so but suppress it, perhaps feeling quietly embarrassed for having such animal impulses.

The Changing Face of Health Care

Since civilized society emphasizes rational thinking over feeling, our health care and education have conspicuously given little attention to the value of touching. Traditionally, hospital births tend to separate mother and child almost immediately following birth. Pediatricians had, at one time, instructed parents to avoid picking up the baby when it cries. Some pediatricians even instructed parents to tie the baby's hands to the crib to prevent it from sucking its fingers. Years ago, kindergarten and first grade teachers were encouraged to "hug every child, every day". As of this writing, one of my patients, a public-school teacher, informed me that she and her colleagues are advised against touching the children.

With increased awareness of the importance of touch, we find that health care practices are changing. Many hospitals are becoming more respectful of mother/child bonding during birth. Some pediatricians have broken with tradition by advocating home births and telling parents to touch the child as much as possible. Some even advocate allowing the little one to sleep with parents — a practice which had been considered perverse by other medical authorities. Likewise, in recent years, we have seen a dramatic increase in the demand for health care practitioners that emphasize hands-on body procedures.

Touching and Emotions

Physical touch is one way of making emotional contact. To maintain inner health and outer harmony, we must touch one another, emotionally as well as physically. Lack of physical and emotional contact contributes to a split in the personality; thoughts are at odds with emotions; logic is at odds with instinct. This split gets projected into many areas of our lives and typically shows up as interpersonal conflict.

The dissociation of the old brain from the new brain may also be looked upon as a defense mechanism of sorts. When feelings are too painful to bear, the cerebrum simply unplugs itself from the source of those feelings. Touching the body is a way of reconnecting the two. When this happens, the traumatic memories and feelings that compelled the

37

separation to occur in the first place may be re-experienced or remembered. This is why deep massage, even if it is not painfully deep, may trigger the spontaneous release of emotions and the remembrance of long forgotten events.

Truthfulness and Stillness

Physical touch is intimately connected to the ability to tell the truth and to be still and quiet. In order for the whole brain to stay in touch with itself, the body must be touched, lovingly and frequently. This establishes inner harmony, allowing the hard-driving cerebrum to be still so that it can listen respectfully and express truthfully the deep feelings rising up from the brainstem.

Truthfulness and stillness go hand in hand. Telling the truth helps us to quiet the mind. Likewise, stillness helps us to get more deeply in touch with our truth and to express it honestly. Sometimes, however, inner turmoil remains no matter how earnestly we try to practice truthfulness and stillness. Quite possibly, what is missing is an adequate amount of loving touch and the emotional connection it brings.

The synergistic blend of touching, stillness, and speaking the truth allows the many warring or neglected parts of the individual to come together into wholeness. Truthfulness, stillness, and loving touch allow the new brain and old brain to function as one brain.

Chapter 5
Pleasure & Pain

Deep inside the brain, at the interphase of the cerebrum and brainstem, is a tiny gray lump of tissue called the *pleasure center*. Though other regions of the brain are also involved in pleasure and motivation, the so-called pleasure center seems to serve as the "Grand Central Station" for all manner pleasantness.

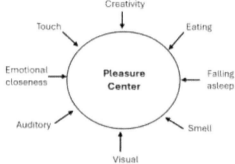

Mother Nature wires the brain so that whatever feels good is also good for us. We are motivated to carry out life-sustaining functions because these same activities stimulate the pleasure center. Therefore, even if we had no education, we would still instinctively do things that keep us alive and healthy. We eat just enough, drink just enough, get just enough sleep, exercise, etc., to adequately stimulate the pleasure center. When these activities no longer stimulate the pleasure center, we stop doing them. The saturation point wherein a given activity no longer stimulates the pleasure center coincides with the point where the same activity is no longer beneficial to the individual.

In one animal study, an electrode was implanted into the pleasure center of a male rat. The electrode was also connected to a lever in the cage so that the rat could stimulate its own pleasure center at will. The result: The rat stopped eating, drinking, and sleeping and refused the company of receptive female rats. It just pressed the lever — as much as 2000 times per day. The animal died. We might argue that the rat died happy, but the point is that it died because its pleasure center was not allowed to fulfill its natural function.

Humans seem to respond in a similar manner. Individuals addicted to drugs often stop taking care of their basic needs, as if the pathways to the pleasure center have been altered.

You Can't Fool Mother Nature

In the years following the rat experiment, some researches tried to apply the same strategy to create a magic button or pill that would bring instinct bliss. Others tried to use it to cure addictions and various psychological issues. Not surprisingly, they did not work. Like the rats in the experiment, these researchers were fooled into taking a short-cut to health happiness.

Apparently, the pleasure center is not merely stimulated by routine life-sustaining functions, but also by other activities, such as smelling a flower or reading a poem. In addition, the emotional areas of the brain (the limbic system) are intimately connected with the pleasure center. This might be why telling the truth and "getting it all out" feels good. Furthermore, the expression of truth opens the door to intimacy with others, which also stimulates the pleasure center.

If we close the door to some of the natural avenues of pleasure, we automatically try to compensate by overusing the remaining pathways. We might do this to the point that the activity in question is no longer a source of health for the body and mind. For example, if we deprive ourselves of the pleasure of emotional connection and emotional expression, we might try to compensate by having sex more often or overeating. If the existing avenues of pleasure are insufficient, we might come up with artificial methods such as smoking, drinking alcohol, and taking drugs. On the other hand, when all naturally occurring avenues of pleasure are open and accessible, each one is likely to be used in ways that promote physical and emotional well-being.

Pain

The pleasure center has a next-door neighbor. It is the pain center. Stimulation of the pain center causes us to feel physical pain or emotional distress. Physical pain is a marvelous invention of Mother Nature. It is a system of alarms designed to motivate us to resolve whatever is threatening our physical well-being. Physical pain is the smoke detector, burglar alarm, and watchdog that stand guard over the body.

If we touch a hot stove, the pain that immediately follows is obviously triggered by excessive heat. In the case of emotional pain, the cause might be more difficult to define and is subject to the unique history of the individual. There is an underlying simplicity, however. A major cause of emotional pain is suppression of those activities that produce emotional pleasure.

As mentioned earlier, a major source of pleasure is the expression of genuine emotions, especially when it is associated with intimacy with others. It follows that a major source of emotional pain is failure to express oneself genuinely and connect intimately with others.

Failure to express the genuine self has an effect on our emotional well-being that is comparable to the effect of food deprivation on the physical body. Emotionally, we are fed by the expression of personal truth and subsequent emotional connection with others. When we deprive ourselves of this soul food, we feel "empty." Chronic emotional pain is a gnawing and aching feeling that often bears a resemblance to physical hunger. Perhaps that is why we often try to fill the emotional hunger by eating more. Likewise, when we express ourselves genuinely, we experience emotional pleasure, which is often described as a feeling of being *fulfilled.*

The Pleasure of No Pain

While I was driving with a friend, she commented that the seatbelt in my car felt very pleasant against her. At first, I thought her comment was rather strange. Then, she went on to say that the seatbelt in her own car pushed against her neck and was therefore very annoying.

My friend's comment underscores the fact that the experience of pleasure or pain is ultimately subjective, involving a delicate balance between the pleasure and pain centers in the brain.

Functionally, the pain and pleasure centers are closely related. Like other pairs of opposites, pleasure and pain define each other. Each derives its identity from the other. Every experience of pleasure is defined by a background of accumulated experience of pain, and vice versa. In fact, if an individual were in constant pain (physical or emotional), the sudden removal of the pain might be experienced as "pleasure." As one former drug user once pointed out to me, what felt so good in taking the drug was "not feeling pain." The "fix" is the blessed relief of not suffering or feeling anxious.

The Agony and Ecstasy of Painting the Fence

There are instances where the pleasantness and unpleasantness of a given activity are clearly a matter of choice, attitude, or conditioning. Painting a house can be a pleasing experience today and very unpleasant tomorrow. In other words, the sensory input is exactly the same, but is interpreted differently in the brain.

In Mark Twain's novel, *Tom Sawyer,* our hero was convinced that whitewashing the fence was a dreary chore. So, through his artistry as a con man, he convinced his friends that whitewashing the fence was a glorious experience that any healthy boy would gladly pay for—which they did.

Similarly, the pain response can be dampened d can be toned down. It still hurts, but not as much. Toning down the pain response is sometimes associated with a similar dampening of the pleasure response. Individuals who seem to feel very little pain also seem to feel very little pleasure. Such an individual does not appear to be bothered very much by the little upsets of life, but at the same time, seems to have a decreased ability to take pleasure in a beautiful sunset or the touch of a loved one. Even the pleasure of sexual intercourse is decreased and becomes restricted to a small region of the body. Once the pleasure center has been toned down through the blocking of the pain center, we then try to compensate by over-stimulating the pleasure center with food, sex, loud music, alcohol, etc.

Getting the Wires Crossed

If the nervous system is allowed to develop naturally, it learns to direct harmful stimuli to the pain center and beneficial stimuli to the pleasure center. Therefore, harmful activities are experienced as unpleasant, while beneficial activities are experienced as pleasurable. This process can apparently be reversed. Certain activities that harm the body can be experienced as pleasurable, while activities that promote well-being, such as expression of genuine emotions and loving touch, are equated with pain or anxiety and therefore avoided.

If a small child, whose neural circuits are still very malleable, is repeatedly punished for self-expression, the result is that the child learns to associate self-expression with punishment. Thus, the very activity that promotes emotional well-being and intimacy is regarded as painful and scary and is therefore avoided.

When the reversal of the functions of pleasure and pain is severe enough, the individual is said to have an addiction. When an addiction is present, activities that harm the body can be experienced as pleasurable, while activities that promote health and well-being are avoided.

The Pleasure of Pain

The blurring of pleasure and pain in their respective functions can be so deep that the individual may appear to be addicted to pain. In one sense, the pain *becomes* pleasure. This can show up in a number of subtle ways. For example:

- Addiction to suffering, tragedy and struggle.
- Taking pleasure in watching others suffer and struggle.
- Addiction to being hurt or victimized.
- Addiction to yearning; the romantic lure of not having what you want.
- The sweet ache of almost getting what you want.
- The pleasurable agony of unrealized potential.

These conditions are more common than we might think. To the extent that we suppress the genuine self, pleasure and pain drift away from their natural functions. When we block the natural portals of pleasure, we might develop an addiction to pain.

I Am Alive

We can untangle the relationship of pleasure and pain by understanding their underlying unity. The commonality of pleasure and pain may be called aliveness, a quality of self-awareness that includes, but is not limited to, our emotions and body sensations. If we close the door on the aliveness, we feel through the pleasure of participating in life-enhancing activities we then seek the experience of aliveness through pain. We might harm ourselves, doing anything that produces physical pain and emotional turmoil, so we can have the experience of *I am alive.* The experience of aliveness is fundamental to our well-being. If denied, it causes us to override common sense and even our basic survival needs.

We perceive opposites through judgment. In this case, the primordial experience of aliveness is separated into pleasure and pain by a gut-level sort of "judgment" that is designed to support health and well-being. It is designed by Mother Nature to make us feel pleasure when we are doing things that promote health and wellbeing, while making us feel pain when we are doing something harmful. However, even when pleasure and pain appear to have strayed from their ideal functions, we must be respectful of their unique expression within us. If we criticize our "taste" with regard to what we find pleasurable and painful, we are, in effect, judging the judgment, which causes us to become even more emotionally tangled.

On the other hand, we can use our judgment more judiciously by simply being honest with regard to what we find pleasurable and painful. Such honesty and self-acceptance result in a gradual transmutation of the pleasure and pain responses. We become more appreciative of their equally brilliant and complementary functions. When we do this, we walk that straight and narrow path that leads to a door, beyond which is the freedom to know that *I am alive* beyond the fear of pain and desire for pleasure. This is the peace that is said to be beyond human understanding, for it is beyond duality.

Chapter 6
Fear & Desire

Fear and desire serve the same functions as pain and pleasure. Fear is the anticipation of pain. Desire is the anticipation of pleasure. When fear is functional, it serves as the protector. Fear directs us away from potential sources of pain and therefore away from whatever might endanger health and survival. Desire directs us toward sources of pleasure. When desire is functional, it promotes health and well-being.

Like other true opposites, fear and desire define one another. Each derives its meaning from the other. And each bears the seed of the other. The obvious presence of one implies the hidden presence of the other.

As with other opposites, fear and desire also complement each other. The healthy expression of fear supports us in fulfilling our desires. Likewise, when we are respectful of our desires, fear finds its proper place as well. Either one might take turns on center stage at any given time, but the visible one is silently supported by the invisible one.

> Functional fear protects. Functional desire promotes health and wellbeing.

Dysfunctional Fear and Desire

Fear is dysfunctional when it is excessive or activated in situations where there is no actual danger. Desire is dysfunctional when it motivates us to seek pleasure in ways that do harm. Both are common in modern human society. Such problems may seem baffling and intractable, until we see how fear and desire dance together in the mind.

When we see the natural relatedness of fear and desire, we can more deeply understand how and why fear and desire become dysfunctional. They can undergo a sort of reversal wherein the individual fearfully avoids things that promote health and well-being, while desiring things that are harmful. When this role reversal is severe enough, the individual is said to have an addiction.

45

Dysfunctional Fear

Why does fear become dysfunctional? Why does it drift from protecting us to imprisoning us? How does the natural guardian of our well-being become a ball and chain that we have to drag around? The answer, in a word, is *programming.*

Fear is instinctual, but, as with other emotions, it can be programmed. Here are four sequences of programing fear so that it no longer serves to protect, but rather to imprison us.

- Avoiding the unknown.
- Sacrificing truth and justice for the sake of safety.
- Assets become liabilities.
- Addiction to fear

Avoiding the unknown can include situations in which the outcome in uncertain, such confrontation or competition. We can be "trained" to engage in confrontation only if we do not have to risk personal discomfort, rejection or failure. We do not play unless we are sure we will win. We might avoid situations where our weaknesses are be exposed. We associate only with those whom we can control or who do not push us beyond our comfort zone. Furthermore, when the fear response is altered so we avoid potentially fulfilling excursions into the unknown, we are also more likely to blindly stumble into dangerous situations.

Sacrificing truth and justice for the sake of safety can also happen when the fear level is high. Consequently, personal relationships might become shallow and dull. On other levels, when we do not value truth, we also do not value justice and fairness. In other words, if we are so concerned about safety that we neglect truth, we also become blind or indifferent to the rights of others. We speak the truth and show respect for others only if doing so allows us to control the situation.

Assets become liabilities when fear is excessive. Talents become tools for keeping fears and anxieties hidden. For example, if I am very articulate but afraid of emotional closeness, I might use my gift-of-gab to avoid intimacy. As a result, persists. This is the reverse of the biblical wisdom that says, "Your biggest weakness shall become your greatest strength." In other words, our talents and abilities, when ruled by hidden fears, become weaknesses.

Addiction to fear can occur because the fear response includes a release of stress hormones and brain chemicals which give us a rush of excitement. A relatively benign example of this would be watching an occasional scary movie or going a roller coaster. An unhealthy example of this would be frequently watching bad news until it becomes automatic. The latter has been described as "fear porn."

The dysfunctional programming of fear usually occurs unconsciously over many years. If we are conscious of it, we would probably not allow it, since it is contrary to our basic desire to be healthy, happy, and free. Likewise, by becoming aware of how our fear response has been programmed, we tend to gradually free ourselves of it.

Dysfunctional Desire

As with fear, desire can be programmed, intentionally or otherwise. Either way, desires tend to become problematical when they are habitually denied, suppressed, or harshly judged. Harsh judgment of a desire is one of the most common ways of unintentionally programming it.

Desires can also be *un*programmed. A simple way to help unprogram our desires is to recognize the associated fears. The more deeply we can see how our desires are linked to our fears, the less we have to "control" our desires.

For animals living in the wild, fear and desire are precisely balanced; therefore, controlling desires is irrelevant. A desire dissolves on its own when it is allowed to fulfill its function. Its function is to motivate the animal to do something beneficial for its survival, or for survival of the species. In a given situation, if fulfillment of a desire threatens survival, fear steps in and overrides it. Very simple.

For humans, things are a bit more complicated. Besides physical survival, a number of other factors determine whether or not we are drawn to something. For example:

- **It is a novelty.** Newness tends to evoke curiosity. Just as fear compels us to remain in the safety of the known, desire compels us to venture into the unknown. One is not necessarily better than the other. Each has its rightful place. When fear and desire are balanced and integrated, we instinctively know when to listen to our fears and stay in the safety of the known, and when to listen to our desires and venture into the unknown.

- **It is scary.** We tend to be curious about anything that evokes fear. Naturally, if the fear is intense enough, we run the other way. However, as long as safety is not too severely compromised, the fear itself can act like an emotional magnet. In other words, since fear and desire are so closely related, we can generate desire in a given area simply by creating the right amount of fear around it. A benign application of this principle is a roller coaster, as previously mentioned. We desire to go on the ride because it is "scary." The emotional part of the brain rings the danger alarm, but the rational part knows that all is well. The result is an artificially induced but benign feeling of excitement. The fear, when openly expressed, produces hormonal secretions similar to those occurring during strong desire and emotional expectancy. In other words, openly expressed fear can easily transmute into excitement or passion.
- **It is forbidden.** When something is outlawed, it tends to entice us. In fact, one of the easiest ways to create desire for a particular thing is to make it taboo. Our innate desire for freedom stimulates curiosity for any forbidden thing. This is the basis for "reverse psychology."

Reverse Psychology

Reverse psychology is often called into play unintentionally by authority figures that instigate an unwanted behavior by rigidly suppressing it or otherwise harshly judging it. This is the case of the teenage daughter who develops a strong desire to date a certain boy because her parents said "no." On the other hand, if the parents simply offered their insight and then set clear and respectful boundaries, the daughter would, more than likely, access her own inner discernment. Since she is not blinded by the thrill of doing something forbidden, she can more effectively assess the young man's attributes.

For example, when I was a teenager, I received some unexpected support in my first clumsy attempt at dating. The support came in the form of my girlfriend's overprotective mother. I met the girl, whom I will call "Debby," while we were both counselors at a day camp. Debby's mother preferred that her daughter date only Jewish boys. In addition, she specifically frowned upon her dating an Italian boy. And, when Debby's mother found out that I was not merely of Italian ancestry, but a native-born Sicilian, she absolutely drew a hard line—which her daughter absolutely had to cross. My new-found sweetie found me that much more appealing. I had it made! Debby was an attractive girl with no shortage of boys who were interested in dating her. But she wanted only me—the one boy who caused her mother to throw a royal conniption fit!

Our Fears Lead Us to Our Desires

"Since, finally, the armored animal, man, is utterly incapable of reaching his most ardent longed-for goal, namely, freedom of his organism from rigidity, dullness, immobility and the rest of the bio-physical straitjacket, he must of necessity fear and hate it; and the less he is capable of reaching it, the more he must hate it… Man's cruelty is directed mainly against what he most longs for…" —Wilhelm Reich, 1950

The above passage is great news. It tells us that we judge, fear, hate, and deny those things we secretly want but believe we cannot have. The more unreachable a thing seems, the more we fear and hate it. The hidden frustration of "I cannot have this," becomes the judgment, "I should not have this," and therefore, "no one else should have this."

So, why is Dr. Reich's insight great news? It is great news because it offers a clue for determining what we really want. If we are afraid of something, we are probably curious about it and perhaps secretly desire to experience it, or something related to it.

Therefore, if we wish to discover our deepest desires, we need only look into our deepest fears. This does not have to be as scary as it might seem. A practical and gentle application of this principle is to simply approach every fear by asking, *"What is the desire behind this fear?"*

If we regard desire is as an empty vessel waiting to be filled., fear may be seen as the lid on the vessel. If our desires become totally repressed and forgotten, the only clue to their existence is the fear that covers them. That fear is a valuable landmark, for it shows us where our deepest desires are buried.

Our Deepest Desires

The big joke is that once we remove the lid of fear that covers the great vacuum, we discover that the vacuum, quite often, cannot be filled from the outside. That which fills the vacuum is already in the vacuum.

Of course, we do receive energy and nourishment from the life around us, but we are not fully satisfied until we have given back more than we have taken. And this we can do only to the extent that we mature in a way that allows us to fill our personal cup from within. Such is the nature of Life. The seed receives nourishment from the earth and sky, becoming a tree that brings forth more seeds, enriching the soil, and providing food, oxygen and shelter for many other life forms.

When we fully alive, we want to bring forth new life. We have a deep desire to give to life more than we have taken. To do otherwise to go insane, escape into addiction, or both.

In summary, our deepest desires can be fulfilled only to the extent that fear is neither hyperactive nor hypoactive. Fear is simply allowed to fulfill its function as the protector; the trusted sentinel of our health and well-being.

We each have a deep desire to give to life more than we have taken.

Chapter 7
The Two Sides of Self-Worth

Self-worth may be said to be a dance of doing and being. In everyday life, doing is about work. Being is about play. Harmony between the two typically means that doing is the vehicle for the expression of our being. In other words, to *be* is to enjoy what you *do.*

Earned and Not Earned

Self-worth based on doing is earned. Self-worth based on being cannot be earned. Doing is about outer results. Being is about inner experience. Self-worth based on doing is tangible and visible. Self-worth based on being is intangible and invisible.

A solid sense of self-worth requires a balance of both doing and being. When one side is denied or rejected, the other loses its meaning. As with any pair of opposites, doing and being define each other and create each other. Doing is the vehicle for expressing our beingness. Likewise, when we allow ourselves to do what we want to do, we open the door to a deeper experience of beingness. When the two are balanced and integrated, each side supports the other.

Since self-worth based on doing is about tangible outer results, it typically involves connecting with others. On the other hand, self-worth based on being involves connecting with oneself. Again, the two are very much related. Connection with oneself supports us in connecting harmoniously with others. The reverse is also true. Connecting with others supports us in connecting with oneself. For example, the self-worth we feel from doing a good job and giving valuable service allows us to relax, go deeply within and nourish our inner being. Likewise, when we are able to put all outer doing aside and just go deeply within, our inner battery is recharged; the life within us renews itself, and we feel inspired to "do" things that translate into reaching out and connecting with the life around us.

Harmony of Doing and Being

When doing and being are in harmony, our intrinsic sense of self-worth (based on being) serves as the foundation of our doing. Our inner being is the canvas on which we create our worldly doing.

Our intrinsic sense of self-worth based on being, typically shows up as the capacity to enjoy what we do. Our beingness also shows up as the capacity to enjoy the tangible results of what we do. In other words, we can appreciate payment and graciously receive acknowledgement for what we do.

On the other hand, to the extent that our intrinsic sense of self-worth based on being is weak, we do not have a strong foundation for our worldly doings. We might dislike what we do, but persist only to get the tangible results. We become heavily invested in getting outer reward. And, paradoxically, we are also less capable of enjoying the rewards and acknowledgment for our worldly efforts.

Doing and being in Disharmony

When we are in touch with our inner being, we are inspired to do, create, and achieve. This drive is usually linked to the desire to receive acknowledgment for what we do. Such a desire is sometimes regarded as a form of vanity, a sin, or a weakness that has to be purged. In truth, it is a simple and natural thing. It is a voice that says, "Look at what I have accomplished. I have put my heart into it and I'm really proud of it." We might be afraid of exposing this desire, it might expose a delicate and deeply emotional place where self-worth based on being is somewhat fragile. In truth, the desire to be recognized for what we do goes hand in hand with the sharing of what we do. To hold back one is to hold back the other.

When we reject or conceal the desire to be acknowledged for what we do, two things happen. First, the suppressed desire for validation becomes the silent ruler of our worldly doings. Like any desire, this one becomes stronger through suppression. We might think we are motivated by caring and selfless love, but are driven by the hidden desire for acknowledgment. Second, by devaluing the desire to be recognized for what we do, that same desire, having become stronger through suppression, will further erode our intrinsic sense of self-worth based on being. A vicious cycle is set up wherein self-worth is eroded on both ends – frantic doing and fragile being undermining each other.

The situation described above is common in the business world, as well as interpersonal relationships. The solution is the cultivation of mindfulness wherein our worldly goals are supported by the path we use to achieve those goals.

The Goal and the Path

When we are goal-oriented, we are in the doing mode. When we are in the doing mode, we put distractions aside and focus on a specific task. To be goal-oriented is to be in a frame of mind wherein we commit ourselves to a certain outcome and (whether we admit it or not) invest a certain portion of our happiness on its achievement. This simply means we will feel the thrill of victory or the agony of defeat. Either way, we *feel*. More specifically, we feel alive. This might be the hidden motivation for emotionally committing ourselves to a goal; it allows us to feel alive—one way or another.

On the other hand, when we are path-oriented, we are in the being mode, which means we allow ourselves to enjoy the journey; to run the race for the fun of it and the joy of being in relationship with the other runners. In the path mode, the journey is a delight regardless of who comes in first.

If the goal and the path appear to be in conflict, we have judged one as more important than the other, and thus, we have lost sight of the complementary relationship of the two. Having a goal simply means we acknowledge what we want and act accordingly. The goal gives us a clear purpose. From an energetic standpoint, a "charge" has been generated; a dynamic tension has been established; a distinction has been made between where I am now and where I desire to be.

When we are emotionally aligned with a specific goal or purpose, we feel *alive*—the aliveness of knowing what we want and going for it. This is so intrinsically fulfilling that the actual achievement of the goal is reduced from a life-and-death situation to the icing on the cake.

Losing Sight of the Goal

As with other opposites, when we judge either the goal or the path as better than the other, the one that is devalued is driven underground and, from there, it runs us. For example, if we declare that the path is more important than the goal, we might convince ourselves that we do not care if we win or lose. This means the part of us that really wants to win is judged as inferior and shoved into the subconscious cellar. Having rejected and suppressed the part that wants to win, we run the race half-heartedly, because if we put too much passion into it, we will reveal the competitor that we are trying to run away from. If we win, we act nonchalant, denying the barbaric thrill of victory. If we lose, we act nonchalant, denying the disappointment of defeat. The bottom line is that by denying the goal-oriented competitor that wants to win, we suppress the very passion that makes the race thrilling. Furthermore, the suppressed competitive tendency is likely to express secretly as passive-aggressive behavior and covert competition wearing the mask of benevolence.

The Goal resembles the Path

When the goal is valued more than the path, there is an assumption that the end justifies the means. This frequently translates into the justification of injustice, killing in the name of God, tyranny in the name of law and order, and deception to keep the peace.

In other words, the achievement of the goal blinds the individual to what is actually happening along the path. We see this in the politician who lies or uses other unethical practices to get elected; health care providers that choose a mode of treatment based on profitability rather than the patient's needs; corporations that bribe public officials or knowingly create conditions that lead to death and disease. The most blatant example of using the end to justify the means is open warfare, where the maiming and killing of babies is justified as a necessary evil for achieving the "greater good."

What is generally not recognized is that the evil (necessary or not) that shows up along the path tends to create a result that is like itself. We often perpetuate conflict and injustice or simply fail to really achieve our goals because we have gone too far in claiming our right to utilize "necessary evil."

The point is that if our goal becomes so important that we are tempted to disregard what we are doing on the path, we would do well to stop and think. We must bear in mind that, as Gandhi pointed out, ultimately, the goal that we achieve tomorrow will resemble the path that we travel today.

If the game is valued more than the player, people become pawns, craftsmen become cogs, and friends become allies who's only worth is their ability to help us achieve our goals. On the other hand, when we walk the path with dignity and honesty, the goal is achieved and the path is a joy. Such mindfulness is natural when being and doing are balanced.

The Brilliant Function of Self-Sabotage

Valuing the goal more than the path means we suffer from too much doing and not enough being. This is when we take our doings too seriously. An excess of doing might get the job done, but as long as we remain in this mode, happiness is not an option.

If we lose touch with the desire to know that we are loved regardless of what we do, nothing we do can truly satisfy us, and no amount of external success or acknowledgment will fill our cup; we simply will not let it in.

The extreme version of this is fanaticism. Fanatics are never happy. At best, they succeed in not feeling their unhappiness. Their insanity is hidden by a thin veneer of stability maintained by the illusion of certainty.

However, most of us do not drift too far into fanaticism because sabotage usually intervenes. What we call self-sabotage might just be our own silent inner wisdom setting us free from ambitions that have become as chains. Self-sabotage might be a way of rebooting the system and untangling our doing and being. In other words, when we lose touch with our inner being, we tend to mess up our outer doing, which forces us to get back in touch with our being.

"I'm not Worthy"

The need to know that we are loved regardless of what we do, might be the basis for the common religious declaration, "I'm not worthy of God's love." This idea probably stems from the recognition that there is nothing we can *do* to win God's Love. To really receive God's love means that we know ourselves as God knows us. In secular terms, this translates into remembering who we are and respecting who we are, which is to say, we have contacted our beingness.

The declaration of "I'm not worthy of God's Love," might seem silly or, at the very least, technically inaccurate. However, there is hidden wisdom here. When the individual really feels his/her inability to do anything to win or earn God's love, the declaration of "I'm not worthy," if it is genuinely felt, might pack a bigger emotional wallop than a more moderate (though technically more accurate) statement, like, "God loves me regardless of what I do."

Chapter 8
Pride & Humility

Self-worth that we earn through doing often shows up as pride. Self-worth felt through contact with one's inner being often shows up as humility.

When we feel pride, there is a sense of fullness. We "swell" with pride. We feel there is more substance to our existence. We spontaneously stand at attention in response to the substance filling us and radiating from us.

While pride is a sense of fullness, genuine humility may be said to be a state of emptiness or simplicity. More specifically, the presence of genuine humility means we are, on some level, in touch with our inner emptiness and are at peace with it; neither rejecting it nor flaunting it as a spiritual badge of honor. If we try to take credit for it, it ceases to *be*.

While healthy pride is a celebration of what we do, humility often translates into serenity regarding the perceived limitations of what we can do. Such serenity is the product of having silently contacted our beingness.

Healthy pride is based on work done with care and attention. Pride in our own accomplishments emerges naturally when we do our best. Any show of humility here is false humility.

Interestingly enough, we can also feel pride in the accomplishments of an individual or group with whom we feel emotionally connected. For example, we can be proud of the accomplishments of our parents, children, brothers, or sisters. There is no logical reason we would feel pride in someone else's accomplishments, unless we consider the possibility that, on a deep feeling level, we regard that person as a part of self.

While pride is based on tangible work, humility is based on the sense of who we are beyond our work, and beyond outer appearance. Humility is based on contact with the genuine self, pure and simple. Any show of pride here is false pride, since the deep awareness of who we "be" includes a sense that we all be passengers on the same bus.

In other words, pride has to do with our unique self-expression as individuals, while humility is based on a quiet realization of our commonality, our primordial kinship, or oneness. Pride is about flesh; humility is about spirit.

Arrogance

Whereas health pride is based on hard facts, arrogance is based assumptions. Healthy pride is a sense of self-worth based on the reality of your own accomplishments. Arrogance is based on the assumption that your accomplishments make you better than others. Arrogance looks upon itself and says, "My form is the best of all possible forms. What I do is more important than what others do."

Arrogance seeks to establish self-worth through comparison, conquest, and dominion over others. Stated differently, healthy pride is earned. Arrogance is not earned, it is stolen.

Healthy pride promotes celebration and sharing. Arrogance promotes brooding isolation. When we feel healthy pride, we feast on the fruits of our own labor which we share freely with others in a joyful celebration of life. When we feel arrogance, we give up that royal feast, and settle for the crumbs stolen from the table of others.

The Origin of Arrogance

The origin of arrogance is impotence. Awareness of one's limitations in the absence of humility can be quite disturbing, paralyzing our capacity to create and achieve. When the experience of impotence is strong enough, it is often associated with shame. As we approach that shame, we might feel intense fear. However, we usually shield ourselves from feeling the shame and fear by covering them with a layer of inflated self-importance or arrogance.

The potential for arrogance is part of our human condition. It can assert itself in any situation where individuality or separateness has forgotten that it springs forth from Unity. Forgetting Unity shows up as loss of humility. Such forgetting of humility, sets the stage for the painful experience of impotence, which we then cover up with arrogance. We can undo this by simply cultivating healthy pride, which then sets the stage for the emergence of our natural humility.

Cultivating Healthy Pride

Healthy pride is rooted in personal truth and physical reality. In everyday life, we maintain healthy pride by practicing truthfulness with regard to what we feel and what we do. We claim what is ours and let go of what is not ours. Genuine pride can rise and swell on the wings of truth. Such pride has no need to restrain or censor itself, for it has done no wrong and told no lie.

When we cultivate healthy pride, our natural humility follows. In everyday life, our natural humility shows up as humor. Humility that is grim and grave conceals a secret pride that takes itself very seriously.

Without humility, there is no humor, except for biting sarcasm or taunting ridicule. On the other hand, humor which emerges from humility can freely laugh at itself without degrading itself. When we deeply contact who we really be, we are likely to laugh (or cry) unashamedly

Union of Pride and Humility

As expressions of doing and being, pride and humility go hand and hand. Pride is the mountain; humility is the valley. The fullness of pride radiates spontaneously from the emptiness of pure humility. When we are in touch with our beingness, we take pride in what we do. Such pride does not fall, for it is securely nested within a deep well of humility.

Pride without humility shows up as arrogance, vanity, and over-concern with superficialities. Excessive pride is an attempt to hide feelings of emptiness that have become too frightening to face, due to years of denial and pretense. Likewise, humility without pride is not humility. It is pious arrogance, false modesty, and ceremonial self-defacement. Such pseudo-humility is an attempt to hide frozen pride.

The harmony of healthy pride and humility is experienced as thankfulness. We are thankful for what we do and who we be. We are thankful for what we have and for what we do not have. We are thankful for our substance and our emptiness. We are thankful for being able to rise up and express the fullness of what we do, and we are thankful that we can relax and gently float back down to the simplicity of who we be.

Chapter 9
Purity & Fullness

Purity and fullness may seem like a pair of abstract concepts with no immediate relevance to our shared human experience. However, this dynamic duo provides a foundation for a deeper understanding other pairs of opposites, such as laughing and crying, described later in this chapter. pride and humility, described in the previous chapter. In addition, other pairs of opposites described in the chapters that follow may be understood more deeply by first understanding the dance of purity and fullness.

Purity

Purity, in the physical sense, refers to uniformity, consistency, sameness or absence of clutter. Purity often translates into the presence of just one thing. For example, in the language of chemistry, a substance is said to be pure when it is singular in its consistency. To a chemist, a chunk of matter is "pure" when it is composed of just one specific type of molecule or atom.

In a broader sense, *pure* can also refer to emptiness, nothingness, silence, and stillness. On the human level, the term *purity* is often used to describe a very high level of personal integrity. It is an absence of pretense or hypocrisy. It is a high level of genuineness, virtually synonymous with innocence. Purity can also refer to an inner state of being, wherein the individual is deeply in touch with what is basic and fundamentally important. In other words, purity is about being in touch with our essential nature, or beingness.

The desire for purity is one of our basic in-born instincts. It compels us to be authentic and congruent. We feel driven to empty ourselves of whatever is false or inconsistent with the genuine self. All our perceptions, beliefs, and behaviors are exposed to the purifying fire that burns off the deception and superficialities that hide who we really are. To chronically ignore or suppress this desire is to invite insanity.

Likewise, to be in touch with our fundamental desire for purity is to have serenity. Furthermore, recognition of our desire for purity, also opens the door to fullness.

Fullness

Fullness refers to a state of abundance and variety. In the physical sense, fullness is abundance and variety of things and activities. On the inside, fullness includes a state of *wholeness*, a condition wherein no part of oneself is neglected, cast out or otherwise denied. Every part of oneself is recognized and allowed its natural place.

Fullness can also translate into *fulfillment*. On the mental level, our understanding is full when all the separate bits of information are well integrated in the mind. On the emotional level, our experience is full when our desires have been fulfilled. When we have fullness on both the mental and emotional levels, we have mental clarity and emotional serenity. We are at peace with ourselves and the life around us. When we have that sublime sense of fullness, we relax, for the journey has been completed, and something new and pure can be born.

The Dance of Purity and Fullness

At any given time, we might feel called to experience purity or fullness. Sometimes we want to experience the richness and fullness of life and sometimes we just want to retreat to the purity and simplicity of the essential self. Each side, however, must give birth to the other. Each side *wants* to give birth to the other. When we have fullness of experience and fullness of understanding, the many small parts of oneself seem to spontaneously merge into a larger and singular self. The many voices merge into the purity of a single voice that cries out, *I Am*. Likewise, when we feel the purity of the singular self, we cannot help but reach out to create fullness and richness.

Purity and Fullness in Everyday Life

In everyday life, the dance of purity and fullness, though ever present, is seldom experienced in its generic form. We usually do not say, "I feel pure today" or "I feel full today."

Neither do we say, "I want to feel purity" or "I want to feel fullness." Our experience of purity and fullness usually takes the form of other pairs of opposites, such as laughing & crying, humility & pride, giving & receiving, will & feeling, fasting & feasting, austerity & wild abandonment, responsibility & freedom, clean & dirty, darkness & light. Each of these pairs is addressed in other chapters of this book.

The play of purity and fullness is also seen in the experience of pain and pleasure, addressed in chapter five. Pleasure, when it is allowed to carry out its natural function, may be described as a sense of fullness or fulfillment. Pain, when it is allowed to carry out its natural function, compels us to purify ourselves of things that are harmful or otherwise obstructive to our health and well-being. Pain has the capacity to empty us of all frivolities and self-deception. Pain makes us focus. It preempts whatever we are involved with at a given time, simplifies our goals and wipes the slate clean so we can make room for what really brings us fulfillment.

Are there ways of contacting our inner purity without creating pain? Certainly. It is not the pain that purifies us, but our capacity to focus our attention. We can cultivate the capacity to focus through solitude, introspection and the daily practice of honest self-reflection and self-expression.

Whether we do it through pain or intention, we are instinctively driven to contact that deep place of purity. Like breathing, we can stop that quest temporarily, but eventually, nature takes over. Sooner or later, the desire to experience inner purity asserts itself. The desire to know our purity, if neglected, eventually overrides all other desires and all other influences, including common sense and logic. Instinctively, we seem to know that the doorway to fulfillment is purity.

If we contact inner purity through pain, the fulfillment that follows will probably take the form of some kind of pleasure. The pleasure will, more than likely, take form in a way that is "symmetrical" to the pain we endured.

If we manage to contact inner purity through a method other than pain and discomfort, we are likely to experience fullness in a way that cannot be adequately described as "pleasure." The purity that is beyond pain and the fullness that is beyond pleasure have been described as the state of *Isness*.

If, however, the attempt to contact Isness translates into a rejection of pleasure or pain, we will repeatedly stumble into alternating experiences of pain and pleasure, purging and bingeing, fasting and feasting. This pattern tends to dissolve when we allow pain and pleasure, and other expressions of purity and fullness, to each have their moment on center stage.

Clean and Dirty

A common expression of purity and fullness is the dance of clean and dirty. Mother Nature wires the brain of many animals so they instinctively practice cleanliness. This is understandable since cleanliness promotes health and safety. Many animals living in the wild clean and groom themselves and each other.

For humans, cleanliness has an additional meaning. Our instinctual leaning toward cleanliness reflects a deeper desire for purity on the consciousness level. The tendency to drift into dishonesty might show up as neglect of one's physical body. As deception and hurts accumulate, we might accumulate clutter around us. Or we might go the other way. The deep-seated feelings of being emotionally or spiritually "dirty" might show up as hyperbolic cleanliness.

Down and Dirty

Though we instinctively seek cleanliness, such phrases as, "Let's get down and dirty," indicate that we equate dirtiness with pleasure. Magazines and movies that are aimed at arousing sexual desire are often referred to as "dirty." This is not surprising. As mentioned earlier, the things we harshly judge or otherwise reject are often the same things we secretly desire.

We can more fully understand the dance of clean and dirty by looking at one version of this duality: sterile and septic. From a purely biological standpoint, there is nothing good or bad about sterile or septic. To a microbiologist, these two words simply indicate the absence or presence of microbial life. However, when these two words are used in nonscientific ways, they are charged with whatever emotional bias and inner conflict that we happen to carry.

As an expression of cleanliness, sterile is considered good, respectable and safe. On other levels, it can also imply lifelessness, dullness, and lack of potential. The soil on which we grow fruits and vegetables is very septic. It is teaming with bacteria, fungi, and worms, as well as their bodily secretions and excrements. This is fertile earth. The blacker the better! The septic tank and compost heap are very dirty and disgusting places, but the revolting biological activity converts the garbage into something useful.

On the social level, the double meaning of the word sterile often sets up an unconscious conflict. We want to be clean and sterile because it is sensible and socially acceptable, but we also equate cleanliness with the absence of vitality. Such inner conflict says, "I want to live life to the fullest, but if I'm full of life, I'm dirty. I want to be clean, but if I'm clean, I'm lifeless."

Unity beyond Opposites

The healthy expression of clean and dirty depends on the harmonious dance of purity and fullness within the mind. The desire to experience the purity of the genuine self goes hand in hand with the desire to live life to the fullest. When the purity of the genuine self is allowed to blossom into the fullness of who we are, we typically allow clean and dirty their rightful place, without obsessing about either one.

Obsession is about guilt and shame. When we harbor a cesspool of guilt and shame, we often protect ourselves by becoming overly logical, while toning down our feelings. Quite often, the only red flag that marks the presence of the hidden emotional burden is obsession.

The inner conflict is resolved when we get in touch with the inner purity of who we really are, beyond pretense and deception. This is the purity that has remained unchanged, regardless of how dirty we think we are. This is the purity that transforms the emotional debris of the past into the rich and fertile soil on which we grow our personal gift to life.

By thus reclaiming our inner purity, the duality of clean and dirty can have its rightful place. We take proper care of the body and the home and we realize that there is a time to be clean and a time to be dirty.

Laughing & Crying

Laughing and crying are two ways of expressing aliveness. They are closely related physiologically. The movements of the abdomen, chest and face associated with laughing and crying are strikingly similar. Even the respective sounds are somewhat similar. And of course, if we laugh really hard, we will, more than likely, shed tears. In addition, when we laugh or cry, many joints and muscles are worked, the internal organs and glands are massaged and capillaries dilate, sending life-giving blood to the deep tissues that previously may have been deprived.

Laughing and crying are also related psychologically. When we laugh or cry, the places inside us that have perhaps been emotionally shut down are awakened. Places that have been in conflict or incommunicado are making peace. Either way, emotions flow freely because we feel connected to ourselves.

Reconnecting

To reconnect with oneself is not unlike reconnecting with a loved one; we are likely to laugh or cry. The connection might also take the form of a meaningful insight. We suddenly become aware of something that we have never been aware of before and respond by laughing or crying. Laughter is often used as a means of releasing emotional tension. Comedy is a way of spoofing our own weaknesses or inconsistencies. Laughter softens the hard angles, smooths out the rough edges and saves us from taking ourselves too seriously.

The great healing quality of laughter is fully realized when we recognize that crying is equally important. Both release tension and move emotional energy. When we do not try to exalt one over the other, each finds its natural expression, surging forward and then yielding to the other with ease and grace.

Purity of Tears and Fullness of Laughter

Though laughing and crying tend to have their healthiest expression when they are given equal importance, most of us would prefer to laugh rather than cry. This is normal and healthy. It is part of the overall instinct to seek well-being and happiness. However, when we cling to laughter and hide the tears, the result is that we limit our capacity to laugh fully.

To laugh fully, we have to feel deeply and purely. When we suppress tears, we cannot feel deeply. The more we suppress our tears, the more we limit our laughter. Specifically, we laugh only when things go wrong in a comical way. When suppression of our tears is severe enough, laughter becomes a toned-down version of satanic laughter, which can only experience pleasure in watching the stumbling and suffering of others. Likewise, the more honest we are about our own pain or sorrow, the higher we can soar in laughter, until we reach the fullness of laughter.

Fullness of laughter is laughter that laughs at no one. It is like a fire that burns clean. Fullness of laughter transmutes everything without consuming anyone, leaving no ashes or charred remains.

Fullness of laughter does not think itself to be better than the purity of crying. Both are expressions of genuineness. The two are intimately related. That is why it is possible to respond to overwhelming happiness by crying.

If we go deep enough into the feeling-mind, we discover that fullness of laughter and purity of crying are separated by an exceedingly fine line that can be crossed again and again without skipping a beat or loss of continuity of expression; each side yielding to the other with the fluidity of two beloved partners in a dance.

We might even reach a place where we seem to laugh and cry simultaneously, unable to distinguish whether we are expressing one or the other at any given moment. In such a place, there are no words to describe what we feel. We might, however, imagine that if the feeling could talk, it might say, *"Here I am... all of me...and I am so thankful to be here."*

Chapter 10
Conscious & Unconscious

"There's no such thing as an unconscious mind," said my friend, "George," as we sat in a restaurant having lunch. "There's only one mind," he said, "and it's entirely conscious; there are simply elements that we choose to temporarily forget."

He said the distinction between conscious and unconscious is artificial. I agreed with him in principle, but I was feeling competitive, so I challenged him. I said, "George, if the distinction between conscious and unconscious is artificial, why did we make it up, and why do we use it so much?"

The obvious answer is that we find it useful. Even when we do not use the words, *conscious* and *unconscious*, we still silently make that distinction every time we use terms like, remember, forget, awake, asleep, intentional, unintentional, known and unknown. I pointed this out to George, and then, feeling a bit mischievous, I added, "Since we obviously find it useful to make the artificial distinction between conscious and unconscious, let's do it consciously rather than unconsciously."

Making the Distinction

The conscious mind holds the thoughts and emotions that we are aware of at any moment. The unconscious mind contains everything else. The conscious mind is in charge of deliberate action, making the distinction what is ours and what is not ours, keeping track of time, making choices and judgments, etc.

The unconscious mind, on the deepest levels, makes no judgment with regard to what is right, wrong or good. It has no concept of time and space, no sense of separation, and is, therefore, in full communication with other minds. It has virtually limitless knowledge that it sends to the conscious mind as inspiration, insight and intuition. Making no clear distinction between oneself and others, it has no sense of territory.

The unconscious mind also stores all the memories and feelings that the conscious mind cannot handle. When the conscious mind tries to get rid of an unpleasant memory or emotion, it simply stores the data in the unconscious mind.

The price for keeping a lid on unwanted memories and emotions is that we also shut the door on empathy, joy, genuine kindness and intuition. Furthermore, the unwanted memories and emotions exert a powerful influence on us. They become the authors of our physical reality. Therefore, the question, how do I really know what I hold in my "unconscious mind, has a simple answer: We just look around at the physical world we have created for ourselves. We look at our bodies, our work and our relationships. Each reflects what really runs us, regardless of what we profess to believe.

In one sense, the physical reality we create may be looked upon as an attempt by the unconscious mind to become conscious. When the conscious mind judges the creations as "bad," learning is blocked. In its harsh judgment of the creation, the conscious mind says, "I do not wish to know this part of myself right now." The unconscious mind simply replies, "Okay," and tries again later.

My Kindly Intentions

During the time that I was writing this section of the book, I had a confrontation with one of the students in my anatomy and physiology class. The issue was a question on a test. The student did not agree with my interpretation of her answer. After we spoke privately about the matter, I still felt that I was right with my interpretation, so I held my ground.

When the class reconvened, the student was still visibly unhappy. There was also a subtle tension in the room. The rest of the class was aware of the little debate between that particular student and me. I wondered if other students had taken issue with my interpretation of the question but were too shy to speak up.

So, I asked the student to express to the class why she was unhappy with her test. I reasoned that her candor would encourage other students to speak up. She felt embarrassed about doing so, but with a little cheering-on from the class, she expressed herself openly.

I told myself that my intention was to communicate to her and the rest of the class that their opinions were welcomed. However, that was not the result of my efforts. Later that day, the student called me on the telephone and stated that she felt terribly upset. She said the experience triggered childhood memories of Catholic School, where she was sometimes humiliated in front of the class for being "stupid."

My conscious intention was certainly not to punish or humiliate her. Yet, that *was* the result. I then looked back and remembered other instances where I (through good intentions) did things that resulted in someone feeling invalidated. Then, I recalled my own childhood and remembered the times I felt belittled and humiliated.

My interaction with that student reminded me that the *results* of our actions reflect what we hold in the unconscious mind. My conscious intention to be a supportive teacher was mixed with my unconscious programming to hurt another human being in the same manner that I had been hurt. And, by a remarkable coincidence, I had picked the one student in the class who was the most vulnerable.

A word of caution: If we become aware of these subconscious patterns while we carry a lot of self-condemnation, the effect can be demoralizing. Therefore, if we choose to examine the subconscious patterns behind our daily interactions, we must remind ourselves to be objective and to have a measure of compassion for all of those who are involved.

Synergy of Conscious and Unconscious

A common assumption is that conscious is better than unconscious. To be sure, the desire greater conscious awareness is natural. In one sense, we might say that the unconscious parts want to become conscious. Such awakening occurs naturally when the conscious and unconscious parts of the mind dance harmoniously. Such awakening has its own timing and rhythm. We really cannot "speed it up." When it

71

looks like we have accelerated the process, we have simply dissolved the blockages that had been slowing us down. Such blockages show up as a tendency to go too fast, probably because we are driven by external pressures, while neglecting our own inner timing and rhythm.

To complicate matters, having convinced ourselves that conscious is better than unconscious; we can then plug in our own notion of what specifically constitutes being conscious or unconscious. We define what it means to be awake, aware, illumined or enlightened. Essentially, those who agree with our beliefs are considered more conscious or enlightened, and all others are unconscious or deceived.

In order to maintain health, the conscious and unconscious parts of the mind must be balanced. On a physiological level, such balance is reflected in the complementary relationship between the parts of the brain that need to rest and those that do not. In order for the individual to maintain physical, mental and psychological health, the conscious mind must rest. The deeper parts of the mind do not need such rest. The cognitive part of the brain needs to rest in order to maintain clarity of thought and emotional stability. The part of the brain that governs instinct and visceral functions does not need such rest; in fact, it is most active when the cognitive brain is sleeping. The more thoroughly we rest the cognitive mind (through sleep, relaxation, meditation, etc.), the more fully we can access the deeper intuitive nature. Likewise, the serenity and inspiration that emerge from the part of the brain that does not sleep, allows the cognitive mind to be at ease, to sleep more deeply and, therefore, function more effectively.

Chapter 11
Will and Feeling

(The Two Sides of Self-awareness)

Our everyday human awareness, like the rest of the created universe, may be understood as a dance of opposites, a dance of Yin and Yang. The Yin side may be called feeling. The Yang side may be termed the will. They dance together to create your unique personality, with all the thoughts and emotions associated with it.

Mental confusion and emotional unrest may be seen as the result of the will and feeling sides of the mind torn asunder. The obvious solution to a troubled mind is to restore harmony between the two sides.

What can we do to promote harmony between these two sides of the mind? Quite simply, we just need to understand them. What is the will? What is the feeling side of the mind?

The Will

The will is our capacity to focus. It is the power to choose. It is the capacity to set boundaries and exercise discernment. The will is our capacity to be proactive. It is about *doing*. It is about setting goals, working and building.

The will includes our intellect, our capacity to learn from the past and plan for the future. Intellect commonly expresses as our everyday thoughts, ideas, perceptions, and beliefs.

The will can show up as courage. Courage is the swimmer who stands at the edge of the water and jumps in, not knowing how deep it is, or what might be swimming around just under the surface. Beyond the raw courage to jump in, the will also shows up as the capacity to keep swimming until the destination is reached. The water is cold, the salt stings the eyes, the muscles get tired and achy, but the will keeps the swimmer moving. The latter is often called "will power," which is the self-discipline and persistence needed to complete a task, even if we don't feel like it.

All of the above qualities of the will can be trained and developed. Cultivating the will can be as simple as reminding ourselves that we have the power to choose. We remind ourselves over and over again of our priorities, though faced with intimidation or tempted by immediate gratification.

Since the will can show up as the capacity to perform a given task even though we don't feel like it, the will may appear to be at odds with the feeling side of our consciousness. In reality, the will cannot exist or function properly without the other side of the mind.

Feeling

Whereas the will is about *doing*, the feeling side of the mind or the feeling-nature is about *being.* The will is linear, sharp, and directed, while feelings are curvaceous and wave-like. The will operates by intent, while the feelings operate by impulse. The will exerts effort, while the feeling-nature is effortless. The will allows us to remain at attention and vigilant, while the feeling-nature allows us to relax, let go, and trust.

The will can be trained and developed, while our ability to feel is not something that we learn how to "do." Feelings emerge spontaneously when we allow ourselves to "be." Expressing feelings is like sneezing. You cannot make yourself sneeze, you just relax and sneeze – when you feel like it.

The feeling side of the mind expresses most commonly as our physical sensations, emotions, and desires. We can feel hot or cold, pleasure or pain anywhere on the body. We can feel emotions, such as happiness, sadness, or anger throughout the day.

The feeling side of the mind also expresses in subtle ways that go beyond body sensations, emotions, and desires. These feelings include intuition, instinct, empathy, compassion, and conscience. These ethereal feelings may or not be associated with the physical body or emotions.

Our emotions may be said to be feelings which are related to the body, while the more subtle and ethereal feelings may be said to be more related to the soul because they have to do with our connection with the life around us. Stated differently, our emotions are based on our experience of separateness, while the other more ethereal feelings are echoes of oneness with the rest of life.

Though we can identify each of the various expressions of the feeling side of the mind, there is an underlying unity. If we try to suppress or deny one part, the others are affected. If we suppress our animal instincts and emotions, our capacity for empathy is decreased. If we suppress our personal desires and urges, our capacity for genuine compassion is decreased.

Another important distinction between the will and feeling-nature has to do with time. The will keeps track of time. The feeling part of the mind does not. The will learns from the past and contemplates the future, while the feeling-nature is ever in the present. The feeling side is, therefore, our wellspring of innocence and spontaneity. On a feeling level, every experience is a new experience. Feelings can seemingly come from nowhere and then disappear into nothing, because they exist only in the present.

Having no existence in the future, the feeling side of consciousness does not plan or plot. Having no past, it is incapable of holding a grudge.

Since the feeling side of the mind is ever in the present moment, it is incapable of learning. The modification of our feelings through learning is made possible by the will, for it is the will that keeps track of time, and thus makes learning possible. For example, our everyday emotions are greatly influenced by our memories, perceptions, and beliefs that are gathered over time by the will.

The Intimate Dance

As with other opposites, the willful and feeling sides of the mind are inseparable. Each is meaningless without the other to define it. Their intimate connection is metaphorically reflected in the anatomy of the brain (Chapter four). The will seems to be focused primarily on the surface of the brain, known as the cerebral cortex, especially in the forehead area. The will, at its best, is very focused and "up front" and "on the surface."

In contrast, the feeling part of the mind is more spread out, further back and deeper in the brain. The outer body sensations seem to be "dispersed" throughout the entire back half of the cerebral cortex, and the deeper body sensations, instincts, and emotions reside in the interior parts of the brain, an area known as the limbic system, which includes the lower parts of the cerebrum and brain stem.

The relationship between will and feeling may be likened to a river. The will is like the banks of a river, while the feeling-nature embodies the water. The banks restrain the water, while allowing it to flow in the direction that it naturally wants to flow. We see this relationship in the brain, where the rational areas of the cerebral cortex censor and modulate the impulses or feelings rising from the deeper parts of the brain.

Without the boundaries provided by the will, feelings may become hysterical, like water flowing with little force or direction, until it dissipates its energy, stagnates, and sinks into the soil of unconsciousness. Likewise, the flow of genuine feelings has a purifying effect on the will, like rushing water smooths out and maintains the banks of a river.

In everyday life, the harmonious union of the will and feeling shows up as mental clarity and emotional serenity. In other words, when the two are in harmony, they complement one another; each one gives shape and substance to the other. The will gives our feelings force, direction, and fullness of expression, while the expression of genuine feelings has the effect of purifying the will, smoothing away its rough and jagged edges.

The harmonious union of the will and feeling-nature occurs when the will disciplines itself to be still and listen to feelings. The more deeply the will listens, the more precisely it can choose. For example, two people might feel sexually aroused by each other and even feel a nice little emotional fluttering in the heart. However, there might also be a deeper instinct that says, *"no, not this one",* or perhaps, *"go really slow."* We may not hear the deeper feelings very clearly if we have habitually ignored them. The result is that we feel "split." One part of us seems to say yes, while another part seems to say no.

In truth, the many different expressions of the feeling-nature tend to coexist peacefully. They are born from the same womb, grow up in the same house, and are very much at ease around each other. The split occurs when the will judges some feelings as good, some as bad, some as useful, and some as useless or inferior.

The split is healed when the will disciplines itself to listen deeply and respectfully to all feelings emerging from within. This is the way the will learns how to make intelligent choices. This is when the will makes choices that *feel* right.

Brother Passion and Sister Grace

When pure will is united with the fullness of feeling, the two give birth to a son called Passion and a daughter called Grace. Passion is forged through intent and attention, while Grace seems to emerge from nowhere in particular, and without effort.

Grace is typically less visible than Passion, but no less powerful. The two are inseparable. Passion is born when the will is purified of pretense and when feelings are allowed to be as they are.

When driving Passion is exhausted, Grace steps in to help her brother. She may or may not actually remove the obstacles, but, rather, allows the drama to unfold more gracefully. Regardless of the situation, she magically appears when needed, often in unexpected ways. This is why Grace is, by her very nature, amazing.

Damning the Flow

Self-condemnation obstructs the flow of feelings. Severe obstruction of feelings results in a loss of will, including the will to live. More commonly, partial obstruction of feelings causes the will to become obscured and shallow, which is to say, wishy-washy, wimpy, spineless, spaced out, and apathetic. The individual has no clear boundaries—no clear sense of self. The mind is cluttered and bogged down with ideas and beliefs, as disapproving voices accumulate in the mind. This is the making of the addict. Or the individual might overcompensate for self-condemnation by erecting a wall of rigidified will which relates to life with a dictatorial certainty.

Whether the person has a poorly developed will (as in the addict), or a rigidified will (as in the dictator), the result is the same: feelings do not flow freely and life becomes meaningless.

The Addict

When an addiction is present, the individual finds pleasure in activities that harm the body, while avoiding activities that promote health and well-being. The same substance that brings short-term comfort also causes long-term damage. This is not surprising. When we conceal the truth, we harm the body. The addictive behavior is, among other things, a way of hiding truth.

Just as the will and feeling parts of the mind go together, so do addiction and harsh judgment. We might hide one and display the other, but both are always present within the mind. An individual who displays an obvious addiction is ruled by hidden judgment in the form of self-condemnation, self-hatred, and unexpressed harsh judgment of others. Likewise, a person who is overtly "judgmental" (hypercritical, dictatorial, controlling) is likely to be ruled by multiple hidden addictions.

Harsh or dictatorial judgment may be looked upon as a twisted expression of the will, just as addiction may be looked upon as a twisted or conflicted expression of feelings. If we wish to resolve that inner conflict, we must understand the nature of that twist. Quite simply, they are twisted because they are incomplete.

In our everyday relationships, when two parties are in conflict, each side typically expresses knowledge that the other represses. The same may be said for the relationship between addiction and the harsh judgment of the addiction.

One of the reasons we may have difficulty removing an addiction, even when it is clearly harmful to the body and mind, is that we do not recognize it as the incomplete awareness of a deep desire. The addict has partial awareness of the deep desire to feel alive, whereas the average person, with no obvious addictions, simply represses the desire and robotically plods along. The addict feels an emptiness and urgently tries to fill it. However, since the addict does not have the will to listen deeply and respectfully to the desire, there is no fulfillment, only a facsimile of fulfillment, a temporary easing of the pain, at a heavy price.

Likewise, one of the reasons we have difficulty in our earnest attempts to remove excessive or harsh judgment is that we do not recognize that the judgment is simply incomplete knowledge. We do not remove incompleteness. We just complete it! The harsh judgment or condemnation of addictive behavior is the incomplete knowing that the "fix" is not what we really want. The desire for the fix is a signal that says, "Pay attention to this desire; this is important!" At the core of the craving is the desire to simply feel fully alive.

Again, harsh judgment of the addiction is simply partial knowing. The rest of the knowing is contained in the addiction itself. When both are understood, they tend to merge into wholeness.

In everyday life, we feel aliveness by eating, touching, laughing, crying, creative expression, telling the truth, emotional contact, and giving of ourselves freely and sincerely. If we close the door on one form of aliveness, we tend to use the others more frequently. For example, if we suppress creative expression or deny the need for intimacy, we might compensate by overusing food or sex. The judgment we then place on the food or sex is the incomplete knowing that we are using them as inadequate replacements for what we really want. In recognizing this, we can do one of two things: We can freely engage in the addictive behavior, or we can abstain from it. Either one can work. It depends on the individual and the circumstance. If the strategy works, both the addiction and the harsh judgment diminish.

In one sense, they do not really "diminish," they merge into wholeness. This might be the hidden wisdom within the sometimes-controversial teaching of twelve step programs; they assert that you never really "get rid" of the addiction. This is taken to mean that you will always have the problem. What it really means is that the problem becomes a blessing; through the process of overcoming the "problem," you are given the greatest of gifts—yourself.

In other words, as long as the will and feeling-nature are in harmony, there is no addiction. However, if the two become dissociated, the same old addiction can come back in full force. In that sense, the addiction never really goes away.

Whether or not the addict is aware of it, the process of undoing the addiction involves a gradual developing of the will. The common practice in twelve-step programs of admitting one's powerlessness might seem contrary to that goal, but is, in fact, based on another bit of hidden wisdom. Admitting one's powerlessness is intended to remove pretense, denial, defensiveness and other patterns of a weakened or rigidified will. Such honesty allows feelings to flow more freely. Thus, the will is gradually purified, sharpened, and deepened. When this is done consistently enough, passion emerges, followed by grace.

Passion sets us free from the addictive pattern—through focused intention and persistence. When passion reaches the end of endurance, grace appears serendipitously as an encouraging phone call, a letter from a friend, a spontaneous wave of inspiration, an insightful dream, a job opportunity, or money that appears just in time to pay the rent or repair the automobile.

The Dictator

Just as the addict appears to have no will, the dictator appears to have no feelings. It is goal-oriented with little regard for the path. The will, cut off from the feeling part of the mind gets the work done, but has no regard for the workers.

To the tyrant, the end justifies the means. It has no conscience because conscience is a function of the feeling side of the mind. The tyrant only has goals which may or may not include respect for truth and justice.

Whereas the addict is afraid of addressing inner conflict, the dictator has no tolerance for peace. In one sense, the dictator is addicted to conflict. In fact, he breeds conflict and uses it as a means of acquiring power and maintaining control.

The tendency described above is not limited to corrupt governments and despotic heads of state. It exists in every one of us. On an interpersonal level, the "addiction" to power and control often shows up as the tendency to criticize and find fault in others. It shows up as the tendency to routinely invalidate or correct others.

Granted, there is value in expressing criticism if we feel violated, or if we genuinely feel the other person's behavior is unethical or destructive. However, if criticism, fault-finding, and conflict become habitual, they act like a drug that produces a temporary high, but ultimately weakens us even more.

The Addictive Cycle and Tyrannical Cycle

The addict is, by definition, out of control. The addict is depleted of energy because the will that is capable of gathering and focusing energy has been weakened.

The addict typically reacts to lack of energy in a way that depletes energy even more. This is one way that the addiction is perpetuated. This cyclic behavior tends to spin more and more out of control, eventually shattering any illusion of being in control. In other words, the individual "hits -bottom."

Whereas the addictive response is characterized by going deeper and deeper into chaos and loss of control, the tyrannical response is to go for even tighter control. Excessive control must breed rebellion—including inner rebellion.

In the presence of the rebellion (inner or outer), the tyrant tightens the reins of control and declares martial law. The tyrant pulls tighter and tighter on the reins, which could culminate in a "reign of terror," wherein the zeal to maintain order results in a complete breakdown into chaos.

We see the above pattern in society, in interpersonal relationships, and within the individual. In the case of the addict and dictator within, the pattern might look like alternate binging and purging.

The Addict and Dictator in Relationship

Just as pure will and fullness of feeling are a complementary pair, so are addiction and tyranny. Each side maintains the other, whether it is within the context of society as a whole, interpersonal relationships, or entirely within oneself.

Within the individual, the dictatorial will, exploits the addicted feeling-nature, but has no respect for it. Likewise, the addicted feeling-nature depends on the will but is secretly afraid of it. This dance is not easy to see. However, we see this inner dance mirrored in the outer relationships. We see it in the relationship between the pusher and the drug addict. On a larger scale, the real-life dictator draws power from the frenzied and fearful mob. The dictator feeds on the fears, cravings and addictions of the masses, while holding them, in contempt.

In other words, rigidified will, having no life of its own, seeks out the addict. The ruling will of one individual harness the chaotic feeling energy of another. The controller uses the fears and desires of the addict to control the addict, just as an unfeeling animal trainer might use food and a whip. Likewise, the addict seeks rigidified will for structure and containment; it is water seeking a channel.

The two parties form a relationship in which the controller has distain for the addict, while the addict is afraid of the controller. They tolerate each other because they feed off each other. Both are content, but neither is free. Freedom comes when each side goes within and discovers the element that is mirrored by the other.

Free at Last

Freedom from addiction or any potentially harmful habit occurs when we no longer judge it harshly. Not judging it harshly allows us to judge it correctly. The desire is seen for what it is. It is a desire for aliveness. In other words, the absence of harshness allows us to experience what we need to experience and learn what we need to learn from the addictive behavior, so that we can be complete with it.

Such completion may not be immediately evident to the casual observer. Nonetheless, a deep invisible change occurs. It is the deeper union of the will and feeling-nature. That union eventually shows up as a greater capacity for calmness on the emotional level and stillness on the mental level. More tangibly, there is a reduced tendency to exhibit behavior that is harmful to the body and mind. The absence of such harmful behavior is an unmistakable sign that the will is getting strong and the feelings are being set free.

The will can develop only when feelings are liberated. There is no will without freedom, and no freedom without will. If we try to externally impose freedom, it is not freedom. If we try to force or con others into developing will, they will not be able to sustain it, for it is not theirs.

A strong and free will includes a boundary that does not violate the free will of others, even "for their own good." Granted, there is such a thing as respectful intervention, but that path must be walked with exceeding care and thoughtfulness, or our efforts backfire. Each of us carries a deep instinct that values free will as much as the survival of the body. An individual may destroy the body if that is the only remaining avenue for freedom.

In the colonial days of the United States, Patrick Henry issued a political decree: "Give me liberty or give me death." His statement had an emotional impact that reverberated throughout the world and is still ringing in our ears. It is a powerful political statement because it is not just political. Patrick Henry was giving voice to the soul's desire for freedom. That desire emanates from a place that does not distinguish liberty from life itself. Patrick Henry and the rest of the colonial rebels were challenging the commonly accepted belief that liberty is a license granted by government. Freedom, though it is a laudable political goal, is not given to us by a political system; it is the product of a will that yields only to the truth emanating from within.

The Will of Iron

We cultivate a will of iron through keen awareness and respect for the truth carried by the feeling side of our awareness. This is the will doing what it does best – listening. Such a will cannot be broken by fear or discomfort. It cannot be distracted, deceived, sidetracked, or seduced by promises of riches, power, special privileges, creature comforts, or sensual pleasures. In the presence of truth, however, it yields completely.

This is how a weakened will develops into a will of iron; a will that does not yield to anything except the truth rising from within. The will that recognizes the true source of its strength is a will that has cultivated wisdom.

The truth that melts and reworks the will of iron is recognized in many cultures. In the Christian world, the truth of oneness carried by inner feelings has been depicted as a newborn infant resting in a stable. Purified will has been depicted as three wise and wealthy men, accomplished and successful in worldly endeavors, and adept in mystical and esoteric knowledge. These three men enter the stable and stand among the farm animals and peasants, bringing to the infant the fruits of their worldly endeavors. In essence, they say, "All that we have accomplished and all that we have built is for you. We stand before you, knowing that, in your eyes, we are not greater than these shepherds. We bow before this truth that you carry." These three wise men personify the will elevated to wisdom and nobility by bowing down and respectfully listening to the truth carried by feelings.

Chapter 12
Thoughts & Emotions

One of the functions of the will is to think. One of the functions of the feeling mind is to generate emotions. Emotions are feelings we can identify as fear, anger, sadness, and happiness. There are many variations or tones of these four basic emotions, but their basic identity is clearly evident.

We also have feelings that we would not call emotions. Instinct, intuition, empathy and inspiration are more ethereal and difficult to define than emotions. Nonetheless, these other feelings typically blend with our emotions. For example, the feeling of empathy may be associated with the emotions of fear, sadness, anger, or happiness. Furthermore, suppression of one feeling seems to result in suppression of all. Therefore, if we wish to sharpen intuition, receive more inspiration, and deepen our capacity to empathize, we must cultivate the ability to honestly address our everyday emotions.

IQ and EQ

Though we may dis agree on how to measure intelligence, it is none-the-less, measurable. Therefore, we can speak of a person's intelligence quotient or IQ. However, to apply similar standards to emotions is folly because, we are trying to judge things that function best when they are not judged.

If we try to test our emotions, they will "fail" the test. If we try to beautify them, they become ugly. If we try to make them more functional, they become less functional. If we push them away, they come back with a vengeance. A person who seems to "pass" an emotional test has simply succeeded in censoring emotions. In that regard, we are not really testing the emotions; we are testing the will's capacity to control emotional expression. We may question and challenge the rational mind because that is how make it sharp. However, with regard to our emotions, there is just one fundamental question - perhaps the only one worth asking: Are the emotions genuine?

In the Beginning

The story of the Garden of Eden may be viewed as an outer dramatization of an internal event. In one interpretation, the relationship between Adam and Eve represents the relationship between our thoughts and emotions.

Emotions do seem to flow in accordance with our perceptions and beliefs. That is why it is extremely difficult to try to change emotions directly. However, if we change the associated perceptions and beliefs, emotions tend to change spontaneously.

It is also true that a particular emotional pattern, once established, exerts a powerful effect on our everyday thoughts. If we look deeper, however, we see these established emotional patterns are maintained by perceptions and beliefs that have become so deeply entrenched over the years that we might not even know we have them.

Relationship of Thoughts and Emotions

The cognitive part of brain (cerebral cortex) works best when the emotional part of the brain (limbic system) is in a calm and happy state. On the other hand, as the emotional mind becomes increasingly agitated, clear thinking, discernment and problem solving become more difficult. This is why we might be taking a test; time is running out and we just can't come up with the answer to a certain question. But when the test is over (and we are more relaxed), we magically come up with the answer.

We can get a deeper understanding of the relationship of thoughts and emotions by, once again, examining the story of Adam and Eve. As the story goes, God created Eve out of Adam, so that Adam would not be lonely. Thoughts are, by their very nature, analytical; they tend to break things apart into ever-smaller pieces, losing sight of the big picture. It is the feeling of the mind which maintains contact with the wordless essence that unites all of life. It is with our emotions that we reach out and create relationship. Without such emotional contact, thoughts become reclusive, alienated and self-destructive

Emotions and Spirit

The importance of emotions in contacting our spiritual nature or essence is indicated by the attention that many religions place on emotions. The drawing power of most religions is not intellect or the power of reason. The typical religion is a set of rituals and techniques designed to access the emotions and cause them to flow in a particular direction. If the religion is ethical, the techniques are used in conjunction with reason to guide the practitioner toward the creation of a harmonious relation with God and the rest of life. This occurs through the natural evolution of emotional energy into spiritual awareness.

If the religion is not ethical, the same principles and techniques are used to emotionally imprint the followers to the religion, keeping them in a state of dependency. The same techniques that can facilitate the evolution of emotional energy into spiritual awareness can also be used to exploit emotional energy and arrest its evolution. Just as an unethical health care provider might not want the patients to get healthy too fast, short-sighted religious leaders may not want their followers to achieve spiritual freedom.

In other words, the followers might be maneuvered in such a way as to maintain emotional dependency on the religion. This is easy if the individual becomes a member of a religion at a very early age. Adults too can be imprinted through a slight-of-hand magic trick in which the followers are given emotionally impactful experience, a sense of wholeness, or a taste of freedom. Since the freedom was apparently provided by the religion, it really does not belong to the seeker; it belongs to the religion and its leaders. To the seeker, the experience of freedom and wholeness is tied to the religion. The experience can only exist within the context of the religious belief that housed the experience. This is one source of the common belief or attitude that says, "My religion is the one true religion."

The above paragraph is not an indictment of any religion or of religion in general. A given religion and its doctrines may be benign and ethical. The religion might be an effective system of techniques and principles for facilitating the natural evolution of emotional energy into spiritual awareness. How those techniques and principles are used is entirely up to the members.

Granted, there is wisdom in being entirely focused on one's own religion, as if it were the only one. Yes, it is the only one. It is the only one for *me*. This makes it easier for the individual to master the principles and techniques of that religion. This is true for any teaching, religious or otherwise. The more devoted we are to a given system, the more it will reveal its secret to us.

Deep devotion to a given religion, practiced intelligently and ethically, results in the cultivation of emotional serenity and spiritual awareness. Therefore, even though the individual is not tempted to "stray," there is a tendency to quietly respect the religions of others. On the other hand, when the methodologies of the religion are used to instill emotional dependency, the individual is likely to adopt the attitude that "my religion is the only true religion, and everyone else is deceived."

Resolving Paradoxes

The close relationship of emotions to spiritual awareness suggests that our emotions are indispensable for resolving the paradoxes we often encounter in religious and metaphysical exploration. Specifically, when we attempt to *think* our way beyond duality (beyond the play of opposites), we frequently encounter paradoxes and unsolvable riddles.

Most paradoxes are really not that mysterious; they are the result of thoughts dissociated from emotions. Paradoxes are the result of the cognitive nature trying to find meaning and understanding separate from the feeling-nature. The more we allow our emotions to dance freely about our well-disciplined thoughts, the fewer paradoxes we encounter. This is because our emotions and our feeling-nature in general, connect us with the great presence of Unity that religion tries to access.

We can begin to bring thoughts and emotions into deep synergy by methodically applying a simple formula: Question your thoughts and accept your emotions.

Question Thoughts and Accept Emotions

The ability to question thoughts and accept emotions is the key for maintaining sanity in daily living. A perception or belief can be either true or false and must, therefore, be questioned for validity. An emotion is neither true nor false; it simply is. When we allow our thoughts and emotions to co-exist in this manner, they tend to complement one another. The willingness to question thoughts allows emotions to flow more freely and genuinely. Likewise, acceptance of emotions gives us the serenity to question our perceptions and beliefs.

When we are at peace with ourselves, we generally do not have to make a conscious effort to question our thoughts and accept our emotions. Both happen spontaneously. When there is inner conflict or confusion, we can help ourselves by intentionally questioning our thoughts or accepting our emotions. It is not necessary to try to do both at the same time. In fact, that would probably be awkward. We need only tend to the one that seems to be calling for attention. The other follows naturally.

There are a number of specific ways of putting this principle into application. For example, if we get upset because the car will not start and we might be late for work, we can repeat over and over again, "The car won't start and I might be late for work." By focusing on the fact or physical event, our perception of it is likely to undergo a subtle change - it does not seem so terrible anymore. As our perception changes, the associated emotions are also likely to change.

The resolution of cosmic paradoxes is one result (and, really, a minor one) of integrating thoughts and emotions. The more tangible results are mental clarity and emotional serenity. Life becomes simple; relationships become simple, spiritual and religious practices become simple.

Simplicity is not well tolerated when thoughts and emotions are disconnected. Simplicity is the natural result of thoughts and emotions in a state of balance and integration.

Such simplicity does not preclude the evolution of complex ideas. In fact, when such learning occurs in the presence of emotional connectedness, the intellect evolves faster and more humanely. This is possible because the intellect is not used as a replacement for emotional connection. It is an *expression* of emotional connectedness.

How do we know we have attained such connectedness? Must we be overtly passionate about everything we do? Not necessarily. One way to know we have such connectedness is that, regardless of how complex our thoughts become, we still have the capacity to delight in simple things.

Thoughts and Emotions at War

When we reject our emotions, the result is a gradual erosion of self-esteem. We then try to compensate by rigidly holding on to our perceptions and beliefs. We see this more frequently and dramatically in religion, but it can also occur in other areas, such as politics, health care, and even in the domain that is supposed to be the bastion of objectivity - science. We also do this in our everyday existence. Just as we put on clothes to hide and protect the body, we put on perceptions and beliefs to protect our sense of identity and cover up our insecurity.

If personal identity and self-esteem have become deeply invested in a certain belief system, we will not stand quietly while it is criticized or questioned. We defend our beliefs like we would defend our mother. We become fiercely protective of our beliefs because they have replaced emotional truthfulness as a source of inner stability. The beliefs have also replaced intimacy as a source of nurturing.

Mental Laziness and Emotional Numbness

The unwillingness to question thoughts and accept emotions often shows up as mental laziness and emotional numbness. These two responses are closely related. What appears as mental laziness (the unwillingness to think for oneself) might be a defense against feeling hidden emotions. The presence of these suppressed emotions disrupts clear thinking. We reflexively close our eyes to anything that might evoke feelings that we do not want to feel. We do not allow our thinking to stray into areas that would trigger unacceptable emotions.

Mental laziness and emotional numbness, once established, tend to be self-perpetuating. It can reduce the individual to a robotic state. On the larger social level, this invites dictatorship. Populations of individuals who are mentally lazy and emotionally numb call forth social and political structures that can spare them from the toil of thinking their own thoughts and save them from the anxiety of feeling their own feelings. As long as everyone thinks and feels the same way, we have a sense of safety. This, however, becomes increasingly difficult as communication and travel encourage the mingling of different cultures and beliefs. As the world contracts, the mind must expand.

If we want to develop the ability to think for ourselves and enhance our emotional aliveness, we need only bear in mind that the two are complementary. Clear thinking supports and enhances emotional freedom. Emotional freedom supports clear thinking. We can see this in the functioning of the brain. The cognitive part of brain (cerebral cortex) works best when the emotional part of the brain (limbic system) is in a calm and happy state.

Worship of Emotions

Acceptance of emotions does not mean worshipping them. Worshipping emotions is the same as being addicted to emotions. When we truly accept our emotions, they gradually evolve into spiritual awareness, which is what they want to do. If this evolution is not allowed to occur, we are likely to become addicted to our emotions.

We can become addicted to anything that gives us a facsimile of serenity or a sense of aliveness. We can become addicted to chemicals, relationships, work and our own emotions. Addiction to emotions simply means they are not felt in fullness. The void that is created from not fully feeling our emotions causes us to silently crave them - we worship them. As with other addictions, the addiction to emotions causes us to become seductive and vulnerable to seduction.

Factoring Out Emotional Bias

When there is a need to interpret data, as in science or legal matters, the ability to question perceptions and objectively examine evidence requires that we factor out our own emotional bias. The way to factor out emotional bias is simply to be aware of it. The more we are in touch with our own emotions, the more capable we are of being objective. A conscientious scientist, who recognizes his own emotional bias or private agenda, is able to be reasonably neutral and objective, or, at least, recognizes that he is incapable of being neutral and objective.

The history of science and politics reveals that such objectivity has frequently been lacking. This is understandable. In the last several hundred years, civilization has placed little or no emphasis on the value of emotional connectedness. As a result, emotionally biased reporting has been more the rule than the exception.

Who's In Charge?

We are powerfully driven by our emotions, even if we think we are not — *especially* if we think we are not. The destructive behavior of the intellect in the realm of politics and technology is simply the result of repressed but still powerful emotions, secretly controlling the overtly dominant intellect. The repressed hedonistic nature of our emotional mind manifests as intellect striving to achieve self-centered political and economic goals at the expense of others. The expansiveness of the emotional nature, when repressed, manifests as intellect on an explosive path of imperialism and megalomania.

In summary, we often try to purge ourselves of our emotions, casting them out because we see them as dysfunctional, treacherous, hysterical and unpredictable. Yet, when we look deeply enough, we see that emotions get that way precisely because they *have* been cast out. The same emotional mind, when integrated with a strong and dependable cognitive mind, becomes quite predictable: it wants to create family and community.

Chapter 13
Intellect & Intuition

Intellect and intuition are the two side of discernment. Together, they serve as the internal radar which we use to navigate our way through life.

Intellect is a function of the will. Intuition is a function of the feeling part of the mind. Intellect is logical and rational, which means it understands things through gathering data through the senses, and then formulating conclusions which are consistent with the data. Intuition is not limited by logic or reason. It can draw conclusions independently of empirical evidence.

The intellect, as a function of the will, can be trained. It is capable of learning; therefore, it may be called our educated intelligence. On the other hand, intuition is inborn, it is part of our innate intelligence.

The intellect asks questions and then formulates answers that fit into the framework of linear time. It can discern how past events might influence the future. On the other hand, intuition does not ask questions. It is non-linear. Its comprehension is not limited by words, time, or space.

One of the functions of the will is to provide safe boundaries for our feelings. In so doing, the rational mind can receive the intuition included within those feelings. We have no tangible evidence to explain how and why we know what we know. We just know, the same way we know when it is time to empty the bladder; the same way we know we are happy or sad. Furthermore, this feeling might be so elusive that it cannot be traced to any specific emotion or body sensation.

Knowledge that is not derived through a balance of the will and feeling-nature remains incomplete or fuzzy. Lack of intellect causes knowledge to degenerate into fearful superstition and blind adherence to dogma. Lack of intellect means that knowledge consists mainly of disorganized information, rote repetition of a few sound bites, unsubstantiated beliefs, vague hunches and "experiences" that do not seem to add up to anything or go anywhere. All of which can have a strong emotional charge that makes it difficult to distinguish fact from fiction. Without intellect, it is virtually impossible to distill reliable objective information from fear, personal bias, and wishful thinking.

Likewise, if there is too much intellect and not enough intuition, knowledge simply grows into an ever-increasing body of information that becomes more complex, becoming lost in minutia, while distancing us from the sweetness and sense of wholeness that allows us to gaze upon Creation and declare, "It is good." The feeling-nature is what connects us to the rest of life. Without it, knowledge is eventually used as a fortress to separate us, and as a weapon to attack one another.

Curiosity

Curiosity is the meeting point of intellect and intuition. Little children, endowed with keen intuition, also demonstrate great curiosity. The child asks questions. The baby is intensely fascinated by mother's eyes, as if silently saying "This huge mysterious creature is myself, and it is different from myself." The baby's intuition knowing and intellect are merged as curiosity. This curiosity diminishes with age but persists throughout life; it is what drives the pure scientist.

In other words, pure intellect, the capacity to question and to gather and organize data, is not far removed from intuition. The drive to understand the world by questioning and looking for proof, emanates from the place within us that already feels its relationship to the rest of the universe, and wants to give birth to that knowing as a body of tangible, provable, recordable data.

When we take the time to understand the relationship between intellect and intuition, the two complement each other. It is not uncommon for scientists to admit that their methodical searching and eventual breakthrough began as an intuitive hunch or a dream. Dr. Einstein reported that he *felt* relativity long before he hashed out the mathematical proof.

Likewise, by using the intellect to question our own perceptions, we cultivate objectivity. Such intellectual honesty feeds back to the intuitive process, so we can distinguish genuine intuitive insights from the many forms of fake or fuzzy intuition, such as:

- *Wishful thinking:* "My intuition says she likes me," which really means, "God, she's pretty, I hope she likes me."
- *Self-fulfilling prophecy:* "I just knew the bank wouldn't give me the loan."
- *Relinquishing responsibility for one's choices:* "I feel we should spend some time together because we have a deep connection," as a cover for, "You have nice legs."

Since intuition rises out of the feeling nature, any sort of bias or unresolved emotional issues can obscure intuition. Intuition is strong and accurate when emotions are reported simply and honestly without condemning or justifying them. Likewise, intuition is influenced by unrecognized fears and desires.

Chapter 14
Sanity

One of my patients once gave me an interesting perspective on sanity. She said, "Sane people think they're crazy and crazy people think they're sane." Though she said it jokingly, the comical value of her statement is at least partially derived from its element of truth.

To say that sane people think they are crazy, calls attention to the fact that a heightened awareness of oneself can be troubling if is not accompanied by kindness toward oneself and others. Likewise, to jokingly say that crazy people think they are sane, calls attention to the fact that the inability to accept reality as it is, can result in a generalized state of denial; we create a facade of sanity to conceal inner chaos. We blind ourselves to inner inconsistencies that might be obvious to those around us.

Most of us have some degree of such inner inconsistencies. They become troublesome only when we habitually try to cover them up with a facade of normalcy and the illusion of certainty. The result of such denial is a gradual erosion of sanity.

Inner and Outer Sanity

We can get some perspective on the sensitive issue of sanity by remembering that it has both an inner and outer component. Inner sanity has to do with how we feel. Outer sanity has to do with how we behave. Inner sanity is simply a state of mental clarity and emotional serenity. Outer sanity refers to the ability to conduct oneself in ways which allow him or her to be free, autonomous, and functional.

The two are obviously related. Inner sanity provides the foundation for outer sanity. How we think and feel determines how we behave.

When thoughts and emotions are sufficiently dissociated or conflicted, perceptions no longer reflect reality and emotions become proportionately unbalanced. This can eventually translate into the inability to function and, perhaps, the tendency to harm oneself and others.

In everyday life, we tend to equate sanity with outer behavior, while ignoring the inner condition. However, in placing the emphasis entirely on outer behavior, our criteria for sanity usually drift away from autonomy to conformity. A person who controls their outer behavior sufficiently enough to fit into society is regarded as sane.

The Key to Sanity

The key to sanity is our willingness to question our perceptions and accept our emotions. These two complementary activities help us to maintain conscious contact with a certain indefinable feeling. It is the feeling embodied by the laughter of a child, the touch of a loved one, a home filled with laughter and trust, and genuine acts of kindness. This silent feeling is the keeper of inner sanity. The feeling is kept alive through the cultivation of honesty. Most of the stressors that challenge sanity are handled by just practicing truthfulness. When we are honest, we tend to question our thoughts and accept our emotions, resulting in mental clarity and emotional serenity.

The Causes of Insanity

As long as we are inwardly sane, we do not have to give much attention to outer sanity. The former organically creates the latter. Likewise, when we chronically neglect to question our perceptions and accept our emotions, inner sanity erodes; we lose touch with that feeling of serenity. Consequently, our perception of the outer world becomes increasingly warped, in a manner reflecting the inner turbulence. We then have to consciously control our outer behavior to keep it in the realm of what is considered sane by the rest of society.

Paradoxically, if we try *too* hard to appear sane, it can make us insane. As we try harder to maintain the outer appearance of sanity, our inner sanity erodes faster. This is likely to happen as long as we give greater importance to the outer appearance of sanity, at the expense of the inner condition.

In other words, we give up inner sanity because we value something else more. As one insightful songwriter once pointed out, "You're giving up your sanity for your pride and your vanity." To indulge in excessive pride and vanity, we must conceal or contort our truth, and live in a perpetual state of pretense. This is inherently stressful, contributing to emotional unrest and mental fogginess.

And yet, excessive pride and vanity are not to be cast out, for they are simply self-respect — distorted external pressure and frozen by neglect — waiting to be set free by truth. Harsh judgment of insanity is probably the single greatest obstacle to sanity. What we do not realize is that our seemingly twisted perceptions and unreasonable urges have within them the very energy we need to maintain sanity.

Even those fleeting morbid thoughts that embarrass or frighten us have the potential to uplift us to greater happiness and deeper serenity. Each of those dark specks of inner insanity contains energy and vitality waiting to be set free. If we curse them with rejection, they become a curse to us. If we bless them with honest recognition and kindness, they become a blessing to us.

Remembering Who I Am

The same songwriter mentioned above, implies that sanity is simply, "the serenity to just remember who I am." The process of discovering who I am or remembering who I am is difficult to evaluate from the outside, especially when we remove the usual outer criteria regarding what is sane and insane. We might be somewhat unpredictable and obey rules and customs only when we want to do so. Onlookers may experience this as a threat because it is difficult to say what the person who is *really* engaged in self-discovery will do next.

Such a person, however, is less likely to steal, kill, rape, cheat, injure or lie. Individuals who are really engaged in self-discovery do so by looking deeply within. The more deeply we look within, the more harmless we become.

Evil Spirit or Troubled Mind

"Evil spirits" means the cause of the problem is external. "Troubled mind" means the problem is internal. Internal and external. Therein is the duality. As with other dualities, we tend to place these two concepts at odds with each other, thus complicating the issue.

Are Demons Real?

Is it an outside job or an inside job? Are we troubled by evil spirits and dark clouds of "negative energy," or do our troubles stem from our troubled thoughts? If we attribute our distress to negative energies or evil spirits that encroach on us, we might light a candle, burn some incense, offer a prayer, or invoke the presence of a deity to kick out the offending spirit or transmute the objectionable energies. And, by golly, we feel better and life seems to flow more smoothly! Or we might look within; we tell the truth with regard to what we did to create the situation and perhaps do something to quiet the mind. And, by golly, we feel better and life seems to flow more smoothly!

In truth, most of us can come up with convincing arguments for either side of this issue. If, however, we cling to one and totally exclude the other, we are likely to face a situation that cannot be adequately explained by the side that we favor. Point of view can make us crazy if we adhere to it dogmatically. If we try to explain troubling or bizarre experiences in terms of psychology, while rejecting astral influences, we will have to conjure up increasingly convoluted psychological mechanisms to explain bizarre occurrences. On the other hand, the tendency to blame evil spirits and externally imposed curses and bad vibes can result in a state of paranoia. The fear simply increases because such eerie experiences tend to re-enforce the belief in astral influences. If we get too preoccupied with trying to keep astral nastiness at bay, we become increasingly entrenched in astral wars. The result of successfully fighting off demons is that we get to fight off bigger demons' next time.

One way out of this loop is to consider both sides. This is possible when the rational mind is in harmony with the feeling-mind. We are then free to dance from one polarity to the other without being inhibited by the fear of appearing inconsistent or fickle. We simply relax, rationally consider the evidence at hand, as well as recognize what feels true in the moment, unrestrained by what we think we *should* believe.

The absence of such externally imposed *shoulds* means the individual is free to gravitate to the side that seems most appropriate, while the other quietly retreats into the background, silently supporting the one on center stage.

Haunted by Guilt

Deep harmony of these two choices can lead to the awareness that is beyond the distinction between inner and outer. However, even before we experience that sublime state of unity, we can see that the two concepts are quite compatible. Those who claim to see or feel non-physical entities often agree that unfriendly spirits and "bad energy" seem to have easy access to a troubled mind. Our struggle with nasty spirits seems to reflect a deeper struggle with our own unresolved emotional issues, especially guilt. This is understandable because when guilt is severe enough, we are likely to obsess about anything, including evil spirits. Any sort of obsession suggests the presence of hidden guilt. The deeper the guilt, the deeper the obsession. When guilt is resolved, obsessions tend to dissolve.

Once the troubling spirits gain entry, (which simply means that they become real to us), it is counterproductive to pretend they are not real to us. Such denial simply deepens the struggle. A more workable solution is to acknowledge they are real to us, and then address the psychological issue (the weakness in our boundaries) that has allowed them to enter.

The nature of haunting spirits is such that we cannot seem to get away from them. This is understandable because guilt does not reside in any particular corner of the mind. Guilt is not just a lump that can be removed. Its influence is distributed throughout the mind, and it affects every aspect of life. We cannot feel guilty in one area without having it affect other areas.

This situation might seem hopeless because, like a haunting spirit that has latched on to us, guilt seems to follow us around and we cannot escape from it, no matter where we go. If we try to expel it, it seems to come back, perhaps stronger or subtler than before. The more we struggle against demons, the bigger they become. On the other hand, when we recognize our guilt without trying to make it go away, it is not so bad anymore.

As we learn to relate to our own troubling thoughts and emotions honestly and with a measure of kindness, we become more effective at handling the nasty spirits and bad energy that seem to haunt us now and then.

Dreams and Nightmares

The most common time to be troubled by unsavory spirits seems to be during sleep. There are two ways of addressing our dreams: from a Western or psychological perspective, or from an Eastern or multi-dimensional perspective.

From the psychological perspective, dreaming occurs during a phase of sleep characterized by rapid eye movements and the production of certain brain waves, known as beta waves. Some schools of thought, such as Jungian psychology, regard dreams as an attempt to integrate the emotional issues of waking life. Not surprisingly, as we handle our emotional issues more effectively while we are awake, our dreams tend to be more pleasant.

As our dreams settle down, we tend to spend more time in the deeper dreamless phase of sleep. This deeper phase is characterized by the production of brain waves known as delta waves. During delta sleep, we experience a deeper rest. It is during this phase of sleep that the body can most effectively regenerate. For most of us, healthy sleep includes a balance of delta sleep for physical regeneration and beta sleep for emotional integration.

If we consider the Eastern or multi-dimensional perspective, our existence can be roughly divided into three planes: physical, astral and causal. The physical plane corresponds to normal waking life. The astral plane corresponds to the beta or dream phase of sleep. The causal plane corresponds to the delta or dreamless phase of sleep. The causal plane may also be called the spiritual or transpersonal plane because we are not identified with physical form or the thoughts that define our personality.

Using the two phases of sleep described above, here are two ways of addressing the spirits and entities that trouble our sleep:

- During the day, we tend to business. We take care of the body, conduct ourselves honestly in our relationships, and do our work ethically and effectively. If we do these three things during the day, we will be more likely to have pleasant dreams during the night.

- Before going to sleep at night, we can give ourselves the suggestion that our dream-time will be used for resolving emotional and relationship issues. We can also give ourselves the suggestion to spend a goodly amount of time in the deeper delta phase of sleep (the transpersonal realm) beyond the reach of the astral drama. This can be done through prayer, meditation, or by just saying "deep delta sleep," over and over.

In other words, we can keep away the real or imagined demons by being very physical during the day and very spiritual at night. We let ourselves be very down to Earth during the waking time, and soar to the restful and dreamless transpersonal realms during the sleep time. The two are quite compatible and mutually supportive. The "higher" we go into the spiritual or causal plane, the more smoothly we flow through our physical existence. The more diligent we are about tending to the physical plane and spiritual plane, the more the astral plane tends to settle down.

Chapter 15
Austerity & Wild Abandonment

Austerity is an act of will. Wild abandonment is surrender to feelings. These two opposing choices dance and sometimes fight within the mind of most if not all civilized humans. We can get them to dance harmoniously, rather than fighting, simply by understanding them.

There is no conflict between them, provided that each is an expression of personal truth, rather than a suppression of truth. As with other opposites, each side ushers in the other. The individual who plunges into the depth of austerity discovers the deep desire to feel *alive.* The individual who is engaged in wild abandonment eventually feels the yearning to retreat.

If one side is not allowed to become the other in its proper time and season, the side to which we cling gradually degenerates. One side becomes a state of struggle, the other a state of yearning. One withers away from lack of use, and the other becomes depleted from overuse.

The two sides of this duality achieve harmony when the individual realizes that the preference for one over the other is just that, a preference. Such preference is to be respected, for it emanates from a wisdom that probably is not apparent to others and sometimes not even apparent to the individual. That same wisdom carries the knowing that our choice to do one or the other does not make us better than others.

Binging and Purging

When one side becomes excessive or dogmatic, it can easily lead to the excessive or dogmatic expression of the other side. The orgies of ancient Rome were followed by the exaggerated austerity of medieval Europe, where Christians engaged in deliberate acts of self-inflicted pain and mutilation. The medieval Christians believed that self-love is evil, and pleasure is dangerous, while poverty and suffering bring the individual closer to God.

Today, we might shake our heads at the pious barbarism of the Dark Ages, however, if we look deeper, we do find a core of truth in those extreme practices. Many individuals who endure great pain often do experience a breakthrough, followed by a sense of peace and fulfillment. Pain causes us to remove frivolities and break the armor of denial, so we can experience who we really are behind the mask. It is not the pain, however, that produces purification. It is the removal of pretense. When we lose sight of this, we arrive at the conclusion that painful penance must precede wholeness. Pain is unnecessary to the extent that we are attentive and truthful. To the extent that we are not attentive and truthful, we invite painful situations, which, in turn, compel us to be attentive and truthful.

Neither austerity nor wild abandonment produces the desired outcome (freedom) if used as a means of escape from truth. Any attempt to escape everyday reality through austerity or wild abandonment result in mutilation of the body. Either way, the individual is unconsciously saying, "I don't like who I am; I don't like where I am." When we chronically hide the truth, we tend to harm ourselves. On the other hand, when we use either principle wisely, there is a natural tendency to respect the body.

Wild Abandonment that Really Feels Good

When we seek pleasure as a means of escape, we typically go through the following dance: we harshly judge our experience of pleasure, thus we do not feel the fullness of it, so we indulge more and more, until we simply saturate our senses. The natural channels of pleasure quickly become insufficient, and we resort to more invasive ways of seeking pleasure.

On the other hand, when the will is pure, which means it is free of arrogance and harsh judgment, we can experience the fullness of feeling in every little moment of sensual pleasure, whether it is the delicate fragrance of a flower, the touch of a loved one, or a fascinating book? Without even trying, we ride the pleasurable feelings to their source, which is the feeling of aliveness beyond pleasure or pain. And we tend to do so in a way that respects the body.

Austerity that Really Works

Austerity, like wild abandonment, is about freedom. The call to do one or the other is simply a question of how the soul wants to experience freedom at any given time. Austerity works if we remember two important principles:

- Judging the opposite as inferior sabotages our efforts.

- If harsh judgment is present, austerity might trigger a crisis wherein we are tempted to go to the opposite pole. For example, a person who wants to lose weight might start craving rich foods and starts binging. The alternative is to persist beyond the perceived limit of endurance, which might produce a breakthrough wherein the person might expose the hidden self-hatred and makes emotional contact with the deeper desires. When we experience this sort of breakthrough, the thing that was tempting us is no longer that tempting. And, if we do indulge, the inclination is to do so in a way that is respectful of the body.

Union

The monk who goes deeply enough into austerity is naturally at peace with the individual who freely engages in sensuous experience. Such acceptance is not patronizing tolerance. The deep experience of austerity is an emptiness that is deep enough and vast enough to embrace all things. It is the silence that allows all voices to be heard. Such purity has so thoroughly let go of everything, and has become so free, that it can allow others to be free. Such austerity can cherish the sensuous experience, as the lover cherishes the beloved. The lover neither envies the beloved nor fearfully tries to convert the beloved into a facsimile of self. Granted, a monk who is a pure monk is likely to inspire others to follow a similar path. Such a monk, however, is simply creating an atmosphere in which others can see themselves. If we really are being ourselves, we allow others to be themselves.

Chapter 16
Change It & Let It Be

One afternoon, I was speaking with my friend. "Richard," who shared with me the following dream. In the dream, he was earnestly searching for truth and purpose. However, he was being followed by a ridiculous-looking creature that was distracting him. It had a greenish complexion and a goofy face that resembled a cow. Its behavior was nonsensical, irrelevant, undignified, clown-like, unpurposeful, and unfocused.

Richard tried to ignore the creature, but it kept following him. He then tried, through various means, to drive it away, but the creature kept tagging along, unoffended and undaunted by Richard's disapproval, continuing to act silly and whimsical, apparently out of touch with reality, and too dumb to feel rejected by Richard's disapproval. Finally, Richard shot him three times with a gun.

The creature bled. However, it did not even have the dignity to bleed properly. It just stood there, still smiling stupidly, with three streams of green fluid comically squirting out of its body. However, as the creature was dying — in a most goofy manner, Richard recognized it as a wise and benevolent deity from ancient Egypt. Richard was horrified. He realized that he had shot and killed the very thing for which he was searching and striving.

The meaning of the dream was clear enough to Richard. The creature represented aspects of his personality that he did not like. It represented all the inferior or irrelevant parts of himself that he was trying to eliminate so he could be the man he wanted to be. In his dream, he had failed to recognize that the things he sought were contained within the same qualities he was struggling to get rid of.

The Basis for All Change

Richard's dream dramatizes an ancient principle for changing oneself. The Bible states, "Your biggest weakness shall become your greatest strength." This principle is the basis for all inner change. It is the key for undoing any weakness, phobia or addiction.

When we are honest with ourselves, truth shows itself with ease and grace. To the extent that we are not honest with ourselves, truth is likely to appear in the guise of something that we might reject. To one who loves, truth appears in the form of the beloved. To one who hates, truth appears as the hated one. To one who is afraid, truth appears in a form that evokes fear. To one who is earnestly trying to change, truth shows up the call to things be.

Our journey through life includes knowing when to change and knowing when to let things be. The signal to do one or the comes through inner listening.

It's About Listening

When we listen deeply, we instinctively know when to initiate change and when to let things be. The side that is actively expressed is supported by the side that stays in the background. Furthermore, the individual who hears the inner call to change feels very much at home with someone who hears the inner call to let it be. They recognize each other and smile.

When we do not listen within, the two concepts appear to be contradictory, no matter how much we try to rationalize them into oneness. In the absence of deep listening, making a change takes the form of rejection, harsh judgment and forcing ourselves to do many things that we do not want to do. Likewise, "letting it be" may take the form of laziness, apathy and stagnation.

The ability to listen, like the ability to observe, is a function of the will. The will becomes the observer when it has been purified and deepened by the rushing waters of our genuine feelings. This observer is a magical observer because, in the very act of objectively observing the truth and letting it be, it changes.

Initiating Change

The science and art of focusing the will to produce outer change is very much a science and an art. It is a science in the sense that it involves a methodology and a set of principles and techniques that are available to anyone who cares to learn them. Initiating change is also an art, in the sense that we get better at it by applying the principles through diligent practice, the same way we learn how to ride a bicycle or hit a baseball.

However, there is a potential trap in using the mind to initiate change. If we consciously affirm, "I choose to double my income", it is quite possible that we are unconsciously affirming, "I choose to double my income because that's what I need in order to feel good about myself." In other words, we are unknowingly re-enforcing the idea that our self-worth is dependent on having certain material possessions or the ability to acquire those possessions. The implication is that if we do not acquire them, we have failed.

In other words, in our attempt to become the creators of our physical reality, we set the stage for the surfacing of our human feelings of inadequacy or impotence. Then, we might conceal these feelings behind a cloak of excuses. We frantically try to hide the shame of not having created the things that any self-respecting god ought to be able to create.

Such an experience gives us a golden opportunity to fine-tune our creative efforts. Our intention changes from, "I choose to double my income (so I can be worthy of love)," to, "I choose to double my income, *and* I am worthy of love." Rather than affirming," I choose to double my income (so that I can be happy)," we affirm, "I choose to double my income, *and* I choose to be happy." The message is clear. Happiness is not based on doubling my income. This perspective brings a measure of sanity and humanity to our worldly doings. Our acts of creation are no longer a brutal self-trial, but a journey of self-discovery.

As we cultivate the understanding that self-worth is not based entirely on achieving our goals, we become more adept at achieving our goals. To the extent that our self-worth is shaky, we tend to use outer achievements and abilities to cover our insecurity.

When we are keenly aware that we are basing our happiness on possession of some material object, we may discover that we no longer wish to acquire that object. The desire for outer achievements has reverted to its primordial form: the desire to simply know ourselves and be true to ourselves. Not surprisingly, in that place of honesty and self-acceptance, the elements yield to our will.

Creating Out of Thin Air

When I was a very young child, I used to try to create objects out of thin air and move things using only the power of thought. Somehow, I felt that I should have been able to do these things.

The above fantasy seems rather funny now, but perhaps the desire to levitate and manifest out of thin air is neither demented nor childish but comes from a deep memory or an ability held in dormancy. Those who have an active interest in such things are perhaps responding to that deep memory.

If the ability to materialize things out of nothingness exists within us, there is probably a good reason why the average person cannot do it. Perhaps, it is for the same reason that (most of us, at least) cannot survive without eating. Perhaps the ability is kept dormant in the quantum nooks and crannies of the subconscious mind because we simply want to experience something else right now.

Nonetheless, we can still be fascinated by the idea of precipitating an apple out of thin air and we would certainly be deeply impressed if we witnessed such an event. Even when we know that the sudden appearance of an apple is an illusion, as in a magic show, we are still fascinated. However, there is also the enjoyment of planting an apple tree; caring for it, watching it change from season to season, and seeing the apples expand as spring changes to summer and summer changes to autumn. When our capacity to feel is fully functional, we regard the apple growing on the tree as no less miraculous than an apple manifested out of thin air.

How to Practice Voodoo

Each of us practices voodoo throughout the day. Every time we have a thought about a fellow human, we are, in effect, creating a voodoo doll of that person within our own minds. We can do all sorts of things to that doll: we fight with it, play with it, bow down to it, have a conversation with it, have sex with it, steal money from it, deceive it, praise it. In essence, we treat the doll with kindness and respect, or we stick it with pins. We have within our minds voodoo dolls of every person that we are in relationship with.

Most of us would prefer to exercise our voodoo responsibly. So-called black magic refers to the intentional use of mind-power to harm or otherwise control another person. Such an act is ultimately self-destructive, for it flies in the face of a basic principle that governs all forms of giving and receiving: Whatever you do unto others shall be done unto you. In Pagan traditions, the act of invoking change begins with "making a circle." The circle symbolizes the inherent unity of the created universe. The universe is "spherical," therefore whatever you project out will return to you in some shape or form.

The only asset to be gained by the use of "black magic" is time. Black magic is a way of borrowing time. The skillful black magician gains more time and is, therefore, able to postpone consequences. And, since more time has been borrowed, more interest has to be paid.

One way we stop the tendency to unintentionally perform voodoo on others is to have no thought of them whatsoever unless we are in their physical presence. When we are in their presence, we can minimize the unintentional voodoo by simply communicating directly and honestly with them.

The alternative is to practice voodoo consciously by neither pushing the thought away nor clinging to it. We can imagine that we are placing that mental voodoo doll upon the current of the ever-present creative flow of the universe, often called the God of our understanding or the ambient and (quite intelligent) energy of the universe. When we do so, the mind becomes peaceful and we might feel a surge of power. If that peace or power could speak, we might imagine that it is saying, "Be not afraid of your own thoughts. Bring your thoughts and emotions of your brother/sister/friend/enemy unto me. And I will love them through you."

This is voodoo par excellence. This is essentially the freedom exercise practiced by the master alchemist/Christian saint/Buddhist sage who has learned the fine art of simultaneously *making the change* by *letting it be*.

Part III
The Outer Dance

Chapter 17
The Two Sides of Relationship

Chapter two describes how opposites interact by competing and complementing. The same may be said of the relationship between two individuals.

However, before we apply the dance of competition and complementing to human relationships, we must again, emphasize that two individuals cannot be "opposites." Opposites define one another. Two individuals cannot define each other. In other words, the wholeness of who you are cannot be understood through comparison with others. Your personality is rich and unique, having qualities which ultimately transcend duality. Therefore, you cannot "know thyself" through comparison with anyone else.

Two people, however, can have some opposing qualities. In fact, any two individuals will have a number of opposing qualities. To the extent that they do, they will recognize one another, as if looking into a mirror. Their awareness might be a nonverbal or emotional recognition, sometimes called "chemistry." This simply means the individuals have the potential to compete with and complement one another.

In a true complementary relationship, the two individuals enhance one another but cannot replace one another. If one party belittles the other or tries to usurp the power of the other, both sides lose. This does not mean that the competitive part of the relationship must be eliminated. It is simply integrated. The two parties can truly complement each other because the competitive part is ever present to question, confront, and challenge one another, so as to promote stability and balance. Such harmony is possible to the extent that each of the two individuals is in touch with a sense of self that is beyond duality, which means, beyond comparison.

When we are in touch with our silent essence, competing and complementing find their rightful place. We can compare ourselves to others and even compete, without becoming nasty or insecure. We can form healthy relationships with healthy boundaries because we sense that our wholeness resides within, not in finding another individual who fits or complements us perfectly. Neither do we frantically try to change ourselves or the other person so as to create a better fit. We can just relax and delight in our differences, allowing our many opposing qualities to reach out to each other and dance the dance of life.

Synergy and Intimacy

A complementary relationship has the quality of synergy, a condition wherein the whole is greater than the sum of the parts. Synergy does not just happen between two individuals. Any two or more people or things can synergize. When there is synergy, there is wholeness. All the parts integrate in such a way as to create something new.

With regard to two people in relationship, the capacity to complement one another goes hand in hand with the capacity to be intimate with one another. Intimacy simply means the individuals share a high level of honesty and trust. When we say that two individuals complement one another, we are describing how they function or work together. When we say they are intimate, we are describing how they relate emotionally.

In other words, when we speak of opposites in general, we say the two sides interact by competing or complementing. With regard to two individuals in a relationship, we can also say the two parties interact through competition or intimacy. Competition and intimacy are not mutually exclusive. The two tendencies flow and ebb organically in a relationship. In general, when the competitive instinct is allowed to express honestly, its natural tendency is to evolve toward intimacy.

The Evolution of Intimacy

The year was 1891. The cold wind blew briskly, and the rain fell steadily, as six men carried the coffin out of the church. Inside the coffin was the body of General William T. Sherman, who, twenty-six years earlier, had captured Atlanta, thus, crippling the Confederate army to end the Civil War.

One pallbearer was a sickly old man who was warned by his doctor not to attend the funeral because, in his condition, he ran the risk of contracting pneumonia and dying.

He attended the funeral anyway. Standing outside in the inclement weather, he even refused to wear a hat, out of respect for General Sherman. As the doctor predicted, the old man developed pneumonia and subsequently died. He had no regrets, however. As he lay on his bed, he was asked why he had risked his life like that. He simply said, "General Sherman would have done the same for me."

Who was that man? A fellow Union soldier? No. He was General Joseph E. Johnston, Sherman's Confederate counterpart in the Atlanta campaign. These two men, who had once tried to annihilate each other, had developed a deep respect for one another.

About one hundred years later, I found myself in a wooded area, northwest of Atlanta, not too far from the place where General Sherman and General Johnston had met in battle. I was holding an air-powered rifle that fired paint-filled plastic pellets that splattered on impact.

I stood with a group of thirty or so goofy-looking men wearing helmets, goggles, and heavily padded ponchos. I said to myself, "This is dumb; I don't want to do this." I soon realized, however, that my reluctance to play paintball had nothing to do with the dumbness of the game but rather my fear of engaging in competition and losing. So, I decided to participate, figuring it was good for me.

Eventually, I found myself running through the forest, sweating, growling, crawling on my belly and diving for cover to avoid the dreaded barrage of paintball pellets. Sometimes my team won and sometimes we lost. Either way, I thoroughly enjoyed the game as I participated in the hasty planning of strategies and attacks on the enemy fort. I even felt the thrill of personally capturing the enemy flag, racing with it through a volley of paintballs and diving over the wall, into the safety of our fort. I was very pleased with myself.

Later, we all sat around a huge campfire and had dinner. I soon forgot who was on which team, and the act of capturing the flag shrank into insignificance.

My experience with paintball showed me that underneath my fear and judgment of competition was a love of competition. This is not surprising. We often judge and fear what we secretly desire. Likewise, once we fully recognize how we enjoy competition, we discover the desire to relate to others beyond competition. When the competitive instinct is expressed honestly, it *wants* to evolve into intimacy. In other words, the element that creates intimacy (the seed of intimacy) is already present in the competitive instinct. That element is passion.

Competition & Passion

I once attended a seminar for men in which the speaker stated that men are driven by the desire to compete, while women are driven by the desire to form intimate relationships. Therefore, he concluded that woman are spiritually more highly evolved than men. Many of the men in the room objected to such a "sexist" idea. They became rebellious and angry — which ironically supported the speaker's assertion.

The speaker also stated that one of the ways men form deep friendships is by first engaging in competition, especially physical competition. This, according to him, is why women are superior; they have the remarkable ability to bond with one another without having to try to kill each other first. In saying this, the speaker was not engaging in "male-bashing. He was not belittling manhood. On the contrary, he was encouraging us to accept and even celebrate our completive nature as men, without trying to sugar-coat it with a pseudo-spiritual veneer.

The above generalization about men and woman is just that - a generalization. None-the-less, it is a useful generalization that highlights an important point. If we (men and women) reject or suppress our desire to compete, we block the road to intimacy. If we try to create intimacy by denying our competitive tendencies, we sabotage intimacy.

Competition is one way of expressing vitality and individuality. In attempting to purge ourselves of competition because we have judged it as inferior to intimacy, we also cut off the flow of our lively self-expression. The result is that intimacy goes out the window.

We are often quick to discard the fighter within us, unaware that the combative spirit has within it the potential for genuine caring and affection. It is like a chunk of metal ore that we might overlook because it looks rough and dirty, and so, we do not see that it contains gold. In our quest for love and intimacy, we (especially men) often perform a funny dance. We discard the fighter, wash our hands, make ourselves look pretty, and then approach the goddess of love and ask, "Where do I find intimacy"? And she serenely responds, "It is in the ground, exactly where you buried it."

To be intimate means we bring into the relationship all aspects of ourselves, including the part that likes to compete. If we keep that part secret, it competes in secret. If we hide that part in shame, it manifests in a way that brings shame. If it is rejected, it expresses itself in a way that creates rejection. If we think it to be destructive and malicious, it manifests in a destructive and malicious way. If we think that it is useless, it manifests in a way that causes us to feel useless. If we express it cleanly and honestly, it evolves into intimacy.

Competition & Self-Knowledge

The hidden motivation for competition is the desire for self-knowledge. In everyday life, competition provides us with the opportunity to experience ourselves by comparing and contrasting ourselves to others. Once we experience ourselves in this manner, the natural progression is to know ourselves within the context of intimate relationship. The latter inspires us the bring forth the deeper parts of ourselves which are beyond opposites, beyond comparison, and therefore beyond competition.

A major reason we might linger too long in the competitive mode is that we judge it harshly. We reject as being primitive and barbaric. On the other hand, if we simply recognize the competitive drive and allow it to unfold naturally, it evolves into the passion for self-knowledge within the context of intimate relationship.

The desire to compete stems from the desire to know oneself.

Compromise

Compromise is the middle ground between competition and complementarity relationship. In a compromise, each side accepts less than full satisfaction in order to accommodate the other.

Compromise is not necessarily good or bad. Compromise is healthy and wholesome when it rests on a firm foundation of values which cannot be compromised. In everyday life, this looks like the willingness to compromise by first refusing to compromise one's personal truth. Compromising truth generally means we are truthful only if it makes us look good or somehow gives us power over others. When we do this, our efforts to compromise break down. We might experience short-term success, but we eventually become inwardly unsettled and things tend to fall apart on the outside.

On the other hand, when we are mindful of our deeper values, compromise tends to work. Though we might make concessions, there is no feeling of having been cheated or deprived. We can happily haggle over prices and logistics, but regardless of the outcome, there is peace because we have not compromised or otherwise sacrificed the pearl of great price. In fact, when we refuse to compromise the pearl of great price, it seems to shine more brightly, emitting a powerful and inexhaustible energy that galvanizes our thinking and enlivens our relationships.

Compromise is healthy when each side has values which cannot be compromised.

Covert Competition

It is important to emphasize that accepting the competitive instinct does not mean that we merely tolerate its presence, as we might tolerate a naughty child. We are speaking here of a gut-level knowing that we really appreciate it.

If such integration of competition does not occur, we invariably try to get rid of it. However, since there is no place to put it outside of self, "getting rid of it" translates into putting it somewhere within oneself where it can't be seen. In other words, it becomes covert or unconscious.

When competition becomes unconscious, its power multiplies. It silently takes dominion. It frequently shows up as passive aggressive behavior. We smile sweetly and compete silently, disguising it as service, religious piety, altruism and other forms of spiritual one-upmanship.

Redirecting Competition

Just as covert competition is insidiously destructive, excessive competition has the obvious disadvantage of destroying both parties. Or they might just replay the scene again and again until they finally catch on.

When we allow competition to evolve into intimacy, we find clever ways of expressing our competitive instinct, so that, rather than destroying one or both parties, it leaves a legacy of relationship. Rather than having gladiators fight to the death, we have football games and pie eating contests. Rather than having feudal wars among power-hungry dukes who plunder each other's treasure, we have colleges competing for trophies and stealing each other's mascots. Rather than having a duel to the death, we have philosophical debates and games of ping-pong. These are all ingenious methods of recognizing the competitive spirit and allowing us to experience it free of harsh judgment, so that its power and potency can evolve into genuine expressions of intimacy.

Beyond Competition

Though most of us have some degree of competitiveness, it is possible to virtually transcend it. In the presence of such a rare individual, the competitive nature within us can do what it secretly yearns to do; it relaxes, for it does not feel diminished or harshly judged by such a master. There is no hidden message of "I'm better than you because you're competitive and I'm not." Obviously, such a hidden message can only be sent by someone who is very competitive and is in denial of it. One who is genuinely non-competitive sends a different non-verbal message: we are equal.

Chapter 18
Holding On & Letting Go

To understand the dance of holding on and letting go, let us ponder electricity. Electricity may be simplistically seen as the flow of electrons from one place to another. They flow because there is an excess of electrons in one place relative to another. The place that has an excess of electrons is said to be electrically negative, and the place that is deficient is electrically positive. The flow of electrons is called the current.

The operation of electrical appliances depends on the current, made possible by the excess of electrons on one end of the wire relative to the other end. This difference in the density of electrons is called the voltage or charge. The greater the voltage, the more intense the subsequent current.

In other words, to establish a flow of electrons, there must be a *holding on* so that a charge can be built up. This is how electrical transformers work. It is an electrical dam of sorts. It absorbs electricity, holds on to it so as to build up charge, and then releases the current of electrons at a greater voltage to do work that could not be done at the lower voltage.

Emotional Charge

On the emotional level, *letting go* is important to our health and well-being. If, however, we assert that letting go is better than holding on, we are setting ourselves up for internal conflict. Whether we know it or not, we routinely hold on and let go throughout the day. There is no formula that tells us when it is appropriate to hold on or let go; when to express and when to hold back, when to speak and when to be silent. We might hold on because of fear or because it seems like the more intelligent choice. Sometimes we do not know why we hold on or let go. We just do so instinctively.

She Tried to Make Herself Let Go

In my office, I once employed the services of a registered nurse/massage therapist. One afternoon, we were standing outside the office, chatting. At one point, she mentioned that she was feeling persistent stiffness and tension in her neck. After she treated the condition with various physical modalities, it still bothered her. So, she asked me, "What else can I do for it? I can't seem to make it let go."

Rather than addressing her question from a structural standpoint, I found myself intrigued by her statement, "I can't seem to make it let go." I had the impression that her choice of words gave a clue as to why the tension was persisting.

She had already pondered the idea that her physical tension was related to something that was bothering her emotionally, but again, her statement was, "I can't figure it out."

I suggested that she change her strategy from, *"making it let go"* to *"letting it let go."* I suggested that she might get to the emotional cause by shifting from trying to figure it out, to just relaxing and allowing the answer to emerge from within.

The following morning, she was radiant. The answer to her dilemma had come to her gradually on the preceding day. Not only had the tension totally released, but she was on an emotional high, feeling as playful as a child. She reported that her neck felt great and her entire body felt energized and limber. In other words, she felt rejuvenated.

She indicated that the tension in her neck was a resentment she had been unknowingly holding for five months—since her last birthday. At that time, her fiancé was not feeling well, and both of them were rather busy. As a result, they were unable to celebrate her birthday.

Like many individuals, she tended to refrain from -mentioning her birthday, while secretly hoping that someone would take charge and organize a party. She had felt very disappointed. However, she judged her emotional reaction as childish and inappropriate, so she kept it to herself and forgot about it.

Shortly after she had that realization, her neck problem cleared up completely and she felt wonderful. In her giddy and playful state, she called her fiancé and said, "I want to celebrate my birthday!"

She not only acknowledged her own birthday, but she had the audacity to ask for a celebration five months after the fact. Such behavior was very out of character for her.

If she had simply addressed the issue when it first came up, it probably would have been handled without much fanfare. Apparently, however, by withholding the truth and holding on to her emotional energy for five months, it silently built up a substantial charge. When she finally did let go, the released emotional energy resulted in a personal transformation that went far beyond the neglected birthday. She used the emotional charge that had built up over a five-month period to break through a wall of fear and inhibition that had been in place for years.

Was this just a temporary high? Apparently not. She remained visibly changed. Weeks later, she stopped what she was doing, and, in amazement, she declared, "I just realized, I love my patients!"

Speaking & Silence

We hold on or let go every time we make the choice to remain silent or speak. As with other opposites, speaking and silence have the capacity to complement one another. When we discipline ourselves to speak words that are honest, the mind can more easily go to the place of deep silence. Likewise, in silence we tend to bring forth words that are honest.

The absence of speech is one level of silence. A deeper level is stillness of thoughts. Such silence is golden, for it brings forth mental clarity. In stillness and silence, we are rejuvenated; we bring forth a sense of newness and a zest for life, as if we are seeing a sunrise for the first time. That sense of renewal is expressed as newfound power and clarity in our communication.

Things Held in Silence Increase in Power

Whether or not our silence on any issue is deemed as healthy or unhealthy, that issue will assume a more powerful presence in the mind. On the positive side, silence allows us to "incubate" and develop an idea before we finally express it. On the negative side, troublesome thoughts and emotions that are kept secret can become the powerful rulers of our reality. This is the reason for the everyday practice of tending to our own psychological health by expressing troublesome thoughts and feelings.

Sometimes, it is wise to refrain from talking about a troubling issue, provided it is done out of respect rather than fear or the need to control others. When a secret remains a secret beyond its time, it becomes a breeding ground for hurtful actions. This applies to all secrets, whether they are personal, social or political.

I Knew it, Until I Opened My Mouth

When silence is used intelligently and respectfully, it allows precious personal truths to rise naturally into the conscious mind. We may experience this during deep meditation, prayer or a quiet walk in the woods. We might awaken one morning with a clear sense of what God means to us. We may have a dream or vision that wordlessly reveals our purpose in life. Yet, if we try to express the vision in words, it often becomes meaningless. This is especially true if our intent is to use the insight to glorify ourselves in the eyes of others, or to belittle someone else.

Even if our intentions are sincere, speaking a truth prematurely can cause it to wither away. Truth, in its primordial form, is boundless and therefore wordless. The moment we speak it; we impose boundaries on it. This is why personal truth might require a period of silence, during which it can gather strength and take shape as words and actions that reflect the purity of that truth.

Chapter 19
Truth

With regard to the practical matter of cultivating sanity and creating harmonious relationships, truth is simple. It is just honesty. You do not acquire it by reading it in a book but discover it by inner listening. If you force yourself to accept an idea that does not ring true for you on a deep feeling level, the result is inner conflict, which then leads to outer conflict.

As described in chapter 1, truthfulness is one of the three great healers of the mind. When we feel a need for healing, we instinctively seek truth.

The Truth Instinct

When we communicate truthfully, we communicate lovingly. If our communication of truth seems to be consistently harsh or hurtful, it is not really truth. In other words, we are not being completely honest. When truth is chronically withheld, the result is that we harm ourselves, while neglecting our responsibilities and commitments to others.

The truth that sets us free is revealed to us when we stop trying to find it as a rational thought separate from feelings. Self-doubt vanishes when the rational mind accepts the simple task of putting words to the feelings rising from within.

Since feelings can change from moment to moment, so does our personal truth. Our truth is not something that we hold on to. It evolves. We give voice to truth as it unfolds before the witness of the rational mind. Personal transformation simply means that our truth transforms. In fact, one of the ways that we hold back personal transformation is that is the tendency to cling to old ideas that no longer serve us.

Truthfulness is instinctual. Mother Nature guides us into honesty by making it pleasurable, provided that the brain is allowed to develop normally. Truthfulness creates a sense of ease and a steadiness of the mind. The expression of personal truth has a simplifying and unifying effect on life. The expression of personal truth dissolves self-condemnation and its byproducts—denial, excuses and defensiveness.

The Boundaries of Truth

As long as we operate in duality, every truth has boundaries beyond which it becomes a lie. Likewise, a persistent lie is typically a truth that has violated its boundaries. Therefore, if we wish to expose a lie, we can do so most effectively by first recognizing its core or "seed" of truth.

To stretch the truth beyond its boundaries is to take things out of context or blow things out of proportion. When a truth violates its own boundaries, it must, of necessity, encroach upon a neighboring truth. When one truth tries to displace another truth, the invading truth becomes a lie. On the other hand, a truth that recognizes the value of a neighboring truth has reached wholeness. Neighboring truths can only be reflections of each other, each bringing to the surface what the other holds in secret. Therefore, to be at war with a neighboring truth is to be at war with a hidden part of oneself.

The concept of the "final battle," is one example of a truth that has exceeded its boundaries, thus becoming a lie. The final battle is the hypothetical event that will eliminate the enemy and bring lasting peace. World War I ("The War to End All Wars") and World War II are two recent historical examples of final battles.

Perhaps the reason we keep falling for the lie of the final battle is that we do not recognize its core of truth. The lie is that we will have lasting peace when we finally defeat the external enemy. The simple truth within the lie is that we will have lasting peace when we no longer *require* an external enemy.

We may be tempted to point an accusing finger at the fanatical groups that push the idea of the final battle, but they are simply acting out a gross caricature of a basic truth the rest of us have denied. There is, indeed, a "final solution." It is the calm recognition of our mutual need to have an enemy, a need that is so deeply engrained and so pervasive that it influences us in every area of our lives, political and otherwise. It is not to be condemned or justified. It is to be simply recognized for what it is: the secret belief and deep fear that if we do not have an enemy to push against, we would have no purpose. No external enemy means we will have no way of establishing our worth. In other words, the absence of an enemy is experienced as the threat of stagnation, no energy, no vitality.

The moment that we simply recognize this hidden belief and associated fear; we begin to tap into a more abundant source of energy. When we experience our primordial aliveness —when the soul feels its worth—we do not need an enemy to validate and enliven our existence.

Another historical example of a truth that has become a lie by exceeding its proper boundaries is the concept of bringing unity to humanity through the advancement of racial purity or perfection. The perversion says that unity can be achieved if the pure and perfect ones among us take power by wiping out, or subjugating the inferior ones. The perversion tries to force its image of unity, purity, and perfection on the rest of humanity. The core of truth within the perversion can be accessed as a simple feeling. It is the feeling of looking at others and seeing oneself. When this feeling shows up powerfully, it is associated with a sense of personal freedom, as well as a sense of warm connection with others; a connection that makes life sweet and precious. Such a pure vision of Unity has been reported in the accounts of saints and sages of various cultures, including heavy hitters like Jesus Christ, the Buddha and Saint Francis of Assisi. It is not unreasonable to suggest that this is the purity and perfection we are all evolving to. Such truth many be called truth with a capital T.

Truth with a Capital T

Truth which can be spoken has boundaries. Truth with a capital T has no boundaries. It resides beyond duality, therefore cannot be fully described in words. Like the God of the ancient Hebrews, it is nameless and faceless. In ancient China, it was called the Toa, but the masters remind us that the Toa which can be spoken is not the real Toa. Like the "living water" described by Jesus, it has no shape or color, but is very much alive.

Truth with a capital T is available to us as a feeling. It is a feeling which makes life meaningful. It makes life worth living. It gives us the will to live. And, it inspires and motivates us to treat others as we would want to be treated.

Since we are social animals, we try to capture that feeling in words, such as the Ten Commandments and the Golden Rule. It has also been codified into political doctrines, such as, "We hold these truths to be self-evident, that all men are created equal, that they are endowed by their Creator with certain unalienable Rights, that among these are Life, Liberty and the pursuit of Happiness."

The verbal rendering of wordless Truth allows us to use put it into practical application. We can use it to guide us in our relationship to each other, and to maintain a stable society. However, the moment we do so, the truth we speak can also be used as a tool for deception.

Deception

Whether we chronically lie actively by distorting truth, or passively by withholding truth, the result is that life seems to become less pleasant. In fact, truth that is habitually withheld often explodes into violence. If it does not lead to overt violence, it lingers as covert hostility, often taking the form of resentment or gossip. Habitual lying produces tension and eventually leads to fatigue, depression, and self-hatred. If we are attentive enough, we may notice a feeling of deprivation. We then devise methods of alleviating the pain and filling the void, such as loud music, drugs, excessive work, excessive play, etc.

Not surprisingly, deception is associated with addiction. In fact, we might say that habitual lying *is* an addiction. If the nervous system is allowed to develop naturally, the individual finds pleasure in telling the truth. Truthfulness is one of the ways we emotionally nourish ourselves. On the other hand, if the individual has learned to equate truth with punishment, the only way of experiencing safety and normalcy is through deception. The approach of truth produces panic and disorientation not unlike an addict withdrawing from drugs.

As mentioned earlier, when a drug is taken as an escape from a painful situation, the experience of euphoria (the "rush") is partially due to the experience of no pain. If a person is in a constant state of physical and emotional pain, the deadening of that pain (by any means) is experienced as "pleasure." Deception creates the same rush of pleasure. It is simply a momentary relief, a sense of safety or power produced by the absence of threatening exposure to truth. This is why addiction of any kind must be accompanied by an addiction to deception, especially self-deception.

Yet, the core desire to express the genuine self is so strong, that it eventually overpowers any attempt to suppress it. To the habitual liar, the thing that is feared the most is the same thing that is deeply desired: recognition. Those who chronically engage in deception eventually start leaving subtle clues. This may be done as an oversight, or intentionally as a way of being cute or clever. The longer we remain hidden, the more obvious the clues become. The liar/criminal, who absentmindedly or mischievously leaves clues, is acting out the baby's need to be recognized and appreciated by mother (Life).

As we might expect, many spiritual teachings encourage us to practice truthfulness and reject deception. However, rejection of deception causes truth to be shallow, while deception silently dominates. With any pair of opposites, the side that is rejected secretly rules. Therefore, if we *really* we want truth to be a powerful force in our lives, we must *understand* deception, rather than merely rejecting or condemning it. We can understand deception by examining it from both the psychological and energetic perspectives.

The Psychology of Deception

Deception is a way of maintaining secrecy. The individual practicing deception has decided that complete candor would not be beneficial in a given situation. He or she is perhaps afraid that the expression of truth will be rejected, attacked, misunderstood, or that it might simply prevent him or her from achieving the desired outcome.

We frequently arrive at this conclusion unconsciously. If we are conscious of it, we do not label it as deception, because deception is considered bad. Instead, we give it other labels: "being discreet," "polite," "considerate," or "shrewd." In other words, our assessment of the situation leads us to conclude that, for one reason or another, full disclosure would not be beneficial. We might very well be right. However, when we judge it harshly, we tend to do it unconsciously, as well as more frequently. The alternative is to do it consciously. Rather than denying that we are engaging in deception, we can simply relax and recognize that sometimes, in our estimation, deception has value. By thus de-vilifying deception, we simply play it out without condemning it, justifying it, or denying it. In essence, we say, "Right now, I'm withholding my true thoughts and emotions." By doing so without condemnation, we begin to resurrect the natural inclination to tell the truth.

Fake it 'til you make it is a way of lying consciously. We know we are faking it; we know we are wearing a mask, and we give ourselves permission to do so. *Fake it 'til you make it* means we are acting. For example, when we act polite, we are acting out the form of love without necessarily feeling genuine love. However, if this is done with no condemnation, justification, or denial, we are performing a powerful shamanic practice; we soon begin to feel genuine love.

The Energetics of Deception

A child dams up the flow of water in a gutter or a creek and lets it accumulate so as to experience the fun of breaking the dam and watching the water rush through with greater force. I have childhood memories of myself as a busy little beaver, joyfully placing rocks, mud, and other debris in the path of a stream, letting the water accumulate into a good-sized pool, and then breaking the dam with one swipe of the hand or foot and watching the water flow furiously out, washing away other debris further downstream. If an adult had walked by and asked me why I was doing that, I would have shrugged my little shoulders. It was just a neat thing to do!

In a similar manner, as adults, we might unconsciously hold back our emotional waters by actively lying or passively withholding truth, to let the energy build up so that we can have the thrill of watching them burst forth at a future time. In other words, holding back the truth results in the accumulation of pent-up energy in the body and mind, setting the stage for the pleasurable release of that energy. This can actually be very therapeutic. The point is; by removing the harsh judgment from deception or secrecy, we can understand and even appreciate it. When we do so, the energy that is bound up in deception or secrecy is set free, which is what it wants. In the presence of love, all things reveal their secrets to us.

Chapter 20
Giving & Receiving

Relationship is about giving and receiving. Ultimately, what is given and received is energy. In order for life to flourish, energy must be given and received. On the ecological level, the dance of life is an intricate ballet of transforming energy, as it moves from one living system to another.

Relationships are harmonious to the extent that giving and receiving are balanced. Balanced means that each individual give and receives what they want to give and receive. It is that simple. However, simple is not the same as easy. How we give and receive in our everyday relationships is linked to our most intimate and private beliefs about ourselves. How we give and receive has roots that reach down to our infantile needs and into the places of deepest fear. Such psychological baggage is mostly hidden; we discover it only when we stumble over it, usually while we are interacting with one another.

The inability to give and receive is quite painful. And rightfully so. Pain is Mother Nature's alarm, telling us that something needs our attention. In order for life to flourish, there must be a continuous giving and receiving of energy. As humans, we are not exempt from that law.

The serious inability to give and receive is like the two edges of the same inner dagger that silently rip the emotional nature of the individual. If this condition is not resolved, it forces us to escape into isolation and addiction. We do anything to numb the pain of not being able to give and receive.

Pure Giving and Full Receiving

Within every one of us is the potential (and the desire) to give purely and receive in fullness. Pure giving is giving with no strings attached. Receiving in fullness is receiving free from any lingering sense of obligation to "pay back."

The ability to give purely and receive in fullness results in a feeling of pleasure which can spill over into a sense of wholeness beyond the usual experience of pleasure and pain. It is simultaneously deeply personal and transpersonal. It is the laughter of a child; it is the tree receiving freely from the earth and sky, and giving freely to the earth and sky; it is two lovers, one penetrating the other, while, on a deeper level, each penetrates and is penetrated by the other; it is the mother giving and the infant receiving, both unobstructed by the notion of indebtedness; it is the divine command, "Let there be light...and let that light take form as the laughter of a child, the fruitful tree, the embracing lovers, the mother nursing the infant, for that is who I am."

When we give purely and receive in fullness, we are fully alive. When we fully alive, we want to bring forth new life. We are programed by Mother Nature with the desire to give to life more than we have received, as described in chapter 6.

Pure giving can only happen in the presence of full receiving. The two are ever united, and, regardless of appearance, they are symmetrical. If person A gives, but person B does not receive it graciously, the giving probably was not as pure as person A believed it to be.

Doing Harm with Giving and Receiving

We do harm to ourselves and others when we try to give with the hand that really wants to receive or receive with the hand that really wants to give. To attempt to receive when the real desire is to give, is to harm oneself through self-indulgence and frantic pleasure-seeking. These are simply attempts to cover the pain of withholding the gifts we are yearning to give. It is like withholding the birth of a baby in the womb. The withheld energy becomes toxic in the system, causing degeneration of the body and mind.

Likewise, to attempt to give when the real desire is to receive is to give from a sense of lack. The act of giving from the place that really wants to receive generally translates into intrusion and interference. When we hide our desire to receive, we become a bottomless pit that cannot ever be filled. On the other hand, when we recognize and embrace the desire to receive, the bottomless pit becomes an inexhaustible fountain of vitality from which we give purely. We find that we are simultaneously giving in a way that does not diminish us, while receiving in a way that does not diminish others. And so, life is enriched.

Things of Value

Things of value may be placed into two categories: Things that can be stolen, and things that cannot be stolen.

Things that can be stolen are tangible items like cars, money, watches, television sets, ships, airplanes, etc. In other words, they are possessions that occupy space and exist in linear time; therefore, they can only be in one place at one time. If we give some of these items away, they are no longer available to us. Therefore, we are mindful of how much of this stuff we give away. When we do this, we are not merely looking after our self-interest. By being skillful and ethical in managing our perishable treasures, we open the door to the experience of treasures that cannot be stolen.

Things that cannot be stolen include joy, laughter, kindness, and truth. Since these treasures do not take up space and are not subject to the limitations of matter, they can be shared freely without being diminished. In fact, they appear to increase every time they are given away.

We might argue that these intangible treasures *can* be taken away, but this can happen only to the extent that our giving has hidden strings attached to it. Those strings may be so well hidden that the giver may not be aware of them, until someone pulls on them.

Giving With Strings Attached

Hidden strings are created when we give with the expectation of receiving something in return. This is not necessarily harmful, unless we our trying to give from the place that really wants to receive. This is when our giving translates into interference. This is when we become heavily invested in having people respond a certain way.

Even when we are not involved in tangible forms of giving and receiving, hidden strings can still be present in the form of emotional expectations. In essence, we invest our happiness in someone else's behavior. If they behave one way, we are happy; if they behave another way, we are unhappy. The more of these strings we have, the more easily our happiness can be "stolen" by others. Likewise, the fewer strings we have, the less likely that anyone can steal our intangible treasures.

However, even if someone does manage to maliciously or accidentally "steal our joy," the thief cannot have it either, because the only way to steal such a treasure is to destroy it, so that no one can have it. The good news is that such a theft is only temporary. Inner joy is like a plant whose roots are exceedingly deep. Cutting the flowers and stems simply makes the roots grow deeper.

I am not implying here that all such emotional strings are unhealthy. On the contrary, when we have affection for others and trust them with our feelings, they, in essence, hold the "strings" to our hearts. Therefore, their scorn or indifference can leave us feeling crushed or betrayed. On the positive side, the vibration of those same strings creates the sweet and tender music of deep intimacy. What we *can* do is exercise some discernment with regard to who we allow to hold our emotional strings.

Giving and Receiving Love

When affection is deep enough, we do not merely feel close to the other person. There is a silent feeling of being part of each other. The emotional strings seem to have no discernable beginning or end.

Furthermore, if we look closely at those very long strings, we cannot help but notice that they seem to carry a quality or essence that can apparently exists independently of those emotional strings, like electricity can exist independent of the wire. The most common name given to that essence is love, which obviously requires its own chapter.

Chapter 21
Love

On the mental level, love is a formless abstraction that we cannot see, hear, taste, or smell. Therefore, if we try to comprehend love on a strictly mental level, it has as much meaning as the color blue to a blind person. On the feeling level, the experience called love is as real as an orgasm. It is typically experienced as a form of vitality, an energetic presence that is given and received. When the feeling part of the mind is sufficiently open, that current of energy can rush through with a force that causes our most cherished ambitions and beliefs to behave like a house of cards in a tornado. More commonly, however, that same energy moves through the feeling-mind like a gentle breeze that rarely calls attention to itself, but shows up as affection, devotion, a flutter of the heart when that special someone enters the room, a sense of being nicely connected to someone, or simply a feeling that life is worth living.

On a more mystical level, all of our words about love ultimately fail us. We can easily describe love if we look upon it as a sort of energy that takes form as our thoughts, emotions, and behavior, just as we can detect the presence of electricity as it morphs into the images on the TV, music on the radio, or the spinning of a blender. However, to describe the *essence* of it is another matter entirely.

The source of difficulty is revealed if we look at one of the more common assertions about love. It is the idea that love, on the highest level, has no opposite. At this level, our perception of love as a kind of energy starts to break down, because energy is not energy without opposites.

Since we think in opposites, it is virtually impossible to describe in words something that, according to mystics, has no opposite. The only way we can even discuss anything that is truly singular is to mentally create, or imply the existence of, an opposite. We do this routinely when we attempt to understand such concepts as God, spiritual awareness, infinity and love. This is entirely acceptable (it has to be we do not have any choice in matter), as long as we realize that, in the very act of naming and defining love, our knowledge of it is incomplete. However, even with such intellectual honesty, any definition of love is likely to be extremely fragile and crumbles in our hands if we hold it too tightly or stare at it too hard.

Love and Truth

The good news is that, on the everyday human level, calling forth love is really simple. Love rides in on the wings of truth. It works every time. To hold back truth is to hold back love. When we are fully genuine, we need not be concerned about having love, for we are *being* love.

On the other hand, when truth is denied, simple acts of love are overlooked. The home is neglected, the body is neglected and work is neglected. The father who denies his truth neglects his family. The mother who denies her truth neglects her children. On the other hand, when we are truthful, we tend to give loving care and attention to the body, the home, and our loved ones.

In the presence of truth, the otherwise formless essence called love takes form as tangible qualities that we give and receive in our everyday relationships, qualities that we can see, hear, taste, smell, and feel deeply.

To know is to Love

From a practical standpoint, love becomes real in our relationships when we see that it is inseparable from knowledge. In the presence of false knowledge, love is also false. We think we love someone when we might simply be infatuated with the false image we have of the person. False knowledge occurs for one of two reasons:

- We have a hidden need to see the person or situation in a certain way. Therefore, we tend to block any information that does not fit our image.
- Defensiveness might prevent us from admitting our ignorance. Therefore, we make up things. We are tempted

to cover the unknown with false or incomplete information.

The unity of knowledge and love also applies to oneself. To love ourselves to know ourselves. The more we know ourselves, the more we can love ourselves, and vice versa.

Historically, love of oneself has been called the greatest love and the greatest folly. Both carry a measure of truth. It is a folly if we attempt to love ourselves without knowing ourselves. Such expressions of self-love typically translate into self-deception, self-indulgence, avoidance of responsibilities and disregard for others. If self-love is understood to be inseparable from self-knowledge, self-love translates into respectful relationship with others. We know what we are responsible for and what we are not responsible for. Commitments toward others are made naturally and fulfilled graciously. And, if our less-than-perfect self-knowledge and self-love, cause us to accidentally step on each other's toes, we can still be awake enough to apologize, make amends where appropriate and move on.

If loving ourselves seems difficult, perhaps we simply do not see the connection between self-love and self-knowledge. Perhaps we do not love ourselves because we have a false image of ourselves. Likewise, if we seem to be having a hard time seeing ourselves clearly, perhaps we are blocking knowledge because we do not love ourselves sufficiently to see the various hidden facets of ourselves without freaking out. Either way, there is a need to see the unity of self-love and self-knowledge.

Unconditional Love

One evening my, then, future wife and I were sitting at the kitchen table talking about unconditional love. At one point in our conversation, she began experiencing something akin to a full-body orgasm (I was not touching her). This was followed by an amazing flow of words from her mouth:

"We do love ourselves, completely, and unconditionally, right now. So, in learning how to love ourselves, we are simply remembering that we already love ourselves, and our very presence here on Earth is an expression of that great love… In the beginning, we were filled with love, and that cannot ever change… Every breath I take has purpose. Every word I speak, every deed I perform, everything I see and hear and feel has purpose. This is way beyond not judging. This is a gut-level knowing that everything I think and speak and do, or witness others think and speak and do, is sacred."

After speaking for a while, she fell silent. I did not say anything, because I was busy writing down her last words. The only sound in the room was the ticking of the clock. Then she resumed.

"Every tick of the clock is sacred," she declared. "Every judgment is sacred! Non-judgment is sacred! We loved ourselves so deeply from the beginning, that we gave ourselves the great gift of this life and every detail in it. When we fully realize what a great gift of love this life is, we are then complete with it, and we move on to the next life which is also a great gift of love…"

I frantically tried to write down her words, as she paced around the kitchen in a semi-trance. I did not dare ask her to slow down.

"…And the whole evolution of life is love," she continued, "which was at the beginning as it always will be, while, simultaneously, it is ever changing and unfolding moment by moment. This is the paradox of love. It is as it has always been, and always will be, even as it unfolds and changes with every breath we take. This knowledge, this amazing awareness, has always been in me. I'm simply recognizing it again right now, in a way that I have never recognized it before."

Just when I thought she was done, she cranked up again. So, I grabbed my pen and resumed writing like a mad man:

"We are simultaneously unique individuals and exactly the same, unfolding and discovering exactly the same thing, each in our own way. This is not a truth that we grasp with the logical mind. It is a feeling that we surrender to, moment by moment. Every thought, feeling, action, inaction is just the truth of God I Am. And this is why we do not really have to eat or drink. All energy and all life emanate from within us, from every cell. We are forever self-sustaining. When we remember this fully while we are within the physical body, our bodies too will be self-sustaining, needing nothing from the outside to keep them going. Our apparent need for food and water is a creation of our beliefs. And this, too, is sacred…it was from love that we chose our human experience."

Unconditional Love in Everyday Life

In everyday life, we can understand unconditional love (somewhat) by comparing it to conditional love. As with other opposites, as long as we do not try to make one superior to the other, both find their rightful place in our lives. Under the light of mutual illumination, we understand that unconditional love is infinitely inclusive, while conditional love has boundaries. Unconditional love is pure giving. Conditional love is giving with some strings attached.

Both have to do with knowledge. It is not so much a cognitive knowing as it is feeling-level recognition. There is a feeling of kinship or connectedness that shows up tangibly as respect, caring, and affection.

Conditional love is a form of partial recognition and, therefore, carries some potential for separation. In other words, there are conditions under which the bond can be broken. Unconditional love is the essence of love that mystics and philosophers speak of or try to. To love unconditionally is synonymous with complete recognition. When we are moved by unconditional love, we have a sense of knowing that is so deep and vast that it can encompass any possible situation that might threaten the connection.

Most of our expressions of love have some conditions. For example, if we give love and it is not gracefully received, we might feel hurt or angry. Conditional love also implies preference, boundaries, and discernment. Most of us would agree that it is healthy to respect one's preferences, but if we have a hidden belief that conditional love is somehow inferior to unconditional love, we are likely to deny that having preferences is synonymous with conditional love. Most of us would also agree that it is healthy to have boundaries and show discernment in giving affection, but we might deny that our discernment is an expression of conditional love.

In other words, although we do the healthy thing of respecting our own preferences, we conceal from ourselves the simple fact that we are practicing conditional love. By not recognizing that our personal boundaries and preference are the same as "conditions," those conditions remain and may become covert power tools. For example:

- We might justify our behavior by calling it "preference," while condemning the same basic behavior in others, by calling it "conditional love."
- We might think that we are being kind to someone out of unconditional love, while we are unconsciously trying to maneuver them into doing what we want them to do.
- Our show of affection toward one person might be a way of buffeting ourselves against another. For example, two or more people may unknowingly bond to one another as a way of forming an alliance against a common enemy, and call it love.

Having thus used love as a control tool, we add to our secret guilt, and therefore have more motivation to keep hidden the conditional quality of our love. Consequently, we look into each other's eyes and say, "I love you just the way you are," even as the chest and tummy get tight, breathing gets shallow, the bowels slow down, blood vessels constrict, tissues are deprived of oxygen and become cluttered with waste products, and the body dies a little.

On the other hand, we might say, "Yes, my love is conditional, and these are my conditions." This is when breathing becomes deep and even, the stomach relaxes, blood vessels dilate and the body regenerates. This is love in action.

How to Cultivate Unconditional Love

If love is energy, unconditional love is "free energy." It flows from a battery that is ever charged. It is the eternal positive pole making love to the infinite negative. It is the product of a holy fullness rushing in to fill the sacred emptiness. The resulting current of energy flows efficiently because the channel has zero resistance—the ultimate superconductor.

How accurate is this model? As accurate as it can be, given that it still depends on the interaction of opposites. However, from a practical standpoint, it will do. We tap into this infinite dynamo when we participate in relationships in which we give to someone with absolutely no strings attached. Or we might imagine that the string is a super-string that is so long and strong that it cannot break or become restrictive. From the energetic standpoint, there are no conditions under which we would block or resist the flow.

If you are aware of such a relationship in your life, just contemplate it, give thanks, and feel the flow. If you are not aware of such a relationship, contemplate it anyway, and it will, more than likely, appear at some point; maybe in a manner that you would not anticipate.

The key is to not force it. Forcing it translates into resistance, which results in a loss of energy. In human terms, the great paradox is that the harder we try to love unconditionally, the more we block it. Unconditional love is about allowing; it needs no help; it simply needs no interference. If unconditional love is preached as a doctrine that we try to force on ourselves and others, it becomes meaningless. In everyday life, the simplest way to invite unconditional love is by allowing it to emerge organically and in a way that is natural for the individual. We do this by just being honest about our conditions.

Chapter 22
Sexuality

Even if there is no sexual intercourse, the inner flow of sexual energy is a dance of opposites. In the case of sexuality, it is a dance between energy that is hot and impulsive and energy that is cool and stable. The two yearn for one another. The hot impulsive energy searches for a home where it can be nested, while the cool stable energy is looking for the spark of life. And, like any dance of opposites within a living system, the flow of sexual energy has to create something, one way or another.

Terror through Denial

Sexual energy can be the focal point of silent terror and psychosis largely due to our repression of it. A number of authors agree that sexual repression contributes to prostitution, pornography and child molestation, as well as subtler forms of sexual abuse. For example, Montak Chia, a teacher of Taoist healing techniques, writes, "In my travels, I have noticed that prostitution seems to flourish side-by-side with the most fanatic religious communities." The same author noted that Switzerland had fairly tolerant attitudes toward sexual expression, as compared to the bordering country, Italy, which traditionally controlled and censored sexual expression. He pointed out that the incidence of sex crimes, pornography, and prostitution were far more prevalent in Italy than in Switzerland.

We might also add that, as of this writing, Sweden, which has a tradition of sexual openness, has the lowest rate of teen pregnancy of any Western nation.

A Source of Power

Montak Chia and other authors agree that if we explore sex on its deeper levels, beyond the shame, power games and exploitation, we discover a source of creative and transformative power that goes well beyond biological procreation and "feeling good."

Through the ages, many religions and spiritual disciplines have recognized this power, and have tried to control or cultivate it through celibacy or the intelligent and ethical expression of sexual energy. They all seem to agree on one thing: we cannot fully comprehend sex, nor can we use it wisely without including the spiritual element. Of equal importance is the need to address the associated emotional issues. If we do not recognize and resolve the murky corners of the mind, they silently rule our expression of sexuality.

The transcendental quality of sex is realized when it is used as a way of knowing oneself, rather than as a weapon for gaining power over others. It can take us to a place that is beyond sexuality and beyond duality. There is a sense of wholeness that can be experienced as a physical sensation, a thought, an emotion, and even as a pure awareness that is beyond physical, mental, and emotional. We might call this experience the fullness of orgasm.

Fullness of Orgasm

The male sexual response is typically brief and self-limiting, characterized by a rapid excitation, orgasm, and ejaculation. The female response is characterized by a slow building of energy, multiple orgasms that increase in intensity, and a retention of fluids (for the most part). Essentially, the male orgasm is governed by a self-limiting negative feedback process, while the female orgasm operates more on an expansive positive feedback principle.

In some systems of sexual cultivation, the man learns to retain the semen and slow himself down to harmonize with the woman's rhythm. In essence, he attempts to cultivate the positive feedback quality of orgasm, inherent to the female sexual experience. The experience is allowed to become increasingly strong, each orgasm paving the way for a stronger orgasm, until the energy level reaches a critical point, and then it breaks through the existing boundaries that define "sexual," giving birth to an experience that is beyond sexual.

There are two obstacles to this. The first is the belief that the male orgasm is synonymous with ejaculation of semen. In reality, ejaculation is what *terminates* the orgasm. The second obstacle is subtler. When the man is faced with the task of changing his sexual response to resemble that of the woman, he (perhaps unconsciously) feels like he is losing his masculinity. In truth, he must cultivate and sharpen his masculine will so as to move beyond his typical self-deflating sexual response.

Fullness of orgasm is possible only when fear, hatred, and the desire to control the other person have been honestly addressed. Such an orgasm is easier to achieve within the context of a long-term relationship that is rooted in mutual love and respect, a relationship that has gone beyond exploitation, beyond the thrill of pursuit and being pursued, beyond conquest, and beyond the barrier of shame.

Within the context of such a sexual relationship, the individual can experience deeper and deeper levels of connectedness, that eventually lead to the awareness that life is singular. As described by Montak Chia, "The man who cultivates his subtle (sexual) energy eventually experiences in his body the fact that all living beings are the same life."

Similar results may be achieved through a lifestyle that is celibate. However, neither sex nor celibacy works in the above-mentioned manner if either one is practiced in a way that denies or rejects the other. As with other choices that function as opposites, the options of sexual expression and celibacy must be allowed to dance harmoniously in the mind. Each one, done in fullness, respects and recognizes the value of the other, and eventually recognizes itself in the other.

If the mind is already at ease, sexual contact can be used to gradually and gracefully discover the bliss that transcends sexuality. The sexual partners simply do what comes naturally. Even when the man is practicing seminal retention, he is doing what comes natural to him: he is developing his masculine will.

If, however, the mind harbors unspoken anger, fear, guilt, or shame, the process becomes more complicated. The intentional cultivation of sexual energy requires mindfulness,

151

attention to ethics and personal integrity. And it requires the determination to be true to oneself. In this respect, the sexual path is the same as that of the celibate monk.

Censorship

In real life, those who advocate control and censorship of sexuality seem to be at odds with those who advocate free expression of sexuality. This is understandable. On the surface, the two sides do appear to be mutually exclusive. Their commonality becomes visible only when we address the human emotions that underlie the two polarities.

The desire to give full and free expression to sexuality comes from the usually unconscious knowing that it is a potent creative force. The fear that compels us to censor sex is based on the same unconscious knowing. It is a sealed memory of the potency of sex. The fear often expresses itself as a moral judgment against sexual expression.

We thus have two opinions: One says, "Sex is a source of great power; let us set it free." While the other says, "It is dangerous; let us tightly control it!"

Each side carries important information. Yet, each remains incomplete as long as it denies the wisdom contained in the other. Those who endeavor to establish laws to censor sexual expression are forever the slaves of sex, simply because we are slaves to anything we fear or suppress. Such individuals are forever battling pornography, prostitution, and other forms of sexual exploitation, as well as their own secret desires to experience those very same things. Likewise, individuals who advocate the free and full expression of sexuality cannot do so (and keep their health and sanity) if they minimize or reject the fear that compels us to censor or control it, because this same fear is the echo of a deep knowing of the potentially explosive emotional and psychic force of sexual energy.

Sexual Preference

One of my patients, whom I will call "Chuck," once attended a seminar for men. Upon his return, he reported that he had sat in a large room with about 250 other men, listening to a slightly overweight man who looked like a truck driver.

He was forceful, authoritative and spoke boldly and bluntly about delicate issues concerning men, women, and sexuality.

During one segment of the presentation, one of the participants asked about homosexuality. The seminar leader immediately responded with, "All gay men in the room stand up, please!"

About a dozen men stood up. "There is a disease in our society," the seminar leader continued in a loud voice. "It is called homophobia. These men now standing are going to help the rest of you conquer this disease."

Chuck was among the few men standing. That was the first time in his life that he had allowed himself to be publicly recognized. He stood looking at the crowd of heterosexual men staring at him, and he wept.

Chuck's story would have been powerful enough, even if it had ended right there. Months later, however, to his surprise, he began to get the notion that maybe he liked women after all!

For many individuals, heterosexual and homosexual do not represent a mere distinction between two personal choices. One side is flatly regarded as good and normal, while the other is regarded as bad and abnormal.

As a very young child, I remember engaging in sexual play with other children of my age, irrespective of gender. At that age, the idea that it was "bad" was meaningless. As I grew older, the child-like sexual play faded away, and girls became increasingly more attractive and mysterious to me. This too seemed perfectly natural. However, the normal developmental process was accompanied by indoctrination. Growing up, many of us were deeply programmed with the idea that sexual play among same-gendered individuals is perverse and shameful. Not surprisingly, we basically pretended that such things never happened in early childhood. This is, apparently, common among children. The experimenting fades away and is perhaps forgotten. If it is not forgotten, it is probably not discussed. It remains as a low-grade fear that quietly disturbs the peace of the adolescent mind.

Admittedly, I was perfectly content to do what most everyone else does, which was to pretend that those early forms of sexual exploration and experimentation never happened. However, as a young adult, I found myself interacting in professional and social circles with a significant number of gay men and women. I saw how inwardly tortured some of them were. This, plus my own unintegrated childhood experiences, led me to ask two questions: Why have they been culturally alienated from the rest of society? And why is there such a strong taboo against same-gender sexual contact? I already had some understanding of how prejudice clouds our ability to reason. I recognized the human tendency to make others conform to our ways. I also recognized our collective need to maintain social order and the integrity of the family. These factors can certainly create a cultural bias against the gay lifestyle. However, the exaggerated fear and loathing of homosexuality was beyond reason. I was puzzled by it. Eventually, it occurred to me that the function of any taboo is to conceal knowledge.

What Do They Know?

Gay men and women know something. For the most part, however, they do not know that they know it, except, perhaps, as a vague feeling. With no social sanctioning to explore their gut-level knowing, they usually bury it, and act it out unconsciously through clandestine encounters or romantic relationships that parallel heterosexual relationships.

They may take on the role of rebels fighting against an unjust society, or martyrs suffering at the hands of the ignorant masses. Since they are usually too preoccupied fighting off the shame projected onto them, they do not reveal to themselves what they secretly know: I am simultaneously both male and female and beyond male and female. This idea is not new. It has been expressed explicitly or through symbolism and by saints and mystics of many cultures. Gay men and women know it as a visceral feeling that they act out, but rarely understand. Nonetheless, they are in a unique position to show us that our deeper identity goes beyond sexual preference and ultimately transcends gender altogether.

154

Sexuality and Identity

As previously mentioned, there are two basic ways that we establish our personal identity. One way is through comparison; we compare opposing qualities—tall, short, fat, skinny, beautiful, ugly, shy, outgoing, etc. The other way is simply to get in touch with the core self which ultimately cannot be understood through comparison because it is beyond opposites. We simply get quiet and feel the core self as a sense of peace that is so deep that it is beyond human understanding (beyond opposites). The more we lose touch with the core self, the more we tend to cling to our identity based on comparison to others.

Gender role is a major part of personal identity established from the outside. Those who choose a gay lifestyle challenge traditional gender roles in a big way. In so doing, they remind us, even if we do not want to be reminded, that the identity given to us by society is like a layer of clothing that covers the deepest genuine self. Like clothing, our externally derived identity is appropriate when it protects and empowers us, allowing us to go places and do things that otherwise would not be possible. However, those same externally derived identities can become a straitjacket that suffocates the soul. Those individuals who choose to remove the sexual role straitjacket remind the rest of us that we are wearing one too.

Adult Sexuality and Child Sexuality

This is perhaps the murkiest and most frightening area of human sexuality. We can begin to bring a measure of clarity and calmness to this issue by first recognizing that "adult" and "child" constitutes a pair of opposites. They define each other, and each bears the seed of the other. The child becomes an adult, and every adult must become a child again. On the practical level, adulthood is about responsibility and childhood is about freedom.

When any pair of opposites interact, there is going to be a flow of "energy" between them. On the human level, the flow may be entirely within the individual or between two individuals. Either way, some of that energy might to be sexual, whether we are aware of it or not.

Children are sexual. In fact, they are sexual from birth. It is equally important to point out that child sexuality is different from adult sexuality. Sexuality in the infant is innocent, trusting and free. On the other hand, adult sexuality typically carries a lifetime of memories and conflicting feelings, and therefore requires containment and responsible action.

Sexual intrusion by the adult can be devastating to the emotional health of the child. The child experiences confusion and chaos because an area that was formally pleasurable and safe is now alien and scary due to the presence of adult sexuality with all of its intensity and contradictions.

There are two ways that adults intrude on the sexual development of the child. Child molesting is the more obvious way. Pedophiles unconsciously act out the strong longing to re-experience the innocence and freedom of early childhood, wherein there are no boundaries placed on the senses, and no distinction between sexual and non-sexual experiences; there is just life communing freely with life. The other less obvious but more prevalent intrusion takes the form of over-zealous parents and other authorities that project their own issues and inhibitions onto the younger generation.

The parents who are at peace with their own sexuality can allow the child's sexuality to unfold naturally. Such parents are unlikely to consciously or unconsciously use the child to act out their own sexual needs.

Arguably, intrusion upon a child's sexuality by hyper vigilant parents or repressive culture can do as much damage as the child molester. Either way, sexual energy can no longer flow in a harmonious manner.

Ending the Vicious Cycle

Repression leads to violation. Violation leads to repression. This is true for any form of repression but is especially damaging when it involves sexual energy. Unexamined, the cycle of repression and violence becomes deeply embedded in the individual's body and mind, and is played out in many subtle, or not so subtle ways, year after year, generation after generation. When recognized and approached with a measure of kindness, the cycle can end.

Breaking the cycle translates into taking personal responsibility for one's sexuality. As self-responsible adults, we neither blame our past nor blindly pass on the wounds to the future. Part of that personal responsibility might involve examining our sexual past. If we get still and quiet enough, we might reconnect with the lost sexual innocence of early childhood. We might even remember the beginning of repression or the intrusion by adult sexuality.

The three great healers of the human mind are truthfulness, stillness and loving touch. In this case, healing is likely to involve truthfulness about childhood sexual wounds. When the memories first start to emerge, there might be some anger. It is natural to get angry when we feel violated. When the violation occurs on such an intimate level, the anger might take the form of rage.

A parent might become enraged if his or her child is violated or otherwise mistreated in any way. Likewise, we might feel the same sort of rage if our own tender and vulnerable (child-like) inner places are violated. If that rage is repressed, it is likely to freeze into shame.

Healing the sexual wounds of the past might involve remembering the forgotten grief, shame, and rage that quietly control our everyday behavior. In order for such healing to occur, the "child" must be free to express. Such freedom is granted by the responsible adult who creates a safe environment in which the child is free to be a child.

Chapter 23
Creativity

Creation is a dance of opposites. This is true for Creation in the cosmic sense, as well as our own personal creative expression. To the extent that our inner opposites dance harmoniously, we tend to create our lives in a way that brings us pleasure. Creativity is a way of expressing the genuine self, which is inherently pleasurable. To the extent that we have inner conflict, our creative efforts have the potential to be painful. This is why we might avoid our creative impulses. Instead, we engage in repetitive or habitual behavior, staying in the safety of familiar territory.

In behavioral psychology, one of the recognized characteristics of neurosis is repetitive behavior. This is obvious in the case of someone who gets drunk every Saturday night to avoid feeling bored or lonely. More commonly, millions of people get up every morning and do repetitive work they do not enjoy because, if they failed to do so, they would have to face the fear of having no money, or perhaps the fear of losing the emotional security of familiar ground.

The key to undoing such repetitive behavior is the capacity to understand, tempered with kindness. If we want to be more creative or to re-create our lives, we cannot do so by attacking the old repetitive routine. More than likely, it is there for a reason. The old behavior probably protects us from being overwhelmed by trying to do too much too soon. The repetitive behavior allows us to remain functional until we receive the inner signal to go into the new and unknown.

When creativity sleeps in the arms of repetitive or known behavior, it does not sleep as a bear in the winter, but as a caterpillar in its cocoon. During that time of staying in the known, the hidden forces of creativity are incubating in stillness and darkness, gathering strength in the domain of the subconscious mind.

Not surprisingly, when we receive the inner signal or are simply forced by circumstances to face our hidden fears and break away from old habits, we often experience a wave of creativity, even if we are not trying to create anything. This is the basis for the myth that all true artists must suffer. However, it is not the suffering that stimulates creativity, but the removal of old patterns of pretense and superficiality, moving away from the safety of familiar but confining behavior.

In fact, the tendency to harshly judge or reject the old repetitive behavior is likely to reinforce it. When we are *really* ready to let go of unconscious repetitive behavior, we do not attack or reject it. We simply give thanks for what was and move on.

The Bipolar Gift

The term "bipolar" refers to the mood swings associated with this condition. The individual can fluctuate randomly from elation to suicidal depression. The high or manic periods include grandiose thoughts, a sense of great power and perhaps a tendency to sleep very little. There is a lack of discernment or disregard for the limitations of time, space, and money. This can show up as uncontrolled spending, a frenzy of activity, and jumping from one new project to another, leaving most of them incomplete. These manic episodes may then be followed by a time of deep depression that might include headaches, chronic pain, and digestive disorders that do not respond to any treatment.

The bipolar individual may exhibit a lack of personal boundaries, which can show up in a number of ways. For example, there might be a feeling of "taking on" the thoughts and feelings of others. The absence of boundaries may also show up in more aggressive ways. For example, the individual might be very invasive, having no regard for the free will of others. There might be a lack of respect for someone else's domain, whether it be money, property, or a spouse. Such an individual, though behaving like an outright thief, is also expressing (in a twisted sort of way) the instinctual awareness that life is singular. In this case, however, the awareness that says, "I am the One Life," translates into, "All things belong to me." Such individuals are as little children in a candy store, taking what they want and thinking nothing of it. Not surprisingly, such an individual can also be fiercely territorial one moment and very generous the next.

If you find yourself identifying with some of the above-mentioned symptoms, relax. Most individuals have some degree of difficulty integrating the boundless realm of Unity or singularity into the tangible world of physical reality, with its many dualities and boundaries. This difficulty is given the medical diagnosis of bipolar disorder only when it has reached a level that significantly disrupts the individual's ability to function.

Furthermore, such difficulty does not necessarily mean there is something biochemically or psychologically wrong with the person. Granted, the situation can certainly be complicated by other factors such as a troubled childhood or a biochemical imbalance. However, the primary difficulty could very well be that the individual's antenna is just very sensitive. The individual sees and feels more than he or she can comfortably handle.

The apparent connection between bipolar disorder and creativity is further supported by the observation that bipolar individuals are often quite articulate and witty. They can spontaneously pull out a clever phrase or rhyme. In addition, they are often keenly perceptive, having a heightened awareness of their environment that may seem to border on the supernatural.

Like the person who intentionally taps into the awareness of primordial unity, the bipolar individual can routinely experience both sides of everything. To do so in a manner that is harmonious with one's personality means that the awareness can take form as creativity, because creation *is* a dance of opposites. However, to do so chaotically translates into a sense of overwhelm, confusion and the supreme frustration of feeling "something" and not being able to translate it into a tangible form. The frustration of the bipolar individual is not unlike that of the artist who is unable to place on the canvas what is felt deeply within.

Psychologists might understandably be cautious about equating creativity with any sort of mental instability. They are concerned that some individuals will use this correlation to justify irresponsible and erratic behavior, rather than honestly facing their personal issues. The individual might use the correlation between creativity and psychological instability as a way of placing a badge of nobility on their condition. Psychologists emphasize that most creative individuals are not mad, and most individuals diagnosed with bipolar illness are not creative geniuses. However, the correlation is strong enough to suggest that many individuals who suffer from bipolar disorder and related conditions might benefit if they are given the time and space to see the hidden gift in their "delusions." They might be helped if their wild flights of thought and emotion are allowed to run their course and then land safely, rather than having them prematurely shot out of the sky and shot up with suppressive drugs.

Sharing the Gift

When we fully integrate the potentially troubling ability to identify with both sides of any issue, it becomes a valuable asset, because it includes the desire to bring the two sides together. To see beyond boundaries is to have a greater potential to genuinely respect boundaries. This is how the golden rule becomes a living reality. We cannot steal from or do harm to others because we will feel it directly and personally. Such a feeling has nothing to do with externally imposed guilt; it is the natural outgrowth of a quiet feeling; the silent knowing that life is singular. One of the ways that such contact frequently shows up is as the urge to create.

Chapter 24
Male & Female

If we address the male/female duality from a purely biological standpoint, it is pretty simple. The vast majority of humans are clearly either male or female. If, however, we include the softer and less tangible aspects of the person, gender becomes less clearly defined.

Some would argue that it is pointless to dwell on what is psychologically and behaviorally male and what is female, because the distinction is heavily influenced by the culture in which we happen to live. As with other opposites, however, the act of denying or minimizing the male/female distinction is just another way of becoming more tangled up in it. If we wish to recognize the "lie" in the male/female duality, we may do so by first recognizing the truth in it, and then we may discern where the truth derails into a lie.

When opposites interact with any degree of harmony, creation happens. The only way for creation *not* to happen is for the two sides to totally annihilate each other…and even then, creation happens, eventually.

Duality establishes a potential difference, a gradient, or charge that allows energy to flow. This is fundamental to life, as we know it. On the human level, the interaction of male and female is just one way of establishing that polarity, so we have energy with which to create. In each other's presence, men and women release their stored emotional energy as romance, deep affection, sexual intercourse, procreation and the establishment of a home. This flow of emotional energy is also redirected and channeled to bring forth spiritual awakening, poetry, dance, music, architecture and other such creations that form our culture.

Duality and Beyond

Comparing, competing, setting boundaries and establishing hierarchies: These qualities tend to be more obvious in males. Maleness also seems to be more analytical, linear and goal-oriented. Male consciousness is on a journey, a mission. It is willing to sacrifice itself for something greater than itself. In this respect, maleness is an expression of duality. In contrast, femaleness tends to be more merging, embracing, non-linear, inclusive, unifying, and, as such, transcends duality.

However, if we look within the embracing, inclusive nature of female, we see cycles, seasons, birth, and death; we see expressions of duality. In contrast, maleness, with its single-minded persistence and power of penetration, is able to break the cycle, stop the repetition, transcending the existing order of birth and death, to ushering in non-dualistic awareness.

In other words, both male and female have qualities that simultaneously express duality and transcend duality. The dualistic nature of one is drawn to that which is beyond duality in the other. This is one of the subtle ways that males and females act as polar opposites to potentize and mobilize creative energy. Maleness disrupts the dualistic (seasonal) nature of female. Likewise, the all-inclusive "Isness" of female absorbs and dissolves the logical hierarchical structure of maleness, thus providing the male with the orgasmic experience of "transcending" his own limitations.

Sperm Consciousness and Egg Consciousness

The very essence of male may be called "sperm consciousness." Sperm consciousness is dumb guts that does not stop or hesitate; it plunges headlong through the obstacle course of life, until it reaches the center of life itself—the great sphere, and then it surrenders totally, for it has reached the ultimate goal. Sperm consciousness is the desire that says, "I want to give all that I have and all that I am to something greater than my finite self."

Sperm consciousness is an extreme expression of a more generalized desire to "belong," exhibited by both males and females. As finite beings, we want to be nestled within something greater than the limited self. This instinct expresses itself in everyday life as the desire of the individual to belong to a family; of the family to belong to a community; and the

164

community to belong to the greater community (culture, religion, etc.).

Sperm consciousness is a fundamental drive. If it is not allowed to express itself freely in relationships and creative work, it can be exploited and twisted into kamikaze pilots, suicide squads and crazed crusaders who unquestioningly sacrifice themselves for thc glory of the empire or some other perceived "greater presence."

Sperm consciousness typically expresses itself more dramatically in men, but it is also present (though more subtle) in women. Sperm consciousness in women is typically hidden within the much more obvious egg consciousness.

"Egg consciousness" is the very essence of female. In striking contrast to sperm consciousness, egg consciousness has no place to go and nothing to do. It does not have to sacrifice itself for life, for it *is* Life. It does not identify itself with the ephemeral seed that is born and then dies; it identifies itself with the essence that goes on and on. Since its consciousness is non-linier, it does not "plan." It simply relaxes into the mystery, which means that it relaxes into self.

Egg consciousness does not perceive that it devours and annihilates the sperm. It carries a vision of life that is beyond the duality of egg and sperm, beyond winning and losing, beyond conquest. Thus, it is able to appreciate sperm consciousness in the only way that sperm consciousness can feel appreciated. Egg consciousness embraces sperm consciousness and says, "Welcome home, Beloved."

Egg consciousness is present in men, though it is typically, not as obvious. It may be likened to a translucent halo, a cool and pastel aura that envelops and quietly stabilizes the fiery passion of sperm consciousness.

Men, Women and Trust

A number of factors determine how much trust two individuals share. One important but usually overlooked factor is the degree of harmony between the will and the feeling nature of each individual. Inner harmony leads to outer harmony. Inner conflict leads to outer conflict. Inner conflict typically involves a clash of the will and feeling nature.

A man's hidden (or not so hidden) belief that he cannot trust women is based on the even more hidden belief that he cannot trust his own feeling nature. Once the feeling nature has been subjugated, repressed, or exploited, it becomes chaotic and unpredictable. Hell hath no fury like feelings scorned! As in other forms of internal warfare, this one is projected out. It often turns into hostility and distrust of women. The mirror image of this internal warfare exists in the woman who trusts men just about as much as she trusts her own will.

Furthermore, once the internal conflict is established, the external conflict is likely to play out in such a way as to re-enforce the underlying belief system. For example, the man who does not trust women is likely to gravitate toward or create situations that will justify his lack of trust.

What about Spontaneity?

For most of us, gender is an important part of our identity. Even if we regard gender simply as a role that we play, we must recognize the strong emotional charge associated with this role.

If we take the gender role too seriously, however, spontaneity is lost and genuine expression is censored. We suppress genuine expression so as to fit the established model of how a man or woman is supposed to behave. The result is inner conflict; information coming from the outside does not match the guidance coming from the inside. For example, it has been stated that women under stress address the issue at hand by talking freely, whereas men tend to prioritize their problems and then develop a plan of action or solution. The woman is said to handle troublesome feelings by just talking about them and not necessarily expecting the listener to provide an answer; while the man handles troublesome emotions by being alone, thinking it over, and then taking the appropriate action.

Granted, these insights can be helpful in creating understanding between men and women. The man can understand that he does not have to solve the problem for the woman. He can just relax and listen, which is probably what the woman really wants him to do. Likewise, when the man feels overburdened and withdraws into himself, the woman can understand that his actions may not have anything to do with her or the relationship. So, rather than frantically trying to draw him out (which causes him to withdraw even more) she can relax while he finds himself in solitude.

They can both relax and realize that each, in their own way, is instinctively carrying out the very useful practice of just letting him/herself be. When a woman talks in a seemingly random manner about her problem, she is letting herself be. When a man withdraws into himself, he is letting himself be.

The general consensus among authors of male/female psychology literature is that women tend to be somewhat more skillful in the verbal expression of feelings compared to men. Even a man who is fairly eloquent in other matters might be horribly inept when it comes to the verbal expression of feelings. This is a point of possible conflict or subtle tension in the relationship. The women might think he does not love her, but he is just being his inarticulate self. To complicate matters, he might sense her dissatisfaction, so he tries to "perform," and goes through the motion of expressing his feelings, basically telling her whatever he thinks will make her happy.

This does not mean that the woman should not ask questions like, "How do you feel about our relationship?" If she feels honestly compelled to ask such a question, it is probably a good idea, as long as she realizes that she might get a less than truthful answer. Experts in the field say that if the woman really wants evidence of a man's love, she should consider his actions more than his words.

Having said all that, here is a word of caution: The above guidelines describing male and female behavior, though useful, can become a hindrance when used rigidly, or when they simply do not match the person's instinctual inclinations. Our spontaneous expression does not necessarily follow these established gender guidelines, or any guidelines.

The desire to talk freely and to be heard is a natural human desire, which tends to show up more obviously in women, but is also present in men. Likewise, the desire to withdraw and go deeply into oneself is alive and well in both genders, though it tends to be more obvious in men. This simply means that the woman need not think herself abnormal or unwomanly if she wants to withdraw and then act in a definitive manner, and the man need not think himself less of a man if he feels compelled to just talk about a troublesome issue without having a specific plan of action. This level of spontaneity, combined with an awareness of how men and women *tend* to behave, promotes harmony and understanding; it allows the fullness of masculinity and femininity to be expressed, and opens the door to the deeper sense of our personal identity, which includes and goes beyond both.

Synergy of Male and Female

The embracing nature of female (egg consciousness) gives equal value to male and female qualities. For the male (sperm consciousness), egg consciousness is the goal. He has to climb for it. When thinking is linear, life is a journey and the path is always upward. The goal is the wholeness and vision of equality carried by egg consciousness.

In other words, male consciousness, at its purest, regards female consciousness as, somehow, "superior." This translates in everyday life as the man who instinctively protects his mate with his very life.

The woman thus feels honored and loved, and embraces the man with deep appreciation, which she can do in a balanced and wholesome manner because of her natural inclination toward equality.

As suggested above, such harmonious interaction between male and female consciousness does not happen by forcing it or pretending that it is present when it is not. Such harmony evolves naturally when we are honest with our fears and desires, irrespective of how we think we are supposed to act. In the presence of such honesty, the wholesomeness of our innate male or female qualities tends to assert itself. In this manner, the synergy between the two genders unfolds and comes to life in a way that is unique for any woman and man in a relationship.

Chapter 25
Mother & Father

While I was attending a support group, I was listening to one of the participants, whom I will call "Jill." She said that she felt guilty about asking us to help her find clarity on a certain major issue in her life, because if she found that clarity she would probably leave the group and move away. She said that in receiving support from us, she felt obligated to stay with us and "pay us back." On the surface, this little confession does not seem extraordinary. It is the sort of thing that people routinely reveal while engaged in discussion that resembles "therapy." When she said it, however, something clicked inside me. "Mother!" I said. I then shut my mouth and, somehow managed to restrain myself while she continued talking. When she finished, I responded by saying, "Jill, to me, there is something very important about us giving support to you even though you will no longer be here to pay us back."

On the surface, my words did not seem extraordinary. When I spoke to them, however, something clicked in Jill. She started crying, feeling overwhelmed, unable to comprehend why she was so emotional about such a simple exchange of words. When she finally did speak, she said—in so many words, "I feel recognized... I feel like I have the right to exist just as I am." She realized that for many years, the care she received from her mother had a hidden price tag on it which had been weighing on her quite heavily. Until that moment, she had been unaware of it.

Her healing involved allowing herself to receive from us even though it meant she would leave "the nest." For those few minutes, we were, in a small way, carrying out the function of the ideal mother.

Mother

Mother gives to the child the experience of receiving unconditionally and thereby imprints into the brain the nonverbal message that silently says, *This is your home, you are welcomed here…You deserve to have your needs met, simply because you were born.* This message is accepted by the baby. A pattern is established for life. Without it, we walk the Earth feeling like strangers. We feel we have no right to claim anything for ourselves. We feel we must negotiate for everything or depend on the good graces of others who are somehow more privileged and powerful than we are.

Mother has the nonverbal vision that allows the baby to be a baby. She asks nothing of the baby, relating to him/her in a way that cannot be understood with masculine business mentality. Mother consciousness needs no practical reason to nurture the new life; she does not weigh the baby's life in terms of profit and loss. She instinctively knows what the life in her body wants to do and she allows the life around her to support her in nurturing the life within.

Mother consciousness does not see her function as an investment. If it were an investment, she would not think twice about putting the child up for adoption if she found a more profitable investment. When a woman does give up her child for adoption, she typically does so because she feels incapable of properly caring for the child. In such a situation, it would be meaningless to say that she was being "selfish," because, as long as she is responsible for the child's well-being, her needs are inseparable from the needs of the child; if she is deprived, the child will also be deprived. It would be reasonable to assume that the same instinct that moves her to bring forth and nurture new life, also lets her know when she is not ready to do so.

When that instinct tells the woman that it is time to bring forth new life, she is transformed into the presence called mother—the nest where the child can simply *be,* without having to prove or accomplish anything. In the safety of mother's arms, the child's very existence is validated, allowing for the development of self-worth in the years that follow.

Now the question is, how does the above flowery description of motherhood relate to the flesh and blood reality of the exasperated young mother who cannot believe that the screaming monster she is holding came out of her own body?

170

She might be tempted to condemn herself as a "failure," or she might get cynical and declare that the above description of mothering is idealistic but not realistic. Another alternative is for her to remember that "mother" is more of a function than a fixed identity. The mother is a person before and after she is a mother. To the extent that she is in touch with her identity beyond mother, she can fulfill her role as mother in a way that is beneficial to herself and her children.

Nurturing can be extended to another person only if it is simultaneously given to oneself. The young mama discovers that her sanity and her baby are saved by allowing herself the same kindness and tenderness that she would extend to her baby. In essence, she is being mother to herself.

Father

Maleness is a focused, linear, driving force. Father is an aspect of maleness expressing itself outwardly to give support and acting in unison with mother as she brings forth and nurtures the new life. Male energy becomes father energy by stopping the established monthly cycle, breaking the earth, planting the seed, thus initiating something new; and transforming undifferentiated female energy into mother energy.

As an expression of the will, the father-function establishes firm boundaries to protect and tend to the physical needs of the mother so that she can have the safety to nurture the child. The father function, however, does not stop there.

Son and Daughter

Father is the child's introduction to the world outside the nest. Father is the source of worldly knowledge. For the male child, father is the more obvious role model of the two parents. Unlike mother, father is not satisfied to just let the child be a child. Father encourages, pushes and sometimes demands that the son be more than he thinks he is. He might also be the brick wall the child must climb over or break through. Through father, the child cultivates resourcefulness, courage, stamina, self-reliance, and will.

For the female child, the mother/father functions are similar to those described for the male child, but are less clear cut, because many of her worldly lessons come from the same parent who does most of the mothering. The mother tends to be more exacting with the details of the daughter's life and tends to be more lenient with the son. In contrast, the father tends to be relatively lenient toward the daughter but demanding with the son. (Note: We are speaking here of general tendencies, not hard and fast rules.)

In truth, for both the daughter and son, the biological mother can fulfill some of the roles that fall under the category of fathering, just as a man can fulfill some of the roles associated with mothering. In fact, in the average home, this is precisely what happens. The loving mother knows where to draw a hard line with her kids. Likewise, a stern father who teaches the child the ways of the world instinctively knows how to temper his lessons with a quiet acceptance that allows for "imperfection."

The expression of the mother and father functions moves along a continuum throughout the life of the child. At birth, there is a dominance of "mother" energy in both parents. At this point, the biological mother provides most of the mothering; she gives birth to the child's body from her body, holds it against her skin, and feeds it with her milk. In those early years, the biological father also does a good bit of mothering. He relates to the baby with undemanding and unquestioning acceptance.

As the baby grows, both parents shift steadily in the direction of fathering. They instinctively become more exacting with the child. Their parenting takes the form of instruction and guidance.

At the other end of the continuum, the child is no longer a child and the parents are no longer parents. Together they have traveled to the realm that is beyond parent/child; they have become equals, joined by a love that is made tender and sweet by the memory of a childhood and parenthood experienced completely.

Both Must be Present

It is tempting to give mothering greater value than fathering, or vice versa, depending on our upbringing and social conditioning. Even when we make a concerted effort to be unbiased and diplomatic, most of us have an emotional leaning toward one or the other.

For the developing child, however, the mother and father functions must both be present, even if provided by the same parent. Mothering, in the absence of fathering, will eventually consume the child, and the nest becomes a tomb. Fathering, in the absence of mothering, looks at the child pragmatically in terms of assets and losses, and will therefore exploit the child. Mother, in the absence of father, looks upon the infant and says, "Oh, you are so precious, so divine, and so delicious! I want to eat you up!" Father, in the absence of mother, looks upon the newborn baby, at first with bewilderment, and then says, "Oh, I see. It's a tube; you put food into one end and shit comes out the other end."

The quality of love that creates a free and happy person is the gift of mothering and fathering acting in unison. Mother is the nest; father teaches the child to fly free from the nest.

Over-identification with the mother or father role takes a toll on the child as well as the parent. The child leaves home, perhaps creating a void in the parent's life. This is not problematical, unless he or she has no well-defined identity beyond the mother or father function.

When the parents have reached advanced age, it is normal and natural for grown sons and daughters to care for them. However, when the aged parents are helpless to the point that they become a drain to their children, the grown children may swallow their guilt and place their parents in a home for the aged. In contrast, individuals who fulfill their parental functions, and then take the opportunity to rediscover who they are beyond the parent role, tend to stay physically, mentally and emotionally healthy and therefore less dependent on their grown children. The bond is still present, but rather than being a reversal of dependency, it is a non-verbal bond of mutual affection in which giving and receiving are done freely.

Chapter 26
Child & Adult

To be an adult is to work. To be a child is to play. The desire to play and be frcc is often called the "child within." That desire can be fulfilled only to the extent that we are willing to work and be responsible.

We relate to children out in the world as we relate to the child within. Likewise, we relate to authority figures in accordance with the condition of the responsible adult. By understanding the inner dance, we can more fully understand the outer dance.

The Inner Dance

The rational and responsible behavior of the adult is an expression of the will. The adult weighs the options, analyzes the past, ponders the future, makes choices, and exercises discipline. The child within the adult is an expression of the feeling side of the mind. It is innocent curiosity flying freely on the wings of unquestioning trust. It is large round eyes that see the world as an amazing mystery, and a heart that knows it is always at home.

The child within says, "I want to be seen." The adult says, "I want to see." The child within needs to be heard and understood, a need that can only be provided by the adult that is capable of listening and understanding.

Whichever we deny unconsciously runs us. As with other dualities, child and adult define one another. The truth felt by the inner child shapes and sharpens the will of the adult. Our innocent curiosity and capacity to feel give meaning to the tasks we assign to ourselves as adults. Likewise, when the adult is present, the child feels safe to be a child. The adult sets the boundaries that allow the child to safely express and explore.

As in other dualities, lack of harmony between the adult and child is the result of judging one as more important than the other. As a result, the one that is rejected is driven into the unconscious and, from there, it silently runs the show, controlling the one that is on the surface. For instance, if the child is seen as greater than the adult, the rejected adult (the capacity for logical planning) is not lost. On the contrary, it takes over and distorts the visible expression of feelings. Thus, the outer child-like behavior becomes a tool of the repressed adult who wants to control and manipulate his/her environment. Likewise, if the child is repressed in favor of a rational adult persona, our so-called rational decisions become the tools of the hidden desires, fears, and fantasies of the repressed child.

The Outer Dance

The adult who stifles the inner child is likely to stifle his/her real-life offspring. Likewise, if the outer adult is not fully present as the responsible parent, the outer child panics and creates chaos.

The stifling of the child within can also show up as the parent who forces him/herself to give from a sense of lack or guilt. When we force ourselves to give, we are also likely to force others to receive. This can happen in any relationship. But when it happens within the immediate family, it is likely to be more serious because the individuals cannot just go their separate ways. The parents' suppressed needs silently suffocate the child, as the parents try to shape the child into something that will bring some semblance of parental fulfillment.

This tendency is undone when the parent takes the time to sort out his/her own needs, rather than projecting them onto the child. Thus, the parent can yield to the deeper instinct that is capable of simultaneously protecting and guiding the child, while setting them free to be more than the parent could have imagined.

Youth and Old Age

Early one morning, I woke up from a dream that gave me an interesting angle on the relationship between the adult and child within. In the dream, I was watching an old man and a teen-age boy. The old man might have been in his eighties, and the boy looked like he was around fifteen years of age.

The old man was wise and learned. He was Oriental, which to me symbolized wisdom and harmony. The boy was impatient, bubbling with enthusiasm. He was a Westerner, reinforcing the symbolism of drive and ambition.

The characters in the dream sat facing each other, as they conversed quietly. They had respect for one another. The boy sat still and respectfully listened to the old sage. Likewise, the old man was generous and patient with the boy. There was a natural easiness in their conversation.

For me, the dream dramatized the relationship between youthful enthusiasm and the wisdom of advanced age; it was harmony between the passion of the teenager and the serenity of old age and the experience that goes with it.

Youth is desire. It wants to reach out, explore, play, build, experience more, do more, and be more. Youth wants to discover itself as it unfolds moment by moment. Old age is tranquility. It is the inner stillness that can allow life to be as it is. Such tranquility emerges naturally when it begins as youthful enthusiasm that is allowed to unfold freely. It is the youthful mind, free to be and do, that eventually evolves into the serenity and wisdom of the learned sage.

Any attempt to devalue or subjugate one in favor of the other results in premature degeneration. Youthful enthusiasm, stifled or exploited, does not mature. Youthful enthusiasm that is not allowed to blossom and bear fruit withers into bitter t old age, unfulfilled and therefore unable to nurture the young. Fear of growing old and fear of death result from youthful enthusiasm not allowed to bring itself into fulfillment.

The sage within is simply our capacity to be still and see the big picture. That capacity hopefully develops with time. Even the hard driving young adult must be able to access that inner sanctuary. The stillness and wisdom of the sage within provides a stable base from which youthful passion can launch itself into the unknown. Likewise, when youthful enthusiasm is allowed to find fulfillment in worldly adventures, it evolves into wisdom and serenity. And so, life goes on, always fresh, always new.

Chapter 27
Responsibility & Freedom

The relationship of child and adult (previous chapter) is one expression of the more general dance between responsibility and freedom. These two qualities are opposites in the sense that they define each other and give birth to each other. When the two are in harmony, responsible behavior allows us to be free, while the desire for freedom motivates us to be responsible.

As with other opposites, they simultaneously compete and complement. When they "compete," each side restrains, subdues and stabilizes the other so as to avoid harmful excess. When they complement each other, they fit together like hand in glove; each side allows the other to flourish in ways that otherwise would not be possible.

On the surface, the relationship between responsibility and freedom appears to require that we compromise. We apparently sacrifice one in order to accommodate the other. However, if the two sides are really in harmony, the sacrifice is no sacrifice, because we instinctively know when to focus on work and when to relax and play: each side yields to the other, without the energy-waste of inner struggle.

On the other hand, if we really believe that we have to give up an important freedom so as to be responsible, we are not really being responsible; we are submitting to something akin to slavery. Likewise, if we feel we must get rid of our responsibilities in order to have freedom, we really do not understand responsibility. We cannot relinquish anything for which we are truly responsible. When we realize that we are truly responsible for a thing, we embrace it freely.

In other words, if we take on a burden for which we feel genuinely not responsible, we are trapped. If we attempt to disown something for which we are truly responsible, we are trapped. We are free when we know we are fulfilling *our* responsibilities, not someone else's.

It is About Relationship

When our relationships are in harmony, freedom and responsibility tend to be supportive of one another. We each have an innate desire for freedom. We have an equally strong desire to be in relationship with those around us. Relationship with others translates into responsibility.

A healthy sense of responsibility reflects our desire for relationship. Such responsibility is easy and natural. It is not a burden imposed from without, but rather a response to a yearning that rises from within. When we really want to be in relationship with someone, we gladly accept the responsibilities that come with it. Therefore, we are free.

Drawing the Line

In everyday life, freedom translates into determining what is our responsibility and what is not. However, when inappropriate guilt is present, responsibility becomes twisted into self-blame, or becomes obliterated under a smokescreen of excuses. There is also a tendency toward abuse or neglect of oneself, while assuming excessive responsibility for others. When the desire to care for and nurture others is done freely, it does not imprison the loved ones but sets them free to blossom into themselves. Such responsibility is not a loss of freedom. It is not self-sacrifice. On the contrary, the very act of giving in this manner is fulfillment and freedom.

However, caring for others can be twisted into *giving to get.* This is a way of living our dreams through our loved ones, pushing them to be the person we secretly want to be.

In general, to the extent that we force ourselves to do things we do not want, we insist that others do the same. Likewise, to the extent that we allow ourselves to be free, we allow others to be free.

Fullness of Freedom and Pure Responsibility

We may not appreciate freedom until someone tries to take it away. However, as long as we require the presence of an enemy to make us appreciate our freedom, we cannot be totally free. Fullness of freedom does not have to be repeatedly challenged so that we know that we have it.

Fullness of freedom is freedom that cannot be taken away because it emanates from the core of our being. Such freedom is possible only in the presence of pure responsibility.

Total or pure responsibility means we are personally responsible for every detail of our existence. This sounds rather cosmic, but what does it really mean? And do we even want it? Let us examine this idea more closely. Accepting total personal responsibility for one's life means two things: no excuses and no self-blaming.

No excuses means we don't defend or justify our perceived failings. Absolute personal responsibility means we do not see ourselves as victims of circumstance. We no longer need to excuse ourselves by blaming the weather, the government, the devil, the drug pushers, the school system, society, the greedy boss, the dishonest salesmen, the sins of our parents, the foibles of humanity, the hypocritical clergymen, the power-hungry capitalist, the dishonest and unprincipled politician, or the limitations of time and space. In other words, every detail of our world is a reflection of what we have consciously or unconsciously called forth. Such removal of *all* excuses can only happen if we also remove all self-blame.

In everyday life, underneath the cover of overt excuses or self-justification is a hidden pool of self-blame. Beyond self-blame is the possibility of pure or total personal responsibility. Freedom from *all* self-blame is fullness of freedom, which allows for pure responsibility.

In Everyday Life

So, how do we move toward that ideal state of deep synergy between responsibility and freedom? Quite simply, we achieve it by just being honest. Truthfulness gradually dissolves self-blame and self-justification. In other words, we do not have to force the process by attempting to surgically remove self-blame or self-justification. Telling the truth sets us free, without necessarily doing anything beyond that. Our hidden feelings of self-blame and the need to make excuses tend to quietly dissolve when we simply express them honestly. When we do so, we deepen our capacity for responsibility and expand our personal freedom.

Chapter 28
Separateness & Unity

Creation is a dance of separateness and unity. We can see this dance in our personal relationships, in the workings of the body, in the ecological dance of life around us, politics, and even in the cosmic dance of Creation as a whole.

The Cosmic Dance

The first step in the cosmic dance of Creation is the separation of primordial unity into polar opposites. Separation is process which allows for the gathering and storing of usable energy. The second step is the rejoining of opposites which allows for the releasing and flowing of energy.

If the primordial opposites make war, they annihilate one another (like the collision of matter and antimatter) and creation stops right there. If they make love, creation bursts forth abundantly and life flourishes.

Since the harmony of opposites is fundamentally important to life, we might ask, what is it that allows opposites to interact harmoniously? We can answer this question somewhat metaphorically by saying that opposites interact harmoniously because each carries a "memory" of primordial unity. That memory translates into an affinity for each other, like the two ends of a stretched-out spring. They are drawn to each other, and they fit together. To the extent that opposites "remember" unity, they make love and thus create life.

The Human Dance

On the human level, the remembrance of unity is what allows us to form harmonious relationships. That remembrance is not a thought in the rational mind. It is a feeling. It is not the rational mind that compels us to create family; it is the feeling part of the mind.

It is important to emphasize that if our goal is to increase our remembrance of unity, progress is delayed if we try to rush it. To deny or devalue separateness is to deny or devalue our individuality, which is an integral part of our humanity. If we deny humanity we delay the natural emergence our divinity. If we want to really expedite the realization of oneness, we can do so by allowing it to emerge organically, here and now, in the world of separateness. Unity is experienced in everyday life as an appreciation of diversity.

Another way to invite the awareness of unity is by recognizing and appreciating how separateness serves us. We express separateness in the setting of personal boundaries, exercising discernment, making choices, stating our terms, and claiming our territory.

We should also bear in mind that the experience of unity is not necessarily an exalted state of peace, compassion and bliss. In everyday life, the subconscious echo of Unity can reverberate through a mind that is congested with emotional issues. It can show up as lack of respect for boundaries. It can show up as the irrational tendency to hurt someone (anyone) in response to one's own pain. The injured party seems to be saying, "I have been hurt by life, so now I will hurt life back." It does not matter who we punish because, instinctively, we know there is just one life. In such a situation, the setting of clear and rational boundaries (respecting our separateness) makes more sense than acting out our twisted experience of unity.

My Thoughts, Your Thoughts

In everyday life, the remembrance of unity can also show up as the ominous feeling that the distinction between one's own thoughts and the thoughts of the other person are not as clear-cut as we might think. We might be sitting quietly next to someone, when suddenly we start thinking about ducks for no reason at all, or we feel resentful toward "George", even though, a moment earlier we were totally at peace with George. Are these "my" thoughts and emotions, or are they the thoughts and emotions of the person sitting quietly close by? There are two ways of approaching this question. One way is to be a true scientist: Don't assume anything! Look the other person in the eyes and honestly reveal who was thinking what and when. The other method is to communicate with no one and just go more deeply into stillness and silence. This method, admittedly, may not help us distinguish between "my thoughts and your thoughts", but it might render the question meaningless.

The Dance within Us and Around Us

The heart is anatomically separate from the lungs, but the two cannot exist apart from each other. The teeth are hard and the lips are soft, because one carries a vast deposit of calcium and the other does not. Physiological aging or degenerative process, boundaries break down; things become more "uniform." A scientist would say that during the aging process, "entropy"" is setting in. Skin becomes tougher and bones become weaker, teeth become soft and arteries become hard, because some of the calcium leaks out of the hard places and settles into the soft places.

Youthful vigor includes the ability to keep things separate within the body. There is a separation of fluids and separation of useful nutrients from waste product. There is separation of electrical charges which keeps our inner battery fully charged. To do all this, our cells, tissues, and organs each maintain their own internal environment, made possible by a distinct border. Each of the hundreds of trillions of cells in the body a border called a membrane, which allows it to maintain its own separate identity, while communing harmoniously with other cells to create a functional wholeness or oneness.

The body as a whole has the ability to separate substances that its needs from the substances it does not need. The useful substances are retained and the potentially toxic waste products are eliminated. The digestive system, for example, separates nutrients from waste products. The liver and kidneys do the same on a more refined level. Without the ability to properly separate things, the body quickly ages and degenerates.

This process of separating the "pure" from the "impure" occurs within the bigger dance of ecological unity. The same substances that we excrete as waste serve to nourish other living things, which, in turn, leads to the production of food and breathable oxygen for us.

Boundaries of the Mind

On the mental and emotional levels, we as individuals are exposed to many ideas and experiences. Some are useful for us, some are not, and some are more useful than others. We separate them accordingly.

One level of separation occurs through making conscious choices. We choose the ideas and beliefs that appeal to us, and let go of the rest. A deeper level of separation occurs silently, without conscious effort. As an analogy, we might consciously choose to eat an apple instead of an orange because we notice that apples make us feel good while oranges give us gas. Once we eat the apple, the body's own wisdom kicks in to extract what it needs and to get rid of the rest. The rational mind does not have to tell the body which parts of the apple to accept and which to excrete.

The more we exercise our own ability to separate what we need from what we do not need, the more we cultivate the serenity to allow others to do the same. This is not the pseudo-serenity of assumed superiority, wherein we bask in the perception of our own enlightenment as we magnanimously allow others to "grope in darkness." Our serenity includes the understanding that what is food for us might be poison for another, and vice versa. It is the understanding that a principle which serves as a guiding light for us might be inappropriate for our neighbor or loved one. It is the understanding that each individual must digest and assimilate a given idea or experience in his or her own way. This is how separateness and oneness can dance the dance of life in our interpersonal relationships. The same understanding can also guide us as we navigate through the social and political landscape in which we live.

Separateness and Unity on the Social Level

We are social animals. Therefore, our health and wellbeing depend on a harmonious dance between our individuality and the community or society in which we live. Maintaining healthy individuality is about cultivating inner harmony. Maintaining a healthy community is about establishing outer harmony.

From a practical standpoint, we as individuals are each responsible for maintaining inner harmony. How we exercise that responsibility will determine how the community affects us and how we affect the community.

If the individual withholds, suppresses, or denies any part of self for the sake of the collective, the community breaks down. We have instead a mutual tolerance of our secret fears and hostilities. This is when we feel isolated and alienated, even though we live in close proximity to others.

In other words, the emotional experience of loneliness — the pain of feeling disconnected from the life around us — is typically the result of its polar opposite — the pain of being disconnected from oneself. We insidiously drift into a pattern of living in a state or pretense in which we deny personal truth so as to fit into the collective.

The stress of living in such pretense drives us to numb our senses so as not to feel the pain of denying the genuine self. We typically escape through food, alcohol, drugs, television, social media, and a frenzy of activity.

The belief that individuality must be sacrificed for the sake of community stems from a poorly developed sense of individuality. On the larger social level, the externally imposed compulsion to sacrifice one's individuality in favor of community translates into a repressive society that demands conformity and does not tolerate diversity of thought or life style. Likewise, to assert one's individuality in a manner that ignores the well-being of the community is to be a miser at best and a pirate at worst. Either way, community breaks down.

A stable community is possible only when it consists of free individuals, because only they have the vitality and integrity to form a thriving collective. The same principle applies for larger political systems, as described in the chapter that follows.

Chapter 29
The Yin & Yang of Politics

Since humans are emotional animals with a tribal ancestry, we can understand why we might easily get pulled into heated political debates. In fact, friends and families have been torn asunder through political disagreement. Furthermore, emotional unrest tends to dampen rational thinking, as described in chapter 11. In this case, emotional charge limits our ability to objectively assess what is happening politically. We can minimize this in two ways:

- Regardless of our political leaning, we remind ourselves that our primary loyalty is to the truth.
- We recognize the dance of opposites at the core of any political system. Specifically, it is dance between the individual and the collective.

Individuality and Community

Politics is ultimately a dance between the individual and the collective. We see this as the so-called right-leaning and left-leaning political systems around the world. The political right typically promotes individuality, often expressed as individual freedom, small government, and low taxes. The political left promotes community, often expressed as the common good and a call for cooperation, justice, and fairness. As with other opposites, neither one can exist without the other. Therefore, the question, "which is better?" has no meaning. The real question is this: are they in harmony or not?

As with other opposites, when the two are in harmony, each side supports and stabilizes the other. In this case, the result is a harmonious society where free and self-responsible citizens provide the energy, vitality, and creative passion that translate into wealth which can then be used to fund public works, as well as institutions that maintain justice, peace, and the rule of law. Likewise, the safety, stability, and conveniences provided by organized society allows each individual to pursue his or her personal dreams and to achieve goals which otherwise would not be possible.

Life Shows Us How to Govern Ourselves

To better understand the harmony between the individual and the collective, as described above, let us consider the workings of the human body. As with other multi-celled plants and animals, the human body consists of trillions of living cells, each of which has a certain degree of autonomy. Each cell has a physical border called a membrane which establishes its identity.

Each cell is responsible for generating all the energy it needs. Each cell also contributes some of its energy and resources for maintaining the body as a whole. In exchange, the well-organized and unified body provides a safe internal environment where the individual cells can survive even under harsh external conditions, as well as accomplish things that would otherwise not be possible.

The natural synergy between the body as a whole and the individual cells includes two fundamental features shared by all life forms. All living systems are designed by Mother Nature to be supremely *conservative* and ever *progressive.*

Life is Conservative and Progressive

Each living cell can generate enough surplus energy to contribute to the body as a whole because each cell is, by its very nature, supremely conservative. One of the commandments of Mother Nature is, "Thou shalt not be wasteful! Thou shalt conserve energy and do things in the most efficient way possible." This is how each cell is able to gather enough energetic capital to contribute to the body as a whole, without depriving itself. Having amassed more energy than is needed for mere survival, life can express its other fundamental quality: to be ever progressive. Life cannot be static. Life, in the very act of living, must evolve. It must expand itself, move forward, and fulfill its potential.

The evolution of life includes a tendency for living organisms to become increasingly conservative and energetically efficient. Thus, even more energetic capital is available to allow life to expand, evolve, and progress even more. In other words, the conservative and progressive elements of life exist in a state of synergy.

190

The Body Politic

The harmony between individual cells and the body as a whole, as described above, also describes the ideal functioning of any political system. The political right typically promotes a conservative approach to governance, while the political left urges us to be progressive.

The conservative right advises us to keep government small and taxes low, while advocating individual freedom. Naturally, such freedom comes at a price. Each individual must be *personally responsible* for his or her own personal wellbeing. In contrast, the progressive left urges us to focus on the common good, so as to allow for the evolution of social and political systems designed to promote a more perfect union, a kinder and gentler society. Naturally, the creation of such a system comes at a price. Each individual must be *socially responsible*, financially and otherwise.

In other words, neither side can energetically exist without the other. The energy needed to create the ever-progressive society must ultimately come from the individual. Likewise, the individual must have the support of the collective to fully express his or her personal right to life, liberty, and the pursuit of happiness.

Though the natural synergy of the two political wings is obvious, the two are frequently in conflict. Such conflict is likely when we lose sight of their interdependence and their natural complementary relationship.

Two Parties in Conflict

When the two sides are in conflict, each expresses its truth in a way that denies the truth of other. Consequently, the fundamental truth presented by each side becomes incomplete and ultimately meaningless. In other words, there can be no sociopolitical unity without individual freedom, and vice versa.

On the surface, political conflict seems to produce social unrest which is random and chaotic. However, when seen through the lens which recognizes dancing opposites, some patterns emerge, and the drama becomes somewhat predictable.

191

Conflict between the two often includes both sides exhibiting some degree of corruption wherein each side violates its own core values and projects its failings on the other side. There seems to be a sort of symmetry in their respective doings. We might notice that the corruption on one side is matched by its mirror image on the other side. For example, the political right can insidiously drift into oppressive, autocratic rule which is the antithesis of small government and low taxes. In other words, the political right insidiously abandons its conservative values; raising taxes, and restricting individual freedom; until the sovereign citizen becomes a cog whose sole purpose is to keep the machine going. Likewise, the political left can drift into a bunch of bloated bureaucracies which insidiously divert public funds to private interests. In the words, the vision of equality and fairness becomes a facade which conceals gross exploitation of the many by the few.

In summary, conservatism gone bad looks like greed and selfness. Progressivism gone bad looks like slavery wherein personal freedom is sacrificed at the altar of the so-called common good. Either way, the result is suffering on the individual level and tyranny on the sociopolitical level. Either way, the rich get richer and the poor get poorer. It does not matter whether the tyranny is labeled as fascistic or communistic. It does not matter whether the boat leans too far to the right or left. Either way, the boat sinks.

How do we keep the boat afloat?

We keep the boat afloat by keeping the two sides balanced. They tend to do so (in the mind, first and foremost) when we simply recognize them as a dancing pair of Yin and Yang. In other words, we recognize their interdependence; which is to say, we recognize the interdependence and natural synergy of the individual and the collective. Their natural synergy has to do with the fact that we are social animals. Therefore, individual freedom and the common good are just two sides of the same coin. Therefore, we recognize and appreciate the natural synergy between personal responsibility (self-interest) and social responsibility.

The Key to Harmony

The key word *voluntary*. To the extent that political unity is achieved through voluntary participation, all is well. Anyway, that is how it would work if the individuals in such a society were free, as well as socially responsible.

Voluntary participation makes sense when we remember that all political power ultimately resides in the individual — whether the individual knows it or not. This is true for the obvious reason that the individual provides the energy and vitality which create the collective.

Governments cannot operate without the energy provided by individual citizens', just as the human body as a whole cannot exist without the energy generated by the individual cells. In addition, we as individuals must have the grace to acknowledge that our personal freedom, prosperity, and fulfillment depend on our willingness to honor our responsibility to the collective that supports us. Such grace is natural to the extent that we are spiritually awake.

The Spiritual Side of Politics

To be spiritually awake translates into awareness of unity. It is the awareness that the life within oneself and the life in his or her fellow citizens is the same life.

Most of us do not have a strong feeling-level experience of the One Life, except perhaps as a temporary peak experience. However, it does show up quietly in everyday life as the inclination to treat others as we would want to be treated. Such an attitude cannot be legislated from without; it must emerge silently and organically from within. Indeed, when we try to force it from without, we kill it before it is born.

When it is allowed to emerge naturally from within, it shows up tangibly as politically minded individuals who passionately support laws and policies which are guided by conscience and higher principles. It shows up as the willingness to challenge laws and policies that violate these higher principles. It shows up as recognition of the harmony between personal responsibility and social responsibility. And it shows up as recognition of the natural synergy between the so-called political left and right.

The Eagle Needs Two Wings to Fly

If we let our imagination soar, we might envision an ideal society wherein each individual is free to pursue personal dreams. Under such circumstances, our natural caring and generosity tends to emerge, because we have both the desire and resources to contribute to the society that supports us. Again, such a system can work only when enough citizens are spiritually awake enough to live by the Golden Rule, which inspires us to *voluntarily* contribute, rather than being forced to do so through threat of violence or incarceration.

Granted, in a society where a significant number of citizens are just trying to survive, a sudden transition into voluntary participation is likely produce chaos. However, the good news is that government starts taking baby steps in that direction as more individuals see the bigger picture. As public awareness changes, government changes accordingly.

Whether we find ourselves leaning to the political left or right, we need only remember that governments can do what they do only when we the people allow it — through our active participation or the passive endorsement of our inaction. Add to this the recognition of the legitimate roles of both the conservative and progressive elements of government (and the complementary relationship of them), and we can avoid getting sucked into energy-draining political battles. Thus, we can gracefully participate in the political process in ways that allow us to maintain our inner peace, while making positive contributions to the body politic.

Political Freedom and Emotional Freedom

As stated at the beginning of this chapter, politics can be a highly charged emotional topic because we are emotional animals. The more we become emotionally embroiled in current events, the harder is it to rationally navigate through the political landscape, and the more easily we are controlled by the powers that be. Therefore, if we wish to harmoniously navigate through the outer sociopolitical landscape, we must be willing to understand our own inner landscape, as described in the two chapters that follow.

Chapter 30
Equality

The desire to have a sense of equality with those around us is not merely a social or political ideal. It is an emotional need. When that desire is not fulfilled, an alarm goes off. We might experience it as anger, emotional pain or a vague sense of uneasiness. If the pain or uneasiness is not resolved, it remains as a silent irritant that does not allow us to rest; like a dripping faucet in the middle of the night; the more we try to ignore it, the louder it gets.

To understand our emotional need for equality, we must understand its relationship to inequality — which also tends to carry an emotional charge that transcends sociopolitical ideologies. We can clear up the confusion and untangle the emotional knots associated with equality and inequality by regarding them as yet another pair of opposites, each having its rightful function in the dance of Creation.

An easy first step in that direction is to consider these two terms in a purely scientific manner. In other words, we use them objectively; free of the notion that one is intrinsically good and the other bad.

Equality and Science

To the scientist, the words *equal* and *unequal* are just numerical expressions of observed physical features, such as length, weight, or volume.

When the word "equal" is used numerically, the scientist frequently qualifies it by saying something like, "These two samples have equal weight, with a possible variation of two milligrams," because he knows that if two objects or measurements are separate, they cannot be absolutely equal; they will vary to some degree. However, the variation may be so small that the scientist might say, "For our present purpose, the difference is negligibly small, therefore, we can regard the two samples as having equal weight."

If two things are separate, they cannot be absolutely equal.

Equality and Social Justice

The social and political usage of the word *equality* is fuzzier compared to the scientific usage because the parameters for the sociopolitical usage are not as clearly defined as the scientific usage Furthermore, in a social or political setting, equality is typically considered synonymous with fairness and justice. For example, in any occupation in which male and female employees have the same level of productivity, fair play demands that they have equal pay and status. In such a situation, fairness obviously translates into equality. However, since we are social beings who value cooperation, fairness and equality are not necessarily synonymous. Fairness implies the willingness to help those in need. Such willingness is easy and natural when it emerges silently from one's own conscience. Therefore, we would not expect a small pregnant female to perform equally in heavy physical work as a big muscular man. Fairness, in this case, translates into special consideration given to the small pregnant woman.

Beyond Social and Political

Again, to understand and fully appreciate the social and political concerns regarding equality, we should remember that such concerns are not entirely the result of social conditioning and political indoctrination. Such concerns have deep emotional and spiritual roots. We seem to have within us an instinct for fairness and justice — which is attuned to perceived equality or the lack there of.

As emotional beings, we want to be treated fairly. As spiritual beings, we want others to be treated fairly. The two are inseparable. As described in previous chapters, emotional energy tends to evolve into spiritual awareness. In this case, when the emotional need to be treated fairly is freely expressed, it evolves into the inclination to treat others fairly.

Ultimately, it makes no difference whether we perceive ourselves as ourselves as being unfairly privileged or deprived. Similarly, it makes no difference whether we perceive ourselves as superior or inferior. Either way, an alarm goes off. The perception of unbalanced scales, the prolonged absence of the basic feeling of fairness in our relationships, can quietly drive us insane. Typically, however, we numb the pain through various mechanisms, from cognitive desinence to drugs.

Doing and Being Revisited

Excessive emotional preoccupation with equality may be understood as stemming from a lack of self-worth. As described in chapter 9, a healthy sense of self-worth is the result of a harmonious dance between *doing* and *being*. Self-worth experienced through doing means it is externally acquired. Self-worth through being means it is internally derived.

A solid sense of self-worth through doing and being results in serenity which shows up as a healthy emotional response to the appearance of equality and inequality. On the other hand, when doing and being become unbalanced, self-worth erodes. This typically happens because we get too wrapped up in our outer doing and thus lose touch with our inner being. The resultant loss of serenity causes us to become even more preoccupied with performance and appearance. This is when we might become preoccupied with equality and the lack thereof. Furthermore, as long as we are in an emotionally vulnerable state, we are also more likely to be programmed (intentionally or not) by the surrounding sociopolitical environment.

The more bring our doing and inner being into balance, the more we tend to relate to equality and inequality as a scientist would: quantitatively instead of qualitatively. We understand that each has its rightful place. When we are emotionally balance, our power of discernment is clear and sharp; and we can see that fairness translates into equality, except when it doesn't.

The interaction of inequalities in people, groups, nations, etc. establishes the driving force which sets energy in motion so creation can happen. Likewise, the silent recognition (the feeling) of equality allows us to look upon our creation and declare, *"Behold, it is very good!"*

197

Chapter 31
Rebellion & Conformity

The choice to rebel or conform is usually not just rational and logistical. It is also emotional. This is true whether the act of rebellion or conformity is on the interpersonal, social, or political level. The choice to rebel is often motivated by anger. The choice to conform is frequently motivated by fear.

The fear or anger behind conformity or rebellion are often influenced by emotional issues which take their origin in one's family history. That is why two individuals may respond differently to the same social and political events. Each person might be reacting to deep and perhaps unconscious emotional issues. This is where "Know thyself" is relevant. This is how we can avoid becoming puppets whose strings are pulled (intentionally or not) by sociopolitical events.

Cutting Emotional Strings

By understanding our own inner world, we invite serenity. Greater emotional serenity promotes mental clarity. Greater mental clarity translates into better discernment. Better discernment means we can navigate through outer events in ways that allow us to maintain inner peace, and maximizing our capacity to have a positive impact in the outer world.

On the rational side, it is normal and healthy to rebel against perceived injustice. It is also healthy to desire some degree of conformity so we can have community. Such conformity is not a denial of free will but rather an expression of free will. Such conformity is voluntary because it emerges organically from the personal aspirations of the individuals.

On the emotional side, when we are fully in touch with our self-worth as unique individuals, we have no strong compulsion to rebel. And if we do rebel, we do so peacefully and intelligently. Likewise, if we are in touch with our sense of unity — our "sameness" — we do not need to conform or force others to conform. There might be the appearance of conformity, but it not motivated by fear, but rather by the desire to connect. Neither is it considered a burden. We do it freely and joyfully as a means of facilitating communion.

Inner Passion and Outer Debate

The desire to rebel or conform may show up in a harmonious way as lively debate. This is possible when our experience of unity, though submerged, still echoes to the surface as the principle that says, "I disagree with your opinion, but I respect and defend your right to voice it."

When we have lost touch with our sense of uniqueness and sameness, rebellion and conformity can get ugly. Nonetheless, each side still needs the other. Each can be sustained only by feeding on the other. The fanatical rebel needs the threat of enforced conformity to justify rebellion. Without enforced conformity, the rebellion quietly melts into the sea of sameness, which is scary if we do not have a healthy sense of identity as unique individuals. Therefore, if there is no evil oppressor to rebel against, the rebel is likely to create one.

Likewise, the autocratic conformist needs rebellion to stimulate reactionary fervor, so as bolster the walls of conformity. Without rebellion, conformity relaxes into a stroll through the garden of diversity, which is scary if we have lost touch with inner sense of unity or sameness. Therefore, those who are interested in maintaining strict conformity will perhaps unconsciously create rebels and "dangerous elements" to burn in the town square.

The Outer Reflects the Inner

If each side is motivated by a sincere belief in their respective cause, and not merely looking for *any* enemy to fight against, they will pay close attention to the hidden dynamics of rebel/conformist. Those who seek conformity may not realize that crushing the rebellion causes it to come back stronger. Likewise, rebellion is successful only if the rebels recognize themselves within the enemy. If this does not happen, the rebels eventually act out the same oppression they were rebelling against. The longer the fight persists, the more we become like the enemy. We can avoid this by using any sociopolitical event as an opportunity to know thyself, especially thy emotional self.

Chapter 32
Hero & Villain

When we are inwardly at peace, we cultivate self-worth by bringing forth the genuine self. We express the genuine self through a balanced combination of doing and being, as described in chapter 9.

To the extent that our doing and being are not balanced, the genuine self is neglected and self-worth erodes. We compensate in a number of ways, such as trying to work harder and achieve more. Or we try to escape through activities that lead to addiction.

One subtle but very common form of addiction is the addiction to heroes and villains. Heroes and villains allow us to feel good about ourselves. They give us an external reference point that we use to establish some semblance of self-worth without doing any purposeful outer work or allowing for meaningful inner communion.

Defining Oneself

The tendency to create heroes and villains can be very obvious or very subtle. We are emotionally drawn to the hero/villain interaction, as indicated by the popularity of movies and novels. The appeal of the hero/villain dance also helps to create a market for newspapers, magazines, and news shows on TV and radio.

We are drawn to heroes because they play roles that we would like to play. The hero provides a model of an individual who reaches the fullness of human potential. The flip side is that we become addicted to hero worship as a substitute to finding our own greatness or uniqueness. Or we decide that the only way we can experience "greatness" is to copy the hero—which is impossible, but we try anyway.

The villain is someone we can blame for our misfortunes. The villain is the person we can compare ourselves to, so we can feel good about ourselves. Just as the hero gives us an image of how we want to be, the villain provides us with an image of how we *do not* want to be.

Whether or not our perceptions of the hero or villain are valid, the common element is our need for them to be good or bad so we can use them as a background to establish our identity. We place ourselves between the hero and villain, thus establishing the boundaries of our identity. "Who am I? I am a worshipper of this hero or that god; I am the enemy of this villain or that evil system."

We insidiously relinquish responsibility for our lives, believing that our well-being depends on the heroics of those who are greater, and that our misfortunes are due to the evil deeds of those who are morally inferior to us. To the extent we deify one, we must scapegoat the other. In fact, the mere presence of the hero might trigger so much hidden insecurity and sense of inadequacy, that we have to create a villain who makes us look good.

In other words, on the surface, we are uplifted by the hero and plundered by the villain. On a deeper level, we give our power away to the hero and try to steal it back from the villain.

The point is that to create a hero is to create a villain, and vice versa. As with other opposites, one side cannot exist without the other: each side setting the stage for the emergence of the other.

If we think ourselves to have transcended the hero/villain duality, there is a good chance that we do it covertly. A simple way to detect the hidden tendency to create heroes and villains is simply to ask, "Do I have an emotional charge on the hero/villain dance?" If the honest answer is yes, the dance, more than likely, occurs within us.

The quickest way to move through this dance is to just dance it. We praise our heroes and accuse our villains. We do it fully and consciously. The next step is that we will not do it at all.

The Fallen Hero

The fallen hero experience is quite common. Such an experience carries an important lesson. It shows us how much of our happiness was vested in the hero. We shift dramatically from feeling content in our admiration of the hero, to feeling confused, lost, or angry when the hero falls. Yet, the person did not really change. Only our perception changed. When we become aware that we were projecting both hero and villain on the same person, we tend to quietly move beyond both.

There are two obstacles that can prevent us from realizing the full wisdom of the fallen hero experience:

- We might make excuses or otherwise deny that we were playing out the hero/villain dance.
- We might condemn ourselves for having been so childish.

Either way, we block learning, and the scene will more than likely repeat itself. On the other hand, when we simply - recognize the fallen hero experience with a measure of kindness to ward oneself, we free ourselves from the need for heroes and villains, which means that we are ready to embrace our own unique individuality.

Beauty in the Beast

Just as the hero can fall, the villain can be redeemed. This is what happens in the story of *Beauty and the Beast.* Deep inside the vulgar beast is nobility. The nobility is allowed to emerge through the tender kiss of Beauty. Beauty is simply truth.

An important element of this myth is that Beauty makes the choice to kiss the Beast without the expectation that her kiss would transform the brute into a handsome nobleman. She saw his nobility first. Her seeing the deeper nobility and accepting the brutish persona compelled the transformation.

The tale of *Beauty and the Beast* illustrates how truth and acceptance transform the villain within us. The villain is driven by self-hatred. The remedy for self-hatred is self-love, not the pseudo-love that attempts to mask the ugliness, but the core of love that regards truth as beauty.

Chapter 33
The Martyr

The martyr is a special type of hero — or villain. Outwardly, the martyr is a hero who is a hero/victim who takes it on the chin for someone else's sin. On the larger social level, the martyr suffers at the hands of unscrupulous enemies or unworthy associates. The martyr is the individual who receives personal injury at the hands of others who stomp on the fruits that the martyr had to offer.

The martyr is the dutiful spouse, mother, father, son, daughter, brother, sister, employer, employee, student, or teacher who goes out of his or her way to be ethical, moral, helpful, and caring, only to be mistreated. Martyrdom can also be weaponized.

Martyrdom as a Weapon

By identifying ourselves with famous martyrs of the past, we place a crown of nobility on our suffering. For example, let us say that I as a teacher put great effort in putting together study material for my students. If some of them do not use it and subsequently do poorly on a test, they might blame me for making the test too hard. I might show outward signs of irritation, but secretly feel elated as I compare my diligence with my student's poor show of character. Now I can sing the blues! I can feel justified in showing resentment (which was there all along). Better yet, I can continue to hide my resentment and embellish my mask of nobility by demonstrating that I still feel "compassion" for my attackers. I can also magnify the drama by comparing my situation to that of well-known martyrs of the past.

Does this mean that all historical martyrs were playing out their hidden need to be recognized as being morally superior? Were they playing out their secret anger at humanity and, even more secret self-hatred? Or was there a combination of a genuine desire to bring forth truth and justice, flavored by an undercurrent of unresolved self-worth issues. These are interesting questions that could stimulate lively discussion or debate, especially since they bring to the surface our need to see the martyrs of the past as perfect or near perfect heroes or saints.

The Martyrs of the Past

Jesus Christ is perhaps the most famous martyr in history. In telling the story of Jesus' suffering at the hands of his enemies, we must make two assumptions: that he suffered and that he had enemies. It may be argued, however, that if Jesus was the fully realized Christ, death and suffering were not his reality, but the reality of his witnesses and followers. The suffering could certainly have been real to Jesus *the man.* Christ, however, cannot die and recognizes no enemies. The mind of Christ can say, "The Father and I are one," without being blasphemous, arrogant or grandiose. The mind of Christ can say, "What you do to the least of your brethren, you do to me" because the eyes of Christ look upon the face of another with the recognition of oneness. Such recognition is not a philosophical ideal, nor a pseudo-pious gesture to someone who is secretly held in contempt. It is a genuine knowing, as obvious as a flower in bloom, as real as a sunrise. This reality is denied by the lingering experience of the martyr.

To accept the reality of the martyr's role, the would-be martyr must consciously or unconsciously declare his or her moral superiority. However, this perception fall apart when we begin to get a hint of the mind of Christ, which includes a sense of equality so profound as to transcend human understanding.

A toned-down version of that awareness exists in every one of us. Without it, we would quietly go insane or kill each other. As the awareness becomes stronger, martyrdom becomes less real to us

Addiction to Martyrdom

Regardless of what was actually going on in the minds of the famous martyrs of the past, the point is that we often use them to justify and ennoble our own feelings of having been victimized.

Granted, it is healthy to honestly acknowledge that we feel violated. However, we cripple ourselves when we habitually use our suffering to elevate ourselves in the eyes of others. We feed on the idea that we are being attacked by our brethren who, sadly, are not ready to receive our gifts. It is especially satisfying when we can compare our suffering to that of Jesus, Joan of Arc, Galileo, etc. We do this as reflexively as a drunk reaching for a bottle.

As with other addictions, the addiction to martyrdom — and victimhood in general — can be a powerful and cunning demon. However, there is a way out. As with other addictions, the first step in freeing ourselves is to just tell the truth about it. Sometimes, that is the only step we need.

The Reason We Suffer

In all fairness to the martyrs of history, even if some of them *were* acting out the unconscious desire to prove they were good and the rest of the world was bad, many of them were, nonetheless, genuinely noble. Given their circumstances, they acted in accordance with their conscience, showing great courage and strength of character, living their lives in accordance with their deepest truth. In times past, personal integrity often translated into the willingness to allow the flesh to be mutilated for the sake of the truth. "You can burn my body, but the Earth still revolves around the sun." In that respect, the martyrs of the past are timeless role models, reminding us to value truth as we value gold. However, while *they* suffered for telling the truth, *we*, in our modern age, typically suffer when we *don't* tell the truth.

When we consistently speak the truth, we tend to treat the body with kindness. Likewise, when the truth is withheld, the flesh is mutilated, through accidents, disease, substance abuse, etc. If truth is withheld, our attempts to heal the body (or our relationships) tend to back-fire. The intent may be sincere and the method may be valid., but if personal truth is kept hidden, we will most likely suffer, physically and otherwise. I am reminded here of a story:

207

She Tried to Out-Martyr Her Mother

One morning, a woman called my office complaining of pain in her lower back and buttock. I had seen this particular patient, whom I will call "Diane", a number of times over the years, and we had developed a good rapport. Therefore, even though I had not seen her for about several months, she spontaneously began talking about the hidden issues that seemed to be associated with her physical condition.

She said that she had been on vacation, visiting her mother. During her visit, the area she visited was experiencing severe flooding. She and her friends were eager to help. They formed a caravan and drove a long way to help fill sandbags to build a wall against the rising floodwaters.

When she first walked into my office, she stated that the physical exertion was the probable cause of pain. As we proceeded to treat the physical problem, she offered more details. She stated that her mother resented being left alone by her daughter, flood or no flood.

While Diane and her friends were away filling sandbags, Diane's mother developed chest pains and was taken to the hospital. Her mother's doctor got word to Diane, who dropped the sandbags and rushed to the hospital, all dirty and grungy and sweaty. When she arrived, her mother seemed to be doing fairly well for someone who had been hospitalized for heart failure. She was alert, talkative and actively displaying how distressed she felt about inconveniencing her family and friends. The attending physician showed subtle but unmistakable disapproval of Diane, treating her like a selfish brat who had given her mother heart failure.

Diane was infuriated. She felt abused by her mother and misunderstood by the doctor. The situation, however, did not lend itself very well to venting her feelings against her mother or the doctor. At that point, her back and buttock began hurting.

The pain waxed and waned for a month before she called my office. As we treated her back, she spoke freely about the emotional implications. Since I happened to be writing this particular part of the book, I mentioned the word martyr. Diane's eyebrows immediately shot up as if a light had suddenly come on in her brain.

Before this latest incident with her mother, Diane had already resigned herself to simply accept her mother as she was. That seemed like a practical solution. However, her declaration of surrender did not register on the emotional level. Mentally, she was saying, "I accept my mother just the way she is," but emotionally she was saying, "My mother is a villain who tries to manipulate me with guilt and attacked me while I was doing a good deed."

In essence, Diane's mother was telling the world, "Look how my selfish daughter gave me a heart attack!" And Diane countered with, "My mother is a pain in the butt!"

Diane realized that she was unconsciously trying to out-martyr her mother, which was bound to fail because her mother was a supreme master of the art. Virtually everyone who knew of the incident sympathized with Diane's mother and vilified Diane.

One of Diane's siblings had confronted her with, "Mother is old and lonely, she's using her sickness to get attention. Why can't you feel compassion for her?"

Diane's sister's real message was: "You are bad because you don't feel compassion for mother." So, I restated her sister's question as a pure question, without the implied condemnation. "What *is* holding back the compassion?" he obvious answer is that we would find it difficult to feel compassion toward someone who is attacking us. It is especially difficult if the attacker reminds us of something within us that we are not particularly fond of. Under those circumstances, rather than feeling compassion, we feel anger. If we suppress the anger, we are likely to feel fear. If we manage to suppress the fear, we might feel indifference or apathy. If we suppress the apathy, we feel nothing at all. As the emotional waters continue to rise behind the dam, internal pressure builds up, until the dam breaks, resulting in a flood of emotions. When such issues are not completely resolved, the emotional conflict is likely to show up in the body.

We go beyond the martyr's role by recognizing the wounded sense of self-worth that underlies the outer behavior. In recognizing the martyr or victim mentality within us, we are more likely to feel compassion for those around us who are acting out something similar.

Chapter 34
Judgement

Judgment is how we perceive opposites. In a more general sense, judgment is how we separate things. We perceive and experience separateness through our unique individuality, often called the "ego."

To judge is to have an opinion on the mental level and a bias on the emotional level. When we judge, we perceive greater and lesser, right and wrong, innocent and guilty. These mental perceptions are likely to be trigger an emotional response, pleasant or unpleasant.

Our judgment of a person or situation is typically based on partial knowledge. Discarding the judgment is like throwing away a piece of a puzzle. On the other hand, to regard our judgment as the whole truth is to remain incomplete. Judgment is transcended, not by stamping it out, but by using it as a step in fully understanding the thing being judged. In other words, we judge consciously.

Judging Consciously

Judging consciously means that we honestly admit that we perceive a difference and recognize our emotional bias about it. When we judge consciously, we understand that we are making distinctions and setting boundaries for *ourselves,* not for someone else. I can say that something is good or bad *for me;* I can say that something is superior or inferior *for me.* That same preference, freely embraced, carries the understanding that our choice might be inappropriate for someone else.

In other words, when we judge consciously, we make choices and express our bias, and allow others to do likewise. Judging consciously promotes a healthy sense of individuality, also called a healthy ego.

The Healthy Ego

The biblical injunction to refrain from judging can be a great stepping-stone to freedom when it sets us free from mental attitudes that rob us of our peace. It is a steppingstone to freedom when it translates into the removal of excessive or harsh judgment of ourselves or others. It is a blessing when it sets us free from the judgments that cause us to assume that our way of thinking is intrinsically superior or inferior to those who see things differently.

On the other hand, if we flatly say, "don't judge" under any circumstance, we have set a splendid trap for ourselves. To literally stop judging completely, we have to stop thinking altogether, as well as eliminating all emotions. In other words, to stop judging means that our individuality or personality must cease to exist.

Such a command throws the ego into a state of turmoil. On the one hand, it is designed to make the mental and emotional distinctions that allow us to function effectively in physical reality, while, on the other hand, we command it to go away!

Even if we understand that "don't judge" means that we simply avoid harsh criticism and assumed superiority over others, we must be careful. We could easily seduce ourselves into believing that we are free of harsh judgment but have merely suppressed it and driven it underground. And so, we might silently strut about, secretly judging others, as we beam them a benevolent smile. The funniest version of this is when we covertly judge others for being "judgmental."

The ego stops being problematical when it is simply allowed to fulfill its function. Its function is to judge. By allowing the ego to judge in situations where judgment is appropriate, it will not do so inappropriately. In addition, we can start to undo the patterns of excessive or inappropriate judgment by being aware of it when it does show up. This becomes easier when we recognize the specific ways that we judge in everyday life. Therefore, the remainder of this chapter is focused on describing the common forms of judgment.

The Two Sides of Judgment

We cannot express judgment in one direction without the other. Every time we consciously say, "This is good," we unconsciously affirm that the opposite is bad. If we regard one thing as superior, we must regard something else as inferior.

The two sides of judgment often take the form of justification and condemnation. Justification literally means that we try to make ourselves or others appear right. Self-justification is typically a shield that hides self-condemnation. It often shows up as excuses, defensiveness or denial, which are used to cloak secret feelings of guilt or shame.

Both justification and condemnation are ways of saying, "I don't like myself." Self-justification is an indirect way of hating oneself, while self-condemnation has the dubious virtue of being more to the point.

When we are ready to break the protective shell of denial, the funny relationship between condemnation and justification becomes all too clear. We see that in the very act of justifying or making excuses for the perceived weakness, we cause the weakness to persist or even amplify. In fact, the defense of a perceived weakness will amplify the weakness more readily than the overt condemnation of it. Overt condemnation is visible and, therefore, more manageable, while justification conceals the condemnation and, therefore, prolongs and deepens its corrosive effect.

Individuals who consciously attempt to overcome an addiction quite often seem to belittle themselves or lament their weakness. This, however, is often a step up, for it is not nearly as crippling as the hard-core addict who denies, rationalizes, minimizes, or defends to the death the addictive behavior.

Mental and Emotional

Judgment has a mental component: "In my opinion, General Custer made a poor decision..." and it has an emotional component: "Green snot! How gross!" The mental and emotional components of judgment are inseparable, though one might be more obvious than the other. Regardless of how detached we appear to be with our perceptions; they are always accompanied by a subtle emotional charge. Likewise, every obvious emotional reaction must be accompanied by an underlying mental perception or belief.

213

Judgment finds its proper place when we regard it as a cognitive skill that we cultivate, as well as an emotional bias that is simply allowed to be. We cultivate the mental aspect of judgment by questioning our perceptions for accuracy. When we do so, the emotional component also finds its proper place.

The Mental Component

The mental component of judgment allows us to make sense of the world around us. It is the ability to establish clear boundaries and exercise discernment. It is our capacity to be objective. It is the methodical scientist who gathers and organizes data, or the impartial judge who weighs the evidence.

Regarding harsh judgment or condemnation, we condemn others because we perceive them as guilty. Likewise, we condemn ourselves because we perceive ourselves as guilty. Any sort of condemnation is about guilt.

The perception of guilt is one way that we justify separation. If we are in favor of the separation, the perception of guilt might be called "discernment." If we are not in favor of separation, the perception of guilt is called "being judgmental."

We might deny there is a link between separation and guilt because we do not wish to be seen as the accusers of our brethren. As a result, we attempt to distance ourselves from those we dislike but deny that we see them as guilty of misconduct. Consequently, the perception of guilt lingers in the mind.

We can certainly want to separate from others without necessarily perceiving them as guilty. We might simply feel incompatible with the person in question. If, however, we do feel violated or otherwise mistreated, a clean separation means we recognize those feelings. Thus recognized, the wound is able to heal, and the perception of guilt can change. The key is that we do not *make* it change. We simply *allow it* to change. As part of this inner change, we might eventually realize that the guilt we perceived in the other reflects our own.

The Emotional Component

The emotional component of judgment is about attraction and repulsion. We read novels and watch movies because we are emotionally drawn in by the interaction of opposing forces. In a similar manner, we judge ourselves and others, thus setting up the drama of opposing forces in our minds. Such drama generates a sense of purpose, a mission, or simply keeps us engaged and entertained.

As we recognize the emotional part of our judgments, we tend to become more objective since the emotional component no longer gets entangled with the cognitive. In fact, when we simply let the emotional component be, without rejecting or trying to justify it, we might discover that it contains subtle intuitive hunches that support our mental awareness.

When the emotional component of judgment becomes problematical, it can take the form of excessive fear, hypersensitivity, prejudice or arrogance. One hidden reason why the emotional component of judgment might become problematical is that we have cut off other sources of aliveness, such as creativity and intimacy. When we are able to reopen these other portals of aliveness, we experience a proportionate decrease in the tendency to harshly judge ourselves and others, and less tendency to seek out drama and conflict.

In other words, the emotional component of judgment is a way of feeling alive or energized. This is true whether our judgment of a given person or situation is favorable or unfavorable. Even if we see that our perception of guilt is erroneous, we might still mentally drift in this direction if it happens to be a major source of aliveness for us. We feel energized by our righteous indignation. Therefore, if our self-esteem is low, we jump at any chance to harshly judge others. On the other hand, when we are at peace with ourselves, we generate feelings of aliveness through intimacy, creative expression and loving touch.

Judgment and Anger

The emotional component of judgment can show up as anger. When we are angry at someone, we are saying, "What

215

you did was bad and I want you to feel guilty about it." However, if we think that the expression of anger is bad, we are likely to pretend that it is something else. Therefore, the anger remains hidden. And, as long as it remains hidden, it remains.

Even if we recognize that the honest expression of anger can be beneficial, we often find it difficult or scary. Therefore, we try to beautify it by denying that anger includes harsh judgment, blaming, guilt-pushing, and the perception of having been victimized. By denying these connections, anger becomes easier to express, but is not experienced in fullness.

Experiencing it in fullness means we recognize the various facets of our anger, including the blaming, the feeling of having been victimized and the desire to make the other person feel guilty. By thus recognizing the anger in fullness, and doing so with a measure of kindness, its energy is released in fullness and is therefore free to change into passion and caring.

A subtle and usually unrecognized expression of anger is jealousy concealed as judgment. We might think we are judging someone harshly because the other person is doing something that goes against our sense of ethics. However, closer examination might reveal that our judgment stems from an underlying resentment that the other person is doing something that we secretly want to do.

Judgment and Projection

We tend to judge others in accordance with our own past experiences. This is especially true when we harbor hidden guilt. We punish others for our sins. When Jesus said to the crowd, "Let he who is without sin cast the first stone," we might wonder if he was aware of the hidden joke in his statement: Only a sinner would cast a stone at another sinner.

A slightly more benign expression of projection is the act of correcting *our* weaknesses in others. We try to teach others the lessons we need to learn. Granted, there is wisdom in this. The ideal doctor to treat diabetes is one who has or had diabetes. Such a doctor has probably studied the disease in detail and has an intimate emotional understanding of it. On the other hand, we would not want to go to a diabetic doctor who treats *all* patients as if they have diabetes.

Judgment as Self-Fulfilling Prophecy

Judgment tends to be self-fulfilling. It tends to change reality in such a way as to conform to the judgment. The person making the judgment might, therefore, feel even more self-righteous than before: "You see, I was right, he's behaving just like I said he would!"

The creative power of judgment is more noticeable when the person making the judgment is adept at projecting his or her intentions or beliefs onto others, or when the person on the receiving end happens to be emotionally vulnerable or open to suggestion.

Again, judgment is partial information. By rigidly holding on to that information as if it were the whole truth, we cause it to blow out of proportion. We then create our external reality in such a way as to validate our judgment. This is one way we deepen self-deception. This is how we create misunderstandings and escalate conflict.

Judgment and Non-judgment

One subtle form of judgment is the one that says, "Non-judgment is better than judgment." This is the last one to fall away before we "shift" into the profound awareness of unity. As we approach this point, we are greeted by the realization that judgment and non-judgment have equal value. This is when the value of the ego is fully recognized. It has been allowed to fulfill its function (effective judgment) and thereby is free to relax and give way to the awareness that is beyond judgment.

Chapter 35
Forgiveness

(The Remembrance of Equality)

Revenge may be sweet in the mouth, but it is bitter in the stomach, toxic to the blood and corrosive to the brain. Equally destructive is the tendency to reject, repress or ignore the desire for revenge by covering it up with the facade of forgiveness. To do so is to bury a bomb in the garden of our relationships. This is not as paradoxical as it might seem. As with other opposites, the key is relationship. If we want to cultivate forgiveness, we must understand its relationship to its opposite.

I'm Sorry

Late one night, my wife and I found ourselves in an argument. We had been married almost a year, which, according to seasoned veterans, is the time frame in which many marriages break up.

Eventually, the defenses came down (partially) and we both told the truth (sort of). On the surface, we appeared to have resolved our conflict. I became suspicious, however, when she repeatedly said, "I'm sorry, will you forgive me?" Why was she apologizing more than me? I was equally to blame!

I knew she was sincere in her apology, but I had a feeling of foreboding. I ignored it, however, because I felt too tired to continue. And so, we went to sleep, thinking we had completed the argument.

In the predawn hours, we awakened simultaneously and silently faced each other. If I had been more attentive, I would have heard the hushed roar of distant thunder. It started as a whimper emanating from my wife. Before I knew it, she came forth with a blistering blitzkrieg of blame, in essence, undoing her apology. I became furious.

In a flash we were nose to nose, firing accusations at each other, as we had never done before. The feelings we had put aside before going to sleep came back with a vengeance. My own rage was so great I felt compelled to remind myself to avoid all physical contact while we were in that state.

In retrospect, the issues we were arguing about seemed to be amplified by a storehouse of unhealed wounds and influences in our lives. These other influences seemed so prominent that the two of us seemed like pawns fighting someone else's battle.

Eventually I started to get dressed, at which point she left the room, apparently to hide both sets of car keys. Undaunted, I got my emergency car key and stormed out of the house. However, her car was blocking mine, and I knew that she would not yield to my request to move it. So, I stormed back into the house, and we argued some more, until she was ready to move her car.

I went to my office, where I thought I would finally get some restful sleep. Instead, I periodically found myself in a half-dreaming, half-awake state, during which I seemed to be arguing on and off with my wife. As the night turned to dawn, the exchange became more peaceful. By the time I got up, the rage had lifted from me, and I had a quiet knowing that it had lifted from her as well.

When we met in person a few hours later, there were no tantrums or accusations, and we had no desire to "hash things out". We spoke quietly and freely, feeling closer to each other than we had since we were first married.

Our discussion that morning included one amazing insight. We discovered that her apologies the night before, though genuine, were a way of sidestepping the fullness of her anger. The "I'm sorry" was a way of preventing herself from going too deeply into her feelings.

A heartfelt apology emanating from genuine feelings of remorse is healing for both parties. More often than not, however, we do not reach fullness of remorse, because we do not express the fullness of our feelings. This is not necessarily a bad thing. When we hold back in this manner, there is probably a deeper wisdom at work, protecting us from expressing more than we can effectively handle at the time.

I Forgive You

Just as a premature apology can be a way of avoiding our feelings, so can insincere forgiveness. When we go through the motion of forgiving someone, we are quite often saying to ourselves, "that person has done me wrong, but I will be big about it and overlook this misdeed." This strategy runs contrary a principle described previously: The key to sanity is to question your perceptions and accept your emotions. This principle reflects the simple harmonious relationship between the thinking and feeling parts of the mind. Our thoughts are clear and our emotions peaceful and joyful when we simply question our perceptions and accept our emotions. In attempting to "forgive" someone whom we genuinely believe has "done us wrong", we are, in essence, clinging to our perceptions of wrongdoing, while trying to force our emotions to change. The resultant inner conflict silently erodes our sanity and can make us physically ill.

Such an attempt at forgiveness, translates into a covert power play. It sounds like this: "I feel that you have wronged me, so I will get even by refraining from any overt act of hostility and thereby show you and the world that I am better than you. I will sit back and let life (God) punish you. And, as I watch you suffer, I will secretly enjoy it, and I will be vindicated." This form of forgiveness is a passive form of revenge. In other words, even though we earnestly try to forgive, we (perhaps unintentionally) project vengeful thoughts, and feel vindicated when things go wrong for the other person.

A Closer Look at Forgiveness

We can get a deeper understanding of forgiveness by first getting a deeper understanding of revenge. The desire for revenge emanates from the deeper desire to experience our equality. (That's why revenge is often called "getting even".)

Genuine forgiveness is very much in resonance with that desire for equality. Forgiveness may be looked upon as the remembrance of equality.

Deep inside, we each have the desire to know our oneness or sameness. In everyday life, this shows up as the desire for equality. When we feel like we have been wronged, the desire for equality translates into the desire for revenge. We conclude that if someone hurts us, the only way to re-establish equality is to hurt him or her equally. This is why we equate justice with revenge. We reach this conclusion on a subconscious level. Therefore, even as we sincerely endeavor to forgive, we are unconsciously plotting revenge to establish equality. When the desire for revenge is not quite conscious, it can often show up as feelings of resentment or hostility.

The desire for equality is so deep that if the attacker is not available to receive our retribution, we attempt to get even (with life) by hurting any other convenient person. This is the origin of the social pecking order in which the husband beats the wife, the wife beats the child, the child beats the younger child and the younger child kicks the puppy. Obviously, this does not solve anything. Yet, if we deny or minimize the desire for revenge or feelings of resentment and hostility, they color and distort our acts of forgiveness.

If we blindly yield to desire for revenge, we simply perpetuate and escalate the violence. Likewise, it is futile to act neutral and pretend that we have forgotten the perceived injustice. We are ruled by the feeling until we allow it to speak. When we do so, we can trace it to its origin. We see that the desire for revenge is a painful and twisted cry emanating from the place within us that yearns to join with the other person in a spirit of equality and fairness.

The straight and narrow path to forgiveness is one that recognizes the desire for revenge; neither repressing it nor acting it out. Through recognition, the emotional energy contained within the desire for revenge can transmute into its primordial form - the desire to know our equality. When we feel the primordial desire for equality, we call forth the remembrance of equality - forgiveness.

No Atheists in Fox Holes

When I was a young bachelor, a friend of mine had a fling with a woman I was attempting to court. I made no attempt to minimize or sugarcoat my feelings of anger and hurt. This was most unusual for me. My typical response was to deny or minimize my emotions and act nice, after which I would isolate myself from others and mentally rehash the drama over and over again, focusing on any detail that would make me look right and the other person wrong. If I could not effectively do this within the framework of the actual facts, my mind would drift into fantasy of how I would have liked it to be.

In this particular situation, however, the events had occurred too quickly for me to pull back and erect my defenses. My emotions were too strong to be hidden behind a mask of neutrality and false forgiveness.

The following morning, as I drove my car, I still felt angry and hurt. The emotional discomfort compelled me to drop the last bit of pretense about who I thought I was. Like a child, I asked God to go to the source of the pain and make everything right. In that instant, a remarkable thing happened. I "located" the source of the pain. I experienced it as a place within me, an infantile place, that made no distinction between what is rational and irrational, sane and insane, civilized and uncivilized. Furthermore, I perceived that in this deep place, there were no clear boundaries between myself and others.

In asking for the healing of that wound, I was, in essence, asking to enter the state of consciousness in which I and my hatred foe were *one*. In everyday language, I simply had the awareness of equality; his blindness was my blindness, his pain was my pain. In asking for healing, I was (unwittingly) asking for equality. My request for equality called forth the remembrance of equality.

Chapter 36
War & Peace

According to Zen teachings, if our social and political goal is *really* peace, we must understand war. We do not have to go to war to get that understanding. If we, however, fail to cultivate such understanding, we will go to war to get it.

Understanding War

War consciousness can be understood on several levels:

- War consciousness is about survival. It says, "you have something I must have, and war is the only way I can get it."
- On other levels, war consciousness says, "I want to join with you, but I'm also afraid of you, so I will conquer you."
- On a still deeper level, when two parties are at war, they seem to be acting out the predicament of a traumatized newborn baby described by Dr. Robert Leboyer, "Don't touch me, please don't leave me."
- War allows us to bring forth qualities and abilities that we do not allow ourselves to develop during peacetime. When our survival is at stake, we tend to forget minor inconveniences and petty arguments. We become single minded and resourceful.
- On the personal level, violence results from the suppression of vitality. Vitality takes the form of playfulness, spontaneity, and creativity. When vitality is suppressed, it accumulates like steam in a pressure cooker. We eventually do harm to ourselves and others. On a larger social level, the result is social conflict and war. In one sense, warfare is a way of collectively letting off steam.

Understanding Peace

Peace is about relationship. If the desire for peace is genuine, its stems from the inner place that says, "I know you. I want to be in relationship with you." We tap into this place

225

through the practice of truthfulness. Truth leads to peace. Truth hidden under the facade of peace explodes into war.

Does peace consciousness ultimately conquer war consciousness? From the perspective of war consciousness, yes, it does (and war consciousness is deeply grateful for being conquered). From the perspective of peace-consciousness, there is no conquest; there is simply the desire to be in relationship with one's friend. In other words, the power to focus, forged during war, is allowed to come home. It is honored. Its wounds are healed. It is allowed to do what it deeply yearns to do - build the foundation for peace.

Allies & Enemies

The enemies are those from whom we try to steal power, or those who can steal power from us. The allies are those whom we enroll to defeat the enemy. Since the bottom line is survival, today's ally can become tomorrow's enemy, and vice versa. When war consciousness encounters a new face, it asks the question, "Is this an enemy, or is this an ally who can help me against my enemies?"

If we are at war, we are in survival mode. Therefore, real loyalty and affection are luxuries we cannot afford. While the battle is in progress, life is reduced to kill and be killed, which means those around us are allies or enemies. Though war can forge the beginning of friendship, we must wait for the battle to end before allies and enemies can become real friends.

We Have It Because We Want It

The outer reality for most of us is a desire for peace and fear of war. The inner reality is often reversed. We secretly desire war and fear peace. As long as the inner reality remains unrecognized, it continues to silently rule. This is one reason that war and social conflict in general seem to reappear regardless of how much we consciously try to stamp them out.

When we no longer condemn war, we begin to understand it. We begin to see our hidden desire for war. We understand why we desire it, and why we have been terrified of peace. We realize that we desire war because we emotionally equate it with purpose, movement, and vitality. We are afraid of peace

226

because we equate it with stagnation. Secretly, most of us regard peace as boring. Underneath the boredom is intense fear of oblivion and death.

The Season of Peace

The season of peace begins when the forces of war reach their peak and have been fully recognized and understood. The season of peace is the time that we look deep inside. It is impossible to harm another while looking within.

To go to war, we must first put armor around our feeling nature, shut off conscience and suspend empathy, so that we do not suffer the death of our neighbor. We might even say that the temptation to harm another is the temptation to forget oneself.

There is nothing wishy-washy about looking within. To do so takes courage, tenacity, resourcefulness and the willingness to be direct and honest with oneself and others. These skills are aimed against any weakness that would tempt us to live parasitically on others; the weaknesses that would cause us to turn away from a royal feast of freedom and friendship, so as to feed on the crumbs stolen from the table of another. Vigilance against such weakness opens the door to the experience of pure power, generated from within.

Looking deeply within allows us to see ourselves clearly and, therefore, to see ourselves in others. This is the man of war, turning his weapons into tools of self-knowledge, thus ushering in the season of peace.

Part IV
Finding Your Way Home

Chapter 37
Time

If time is the canvas upon which we create, timelessness is the floor on which it rests. The flow of time is an integral part of the dance of opposites, while timelessness is, technically, beyond duality. However, the moment that we speak or think of timelessness, it becomes part of the dance of opposites in the mind.

Time and the Mind

The thinking part of the mind operates in linier time, while the feeling part of the mind gives us a window into timelessness. In other words, the experience of timelessness is likely to show up as a *feeling*. We might not have any words to describe this feeling, but if we did, we might say that it is deep tranquility. We might say that it is the capacity to hold our peace and give our joy. We might say that it is the capacity to look upon the created universe, and declare, "Behold, it is all very good."

Ultimately, the timeless realm is beyond the understanding of the thinking mind. Regarding timelessness, the thinking mind is a blind man, and the feeling mind is the seeing-eye dog. To the extent that the two are in harmony, we are sane, functional and happy. We feel warmly connected to the life around us. The thinking mind can do its job, it can reflect on the past, plan for the future, and take action in the present moment, focused and fully engaged with the task at hand. And the feeling mind makes it all worth doing.

Time and the Physical Body

The body responds faithfully to whatever feelings and beliefs that are consistently held in the mind. In fact, according to some authors, we can slow down or even *stop* the aging process by maintaining a peaceful awareness of timelessness.

Whether or not we agree with the above assertion, studies done on long-lived individuals suggest that a strong spiritual connection supports us in aging more slowly and gracefully.

Such awareness, when it is genuine, is likely to show up as a feeling. And that feeling might be as simple as serenity, a sense of peace which is likely to show up as an absence or toning down of fear; most notably, absence of the fear of death.

Physiologically, the toning down of fear means the nervous system calms down. More specifically, the sympathetic system tones down, while the parasympathetic system is activated, allowing the body to go into regenerative and restorative mode, which support health and longevity.

The same inner peace which supports physical regeneration also invites emotional healing. The individual is able to let go of painful memories or resentments from the past because these time-bound events are experienced against the background of the bigger picture — timelessness.

Release the Past/There is No Past

At this juncture, we might encounter a seeming paradox or contradiction. How can we release the past if there is no past? If we approach this contradiction light-heartedly, it might lead to a fascinating debate between those who advocate remembering and releasing memories of the past and those who insist that these "memories" are not memories at all, but stories we make up here and now.

In other words, one side advocates looking at current behavior and correlating it to childhood experiences. The other side states, "We create all experiences here-and-now, including the experience of 'memories.' The painful memories are not memories at all. There is only now and the choices we make now."

A simple way to resolve this contradiction is to not try to resolve it all. We simply look at it pragmatically by asking, "Which model is more useful to me right now?" One or the other, used properly, could help us navigate through life, depending on the circumstance.

Granted, the above solution might seem like "cheating" if we are looking for the absolute truth which we can cling to in any circumstance. However, that same rigidity is also likely to cause us to misuse either model. For example, both could be used to avoid taking responsibility for one's life. One side might deny the existence of the past so as to deny memories that are too uncomfortable to contemplate. The other side might dwell on the past to avoid the present and to remain stuck in victim mode.

Bottom line: The experience of linier time is part of our human existence — but not all of it. How we navigate through our own personal experience of time will determine how we experience timelessness. For example, remembering and healing wounds from the past opens the door to the perception of the eternal now. Likewise, to directly seek a transcendental experience, such as timelessness, can very well open the door to unresolved emotional issues from the past. In fact, to force such a transcendental experience, through psychotropic substances or other means, while still harboring unresolved painful memories, can produce psychological disorientation or psychosis.

Time, Space, and Sanity

The "untimely" experience of timelessness can be disorienting because our everyday thoughts function within the framework of linear time. The same holds true for our everyday emotions. Furthermore, as professor Einstein pointed out, time and space are inseparable.

The interrelatedness of time and space has been demonstrated repeatedly. Mathematical models and experimentation have revealed that time and space are basically two expressions of the same basic phenomenon. In addition, their connection has also been reported by mystics, saints, and countless individuals in and out of mental hospitals.

Since time and space are inseparable, a change in one affects the other. Therefore, if the mind dives into a strong experience of timelessness, the normal experience of "space" also goes out the window. Boundaries dissolve, whether we want them to or not. We lose the friendly and familiar frames of reference, such as up, down, left, right, front, back, large, small, self, and other.

Carl Jung coined a phrase to identify the timeless/spaceless realm of the mind. He called it the *collective unconscious.* He once told the story of a client, a levelheaded military man, who was exploring the collective unconscious. This client also had a daughter in a mental hospital. Through his work with Dr. Jong, the client learned that both he and his daughter were tapping into the same collective unconscious. The man therefore wanted to know how his own experience was different from that of his daughter. Why was his experience orderly and harmonious, while his daughter's experience was so chaotic and disorienting that she was not able to function? Dr. Jung replied, "You dove in; she fell in."

Just a Moment Ago

The experience of timelessness does not necessarily have to be dramatic or disorienting. When the perception of time and experience of timelessness are in harmony, the mind can proceed on its journey through linear time, as it quietly gets hints of timelessness — which typically show up as feelings.

These feelings may present themselves as a sense of wonder; the world takes on a newness or brightness; everyday events seem astounding — in a quiet sort of way. If we are attentive to these subtle feelings, they grow. We look at the same oak tree every day, appreciating its majesty, and one day, we may feel something new. If that feeling could speak, it might say, "That oak tree…wasn't it an acorn just a moment ago? Behold the mountain; it was a valley just a moment ago. Behold the grass-covered plain; it was an ocean floor just a moment ago; and in yet another moment, it will become a deep canyon. Behold the star; just a moment ago, it was a nebula; in another moment hence, its energy and matter will be transformed into a flower."

The scientist who looks at the ordinary landscape and marvels at what is, what was, and what will be, has merged the rational perception of linear time with a subtle feeling of timelessness. By the calendar, eons have passed since life first appeared on Earth. Yet, when the feeling mind is open, the event is stunning and miraculous, as if we had witnessed it just a moment ago.

Chapter 38
Birth & Death

Linear time makes birth and death possible. Timelessness makes possible awareness of life beyond the boundaries of birth and death. As suggested in the previous chapter, the awareness of timelessness does not have to be disorienting. It can show up as a quiet feeling of serenity, or a perception that says, "I was born into this body just a moment ago. And, in another moment hence, I will fly free from it."

How do we invite that timeless quality of life beyond birth and death. One way is to simply recognize both as partners in the dance of creation.

As with other opposites, we are ruled by the side that we reject or resist. Such resistance shows up as fear or grief.

Fear

Fear of birth is fear of the new and unknown. Fear of death is pretty much the same thing. An important part of our journey through life is the letting go of the old and bringing forth the new. When we fear letting go of the old, we obstruct emergence of the new and therefore restrict creative expression and passion for living. The more easily we let go of the old, the more easily we bring forth the new.

Fear of death is fear of the unknown. As described in chapter six, fear of death is normal expression of our instinct for survival. However, fear of death suggests the presence of unfulfilled desires. In other words, fear of death may result from not having given ourselves the opportunity to give birth to that which is waiting dormant within. We feel that we have not yet sung the song we were born to sing. We are driven by the fear that we will die before that child is born and that song is sung.

When we allow ourselves to express our creative urges and aspersions, we do not fear death; we do not fear letting go of the old. There is simply a quiet sense of completion. To experience death from that perspective is not unlike graduation, or saying goodbye to a house we have outgrown. In saying goodbye there might be a touch of sorrow, but it is a sweet sorrow, inseparable from joy.

Grief

Difficulty in feeling complete can show up as lingering grief. Grief associated with the death of a loved one is normal and healthy. This is how emotions "catch up" with external reality. When a loved one dies or, for that matter, when an emotionally significant relationship comes to an end, a part of us seems to die also. To the extent that we respect such an experience of "death," we usher in the birth of a new part of self.

In other words, grief can serve as an emotional bridge between death and rebirth. The more sudden or unexpected the death, the longer the period of grief. Persistent grief means that the individual is stuck between death and rebirth. Persistent grief is the inability to feel the completeness of an experience.

However, we must be cautious about arbitrarily concluding that we have grieved "too long." We must be even more cautious about deciding for others that they have grieved too long. As with birth, grieving over a death has its own timing and rhythm. If we try to rush or censor the process, the unresolved pain is likely to remain, preventing new life from emerging.

Grieving is complete when the relationship or the life of the departed loved-one is felt as a precious and complete experience. At that point, the grieving individual experiences a "birth" or renewal.

Every day, we start and finish things. It is relatively rare that we experience grief over it. We start and finish in many small ways and a few grand ways. How gracefully we move through this cycle depends on how gracefully we embrace the unknown.

Again, fear of birth is fear of the new and unknown, as is fear of death. As with other opposites, we are ruled by the side that we reject or resist. To experience both as partners in the dance of creation is to invite the timeless quality of life beyond birth and death. Which reminds me of a story:

The Old Tree

I awoke at about 3:30 AM and found myself curled up on a couch in the waiting room next to the intensive care unit of a hospital in northeast Pennsylvania. My father was in critical condition. My oldest brother was sleeping on another couch in the same room. His snoring was thunderous, and I was feeling restless anyway, so I went for a stroll.

For a while, I walked slowly through the dimmed corridors, my footsteps echoing softly on the linoleum. To my surprise, I remembered a cartoon I had seen at the age of ten. It was a TV series that aired every day after school. The show was about a community of animals ruled by a young lion named "Kimba."

I had long forgotten the actual contents of the show, but as I walked through the corridors of the hospital, I clearly remembered one particular episode. It had to do with a large, ancient tree standing in a clearing in the midst of the jungle. For the animals in the community, the tree was a common gathering point. For many of them, it was a source of food or shelter. It was far older than the oldest animal in the community. From season to season, through countless storms and droughts, it stood steady and firm. The tree was their home base, the center of their universe. It defined them as a community.

When the animals realized the old tree was dying, they frantically did everything possible to keep it alive. Eventually, they resorted to tying strong vines around its trunk and branches to prevent it from breaking apart. In the end, however, the old tree broke the restraints and began to crack in various places.

The animals stood in a circle around the tree. They watched as it crumbled to the ground. In a matter of seconds, their lifelong companion was reduced to a heap of splintered logs and broken branches.

For a while, the animals stared in silence at the remains of the tree. Kimba stepped forward, fell on the debris, and sobbed. And then, in the depth of his grief, Kimba looked up and fell silent. He walked slowly to the center of the rubble. There, he saw a single tiny seedling. That was when Kimba understood. The old tree wanted to die. It wanted to make room for new life. Their old friend had become a new friend.

Beyond Birth and Death

I stood in the darkened corridor of the hospital, looking out the window. Thirty years had passed since I had seen that cartoon. As I gazed down at the snow-covered rooftops and the rows of glowing streetlights, the images continued flashing through my mind. I recalled the cartoon vividly, as if I had seen it just a moment ago.

Later that day, as my father took his last breath, my brothers and sisters and I stood around his bed. All seven of us wept, some of us loudly, some of us quietly. Yet, as I let myself feel the loss, I also became aware of something new and innocent in our presence. The feeling was subtle, yet quietly overpowering. I was experiencing both death and birth, and something beyond both—Life, ever-changing and always the same.

Chapter 39
Order & Chaos

Order and chaos are yet another expression of duality based on the presence and absence of something. The dance of order and chaos may seem abstract and far removed from the practical world, but it is actually an integral part of your everyday life which shows up in many different ways.

Order and chaos show up as rigid and flexible, regimented and spontaneous, organized and disorganized, harmony and disharmony, focused and scattered, responsibility and freedom, work and play, purposeful and random, planned and spontaneous, committed and uncommitted, sane and crazy, known and unknown, etc.

We choose the pair that conforms best with our judgment of the situation in question. If we favor order, we use words like *harmony, organized, responsible, purposeful, focused, sane*. We say, "I want to be organized, I want my actions to be purposeful. I want to walk with intention and focus. I choose to be sane."

If we favor chaos, we probably will not call it that, since the word has an unfavorable association for most individuals. Instead, we use words like *spontaneous, flexible, and freedom,* We say, "I want to be spontaneous; I want to dance in accordance with my own inner flute, not march to the beat of the collective drum. I want to play; I want to be free." However, we might be reluctant to acknowledge that freedom may appear to be chaotic or even crazy. In the words of Zorba the Greek, "A man must have a touch of madness or he will never be free."

Order and chaos follow the same pattern of other dualities. To cling to one side is to fear the other. To judge one as better, is to make the other the silent ruler. Likewise, when we understand each side, we allow the two to function as partners in the dance of creation; each side asserting itself and yielding to the other in a harmonious way that allows life to flourish.

And, as with other opposites, their interaction results in the emergence of new life.

The Secret Desire for Order

Most of us would agree that the exaggerated need for order generally stems from fear. Paradoxically, if a person is playing out an exaggerated preference for freedom or chaos, there is often an unrecognized desire for order. and the associated need for safety. And containment This is the child who creates chaos, sending to the adult a nonverbal message: "Please give me structure; build a fence around me; I want to know my boundaries so I can feel safe." Adults can display a similar tendency, acting sort of crazy as a way of playing out the secret desire for containment.

The Secret Desire for Chaos

There are a number of reasons we might secretly desire chaos. Random and chaotic events, seemingly beyond our control, give us an excuse for not achieving our goals. It is uncomfortable to think that we have not become wealthy because we are not good at business or some other hidden flaw in our character. However, failure is more socially acceptable if it is due to the "unstable economy," or some other random or chaotic event that has nothing to do with us personally.

If we feel bored with life or if we feel restrained or trapped, we might secretly desire chaos to reshuffle the deck so that we can feel free to do something else. In this case, chaos translates into freedom.

Whatever the reason, the very fact that we secretly desire chaos means that we are likely to invite it. We secretly call forth the random or chaotic event. For example, if I want to move my office to a different location, but am afraid of making a move, I might procrastinate indefinitely. However, if a flood destroys my office (which it did), I am pushed to do the thing that I was afraid to do on my own initiative.

On the other hand, if we recognize the hidden desire for change, we can simply do it intentionally. We can consciously initiate change, rather than unconsciously wishing that a random/chaotic event beyond our control forces change.

Chapter 40
Known & Unknown

One of the most common ways that we seek order is to seek knowledge. Gathering knowledge, whether through intellect or intuition, is a major way of bringing order into our world. Likewise, the absence of knowledge implies the absence of order and, by implication, the presence of chaos.

As expressions of order and chaos, The known and unknown dance within us in the same manner as any pair of opposites. Each side defines the other and bears the seed of the other. The dynamic tension between the two drives us to create.

Harmony within the mind includes harmony between that which is known and that which is unknown. The manner in which we create the future is, among other things, a dance of the known and unknown. The dance tends to be harmonious when we are mindful enough to apply what we know and respectful enough to recognize what we do not know. The known gives us the power to act, while the unknown restrains us from acting too quickly. For example, if I want to invest in the stock market, my decisions will obviously be influenced by what I know and what I do not know.

Since knowledge allows us to be somewhat in control of our future, most of us prefer knowledge over ignorance. Occasionally, however, we turn our eyes away from knowledge that is available to us. In fact, the same fear that might compel us to cling to the known, can also cause us to turn a blind eye to whatever we do not want to see. This is a major reason why the future often does not unfold as smoothly as we would like. We are fearfully preoccupied with gathering too much knowledge so we can anticipate every possibility, or we are afraid of looking at the facts. The two are inseparable. The obvious presence of one point to the hidden presence of the other.

The balance point is where we allow the known and unknown to dance harmoniously within us. We accept the knowledge that is available, while trusting ourselves to proceed (with appropriate caution) in the presence of the unknown.

Our preference for known over unknown might show up as pretending to know in order to hide our discomfort or embarrassment with not knowing. Such pretense, when practiced habitually, contributes to emotional unrest and mental fogginess. The healthy alternative to pretending to know is to admit that we sincerely do not know.

Knowledge and Wisdom

Aas mentioned earlier, we can know things through intellect or intuition. The knowledge conferred by intellect is learned through time and organized in a linear fashion. The knowledge conferred by intuition is not limited to linear time. The intellect stores and organizes information that begins at birth, while intuition draws on information beyond the boundaries of birth and death. The knowledge gathered by the intellect is rational and tangible and can easily be communicated in words, while the knowledge emerging from the feeling nature may be so mysterious as to defy verbal description.

When the bits of knowledge conferred by the intellect and intuition are deeply integrated, the result is wisdom. Wisdom is subtler than knowledge. Knowledge is simply information, which we can gather fairly quickly. On the other hand, wisdom tends to evolve gradually. We cultivate wisdom over time, through the relationship of our intellect and intuition.

To the extent that the two are not harmoniously blended, knowledge remains incomplete. Incomplete knowledge does not have to be false knowledge. False knowledge means that our perception is erroneous because it is based on inaccurate data, emotional bias, or some private agenda that values personal gain over truth. Typically, incomplete knowledge becomes false knowledge when we trick ourselves into believing that we are seeing the entire picture. When we mistake incomplete knowledge for complete knowledge, we are prejudging or misjudging something or someone.

To Love is To Know

To love completely requires that we know completely. The reverse is also true. Total knowledge of a thing becomes available only if we are willing to love it totally. We see a version of this in interpersonal relationships. If we profess to love a person totally (unconditionally), the implication is that we know the person totally. If we withhold love from any part of the individual, our knowledge is incomplete.

The inherent unity of knowledge and love also applies to oneself. To love ourselves is to know ourselves. The more we know ourselves, the more we can love ourselves.

Some schools of thought regard self-love as a vice. Others regard it as a virtue. Both carry a measure of truth. Self-love is a vice if we attempt to love ourselves without knowing ourselves. Such an expression of self-love translates into self-deception, self-indulgence, avoidance of responsibilities, and disregard for others. If self-love is understood to be synonymous with self-knowledge, self-love translates into loving relationship with others.

In other words, the key to loving ourselves is to remember that self-love and self-knowledge are inseparable. Loving ourselves more deeply is possible when we are willing to know ourselves more deeply. Likewise, we can deepen self-knowledge only if we have enough intrinsic self-love to see the hidden parts of ourselves with a spirit of gentleness and kindness.

Complete Knowledge

Fullness of knowledge or complete knowledge (which goes hand in hand with fullness of love or unconditional love) is not as difficult or unworldly as it might seem. It is possible to cultivate fullness of knowledge on the human level. The key is to remember that cultivating fullness of knowledge (in a stable form that does not overwhelm us), typically takes time. We might even say that cultivation of complete knowledge is what time is for.

The other key is to remember that fullness of knowledge is not just a mental thing. Since fullness of knowledge is synonymous with unconditional love, it must also include the feeling part of our awareness. Fullness of knowledge shows up as a mental perception and an emotional experience — and beyond.

Incomplete Knowledge

Most of our knowledge of ourselves and the world around us is incomplete. Nonetheless, incomplete knowledge has value, provided we know that it is incomplete, or that, at the very least, we are open to the possibility that we are not seeing the entire picture.

Incomplete knowledge is false knowledge when we trick ourselves into believing that we are seeing the entire picture. We look at the horizon and regard it as the end of world. When we mistake incomplete knowledge for complete knowledge. This might show up as prejudging or misjudging something or someone.

In the presence of false knowledge, love is also false. We think we love someone when we might simply be infatuated with the false image we have of that person.

False knowledge occurs for one of two reasons:

- We have a hidden need to see the person or situation in a certain way. Therefore, we tend to block any information that does not fit our image.
- Defensiveness might prevent us from admitting our ignorance. Therefore, we make up things. We are tempted to cover the unknown with false or incomplete information.

If we pretend to know, there is no room for new information. The fullness of knowing is born in the place that is pristine and untarnished by the pretense of knowing. The purity of not knowing is state of innocence, free of judgment, and free of pretense. When the unknown is allowed to be itself rather than hiding behind false or incomplete knowledge, it becomes the empty vessel which we can fill with knowledge. It is a clear canvas for creation.

Chapter 41
Motion & Stillness

(Self-worth Revisited)

As described in chapter 7, self-worth has two sides: doing & being. Self-worth experienced through doing is earned. Self-worth experienced through being cannot be earned.

We can get a deeper understanding of doing & being — and bring them int deeper harmony — by regarding them as an expression of motion & stillness.

The experience of self-worth through doing is about motion. The experience of self-worth through being is about stillness, because it is in stillness that I connect with who I am.

The Relativity of Motion & Stillness

As with other true opposites, motion and stillness define each other. In the physical universe, there is no absolute motion and absolute stillness. Motion and stillness are relative terms. Their relativity is a foundational feature of Einstein's Theory of Relativity.

Another sign that motion and stillness are true opposites is that each side emerges from the other. Motion comes from stillness and then returns to stillness. The latter point is relevant, having practical value for those who wish to cultivate inner stillness and outer success.

"Stillness is the root of all motion." — Lao Zhu

Motion & Stillness in the Mind

On the mental level, motion translates into our moment-to-moment stream of thoughts, and stillness translates into the capacity to focus, and to listen.

On the emotional level, motion translates into *e*motion — the flow of emotional waters in response to our mental perceptions. Likewise, emotional stillness translates into the peace we feel when the thinking mind quiets down.

Cultivation of inner stillness provides practical benefits for body and mind. On the physiological level, mental stillness, and the emotional peace that goes with it, translates into the toning down of the sympathetic nervous system and up-regulating of the parasympathetic system, which allow the body rest, heal, regenerate, and rejuvenate.

Regarding our worldly activities, as we cultivate the ability to enter into stillness, the mind becomes more creative, efficient, and productive.

The simplest way of inviting inner stillness is to effectively manage the mind when it is actively in motion.

Managing Motion

As a young child, prior to migrating to the USA, I did not watch television because we did not have one. Neither did I spend hours on the internet, because that technology had not been developed yet.

After moving to America, we eventually got a television. And I was thrilled! I quickly got into the habit of watching hours and hours of cartoons, The Lone Ranger, The Three Stooges, Abbot and Costello, and anything having to do with rockets, space travel, and dinosaurs.

When our city experienced a power outage, I felt a strange sense of uneasiness during the evening. I didn't know what to do with myself. Having no other recourse, I sat down at the living room table with a piece of blank paper and some crayon and drew a picture. And that is how I kept myself entertained for the entire evening.

After having been engaged in my artwork for about 30 minutes or so, I noticed that I was not bored anymore. And the sense of uneasiness was gone. I was fully emersed in my project and was feeling rather peaceful. Even at that young, I noticed that I felt a calmness which was very different from the pacified stupor induced by Bugs Bunny. In retrospect, I suspect that I also slept very deeply and peacefully that night.

As an adult, I have consistently noticed that I am more likely to wake up feeling refreshed and renewed in both body and mind when I am physically active, creative, and productive during the day, and refrain from watching the news or otherwise stare at a screen for the last one or two hours prior to going bed. On such mornings, I also find it easier to sit in stillness. In other words, how I manage my outer motion has a profound effect on my capacity to enter into stillness.

How to Cultivate Stillness

If you find it difficult to sit still, you probably find it even more difficult to bring stillness to the mind. In fact, if you are like most folks, you find it virtually impossible to sit still and not think about anything — and trying to make yourself do so just makes the mind more agitated. We can get around that by remembering that motion and stillness are relative of terms. This is certainly true for motion and stillness in the physical world. It is also relevant for the workings of the mind. In other words, when we sit down to meditate and endeavor to "practice stillness," we are not trying to stop thinking altogether. We are simply allowing the mind to tone down mental activity. This principle is important because it sets us free from unrealistic expectations and harsh judgment of ourselves when the mind is not as quiet as we think it should be. Such harsh judgment and self-recrimination for failing to go into stillness is in fact a major obstacle to the cultivation of inner stillness. Such harsh judgment is likely to happen to the extent that we have an addiction to motion and aversion to stillness.

Addiction to Motion and Aversion to Stillness

These two patterns are very common. They are also obviously interrelated. Addiction to constant activity (physical or mental) leads to aversion to stillness. Likewise, by avoiding stillness and quiet time, we become more dependent of perpetual motion in order to feel "normal."

When we first try to stop the outer activity and enter into stillness, we might feel emotional unrest. Such unrest might be compared to the physical discomfort associated with giving up caffeine. To complicate matters, as with other addictions, harsh judgment and self-recrimination seem to exacerbate the problem. This is why twelve-step programs encourage recovering addicts to let go of the demand for perfection and to avoid self-recrimination. And this is the attitude which allows us go through the "withdrawal" phase of cultivating stillness.

Be Still and Know that I am God.

When we spend time allowing the mind to quiet down, a portal of sorts opens up. It is a doorway to the deepest genuine self. That door typically opens gradually. There might be high times and low times when the door opens wide only to slam shut. There might be a "peak experience" followed by a let-down. However, over time, the battle ground in your mind becomes a field of peace where the small self — the so-called ego — can rest a while in communion with the bigger self. Over time, we might experience the bigger self as an actual "presence" which resides in stillness.

From a practical standpoint, the daily practice of inner stillness is a time of plugging into our own personal source of vitality. The inner battery is recharged,. We cultivate mental clarity and emotional serenity.

The moment-to-moment practice of stillness usually translates in simply watching your thoughts and the associated emotions as they emerge on the screen of conscious awareness. This seems to be easiest to do early in the morning, after a night of deep restful sleep.

One of the challenges associated with watching your thoughts is that it is a passive process. We can make it easier by changing into an active process by giving the mind something to do. For example, while watch your thoughts and emotions, bless them! If your mind wanders, bless the wandering. If you feel harsh judgment for your lack of inner stillness, bless that too. If you dose off, bless the dozing. If your feel impatient, bless your impatience. In other words, when you bless the state of mind which seems to be disturbing your inner stillness, remember to bless the disturbance, and it will serve as a doorway into deeper inner stillness.

When we bless the motion, we invite stillness.
When we commune in stillness, we bless the motion.

.

.

Chapter 42
Darkness & Light

"All creativity awakens at the primal threshold where light and darkness test and bless each other." – John O'donohue

To perceive light and darkness as separate is to be in duality. To see them as one is to experience unity. The perception of their separateness is a thought. The experience of their unity is a feeling. When our thoughts and feelings are integrated, we can recognize the separate identities of light and darkness, as well as their intimate relationship in the dance of creation.

Light and darkness are often used to symbolize two primordial qualities that are otherwise difficult to verbalize without using a heavy dose of flowery metaphors and far-flung teleological abstractions — which I will do in the pages that follow. Such abstract descriptions can become as far removed from our day-to-day reality as the equations of a theoretical physicist. Yet, like said equations, they do have value, simply because light and darkness are deeply meaningful for us. Light and darkness symbolize the two primordial forces that emerge from Unity and then give rise to everything else.

For most humans, the dance of light and darkness in Creation holds emotional charge and perhaps some confusion. Ultimately, the confusion and emotional charge stem from our deep cultural programming that places opposites at war with one another. Because of that tendency, the natural relationship of light and darkness is torn asunder. That relationship is reestablished as we gradually cultivate an appreciation for the dance of opposites that makes life possible. In the meantime, we can begin to clear up some of the confusion, and tone down the emotional charge, by first understanding light and darkness from a purely physical standpoint. In other words, let us first consider light and darkness, as a physicist would.

The Physics of Darkness & Light

Light is the fundamental energetic stuff of the created universe. Darkness is the absence of that stuff. Light is motion. Darkness is stillness. More specifically, light is a vibration of something. Darkness is the absence of that vibration. In that sense, darkness embodies absolute stillness and emptiness.

The exact nature of that vibrating substance is open to interpretation. However, whatever it is, it is definitely vibrating. We also know that light moves very fast. It travels through space at a velocity of about 186,000 miles per second, which is the fastest movement that physicists have been able to measure thus far.

Furthermore, the vibrating and rapidly moving energetic stuff which we perceive as visible light, is but one form of a more generalized energy called electromagnetism. Other forms of electromagnetism include infrared waves, radio waves, microwaves, ultraviolet rays, x-rays, and gamma rays.

Electromagnetism may be understood as yet another dance of Yin and Yang. The Yin side is magnetism. The Yang side is electricity. As with other true opposites, electricity and magnetism are inseparable. They are two sides of the same energetic coin, each side giving birth to the other. An electric current generates a magnetic field. Likewise, a rotating magnetic field can be used to induce an electric current.

Physicist describe light as the product of magnetism and electricity rapidly transforming into one another. The difference between visible light and other forms of electromagnetism is the frequency. Ultraviolet light, x-rays and gamma rays vibrate at higher frequencies than visible light. Likewise, visible light vibrates at higher frequencies than infrared waves, radio waves, and microwaves.

Beings of Light

Higher frequency translates into higher energy. Large doses of ultraviolet light, x-rays and gamma rays are harmful to life because they pack more energy than most living organisms can tolerate. On the other hand, the energy of visible light is mild enough to be harmless to life. In fact, plants use visible light to build the organic molecules that we and other animals consume as food. In one sense, our bodies consist of light energy stored within the molecules of life.

Light as Information

With the invention of radio and TV, we learned that electromagnetic waves can be used to carry information. So, using a bit of poetic license, "light" becomes a metaphor for knowledge, while darkness is a metaphor for the absence of knowledge.

Our language reflects the fact that we equate light with knowledge, and darkness with the absence of knowledge. To "see the light" is to be in the known; to be "in the dark" is to be in the unknown. To become "illuminated" is to gain knowledge.

We prefer light over darkness because we prefer known over unknown. This is quite understandable; the desire for knowledge or "en*lightenment*" is instinctual. If that instinct is not expressed freely and naturally, it might show up as a tendency to cling to light and reject darkness, or vice versa.

Fear of the unknown shows up as fear of darkness. The unspoken assumption is that light is good and darkness is bad. The light is perceived as something that dispels or banishes the darkness. This creates an insidious split in the mind. We prefer the light because it is visible and known and, therefore, predictable and safe. Yet, we also long for the stillness of darkness; for it is the domain of infinite possibilities, the womb that brings forth all things new and pristine. We yearn for it, for it is the source of innocence. However, most of us are also afraid of it, because of our tendency to place opposites at war with one another.

This inner split is so deeply repressed that it is barely noticed by most light-skinned people. However, it is much more real and much more personal for dark-skinned people living in a predominantly light-skinned society. This is especially true in an orthodox Judeo-Christian setting where light symbolizes good, and darkness symbolizes evil. In the presence of this deep cultural bias, a dark-skinned individual might feel uneasy, because a part of self is being rejected or

251

cast out. The uneasiness if it could speak, might say, "Light is good and dark is bad. I have dark skin. Hmmm..." Consequently, dark-skinned people living in a predominantly light-skinned society are uniquely qualified to see this preference for what it really is—a rejection of one's very soul.

The Metaphysics of Light and Darkness

As with other pairs of opposites, light and darkness have meaning only in the presence of each other. They define each other and give birth to one another.

The light shines in the darkness because that is the only place it *can* shine. In the physical sense, the "speed of light" would have no meaning, if there were no darkness in which the light could move. The light emerges from the darkness and maintains its identity by being nested in the darkness.

Darkness is synonymous with the unseen, unknown, and unheard. It is silence, stillness, vacuum, the void. To our senses, darkness is a box into which we cannot see. To the intellect, it is the absence of all information; it is utterly *nothing*. In that sense, the idea of "casting out" or "banishing" darkness seems rather bizarre. How do we cast out emptiness? It is not a space-occupying lesion that we can just amputate. We do not "cast out" emptiness. We fill it.

Just as darkness is emptiness and stillness, light is visible; it can have shape, form, color, and texture. It is forever moving, vibrating, and expanding.

Light and darkness symbolize the two primordial forces that emerge from primordial unity and then give rise to everything else. This grand dance of creation ultimately defies description. We can, however, make it somewhat real to us by describing it in human terms. The many creation myths that abound in various cultures attempt to put into words that which is beyond words. Some of them describe it as a war, and other depict the harmonious dance of creation. For example, pure darkness may be said to give birth to the fullness of light. And, thus, the darkness is able to look upon itself in the light of its own creation and it declares, "I am!" This is unity restored. In declaring, *"I am,"* the fullness of light knows itself to be the purity of darkness made visible. It is simultaneously the purity of darkness and the fullness of light, eternally still and ever expanding, deeply mysterious, and fully realized.

In other words, the relationship of primordial light and darkness may be likened to that of the womb and the baby. This analogy, however, is limited. When light becomes "old enough" it unites with darkness in a different way. In this union, the light "cools down" a bit, allowing it to condense into form which we call protons, neutrons and electrons, which come together to form stars, planets, and sentient life forms. These created realities embody the infinite diversity and primordial wholeness of *"I am."*

One variation on this creation myth shows light and darkness making war instead of love. Since this war takes place beyond linear time, we cannot speak of a "first cause." In rough human terms, we might say that the darkness judges itself harshly and gives forth a blinding light. Why does the darkness judge itself harshly? Because it cannot see itself in the blinding light. This is where linear thinking or intellect reaches a ceiling. As with other attempts to intellectually describe our spiritual origins, this one seems to end with a paradox.

"The light shines in the darkness, and the darkness comprehends it not." It does not comprehend that it is looking at itself made visible and tangible.

This paradox would be quite tolerable if it were just an intellectual puzzle that we kick around at a party. However, when the awareness is more *experiential,* it is likely to include a rather intense emotional component. The confused combination of judging darkness and blinding light screams out, *"I am not!"* This is the scream of primal terror and shame. It is the terror of total annihilation; and the shame of perceiving oneself as split from oneself. It is the ultimate accuser and accused rolled up in one. It is a dance of cosmic insanity, in which the angry accuser does not realize it is attacking itself. And the terrified accused does not know it is being attacked by itself. Perhaps all human battles stem from this one.

253

The Psychology of Darkness and Light

The above metaphysical description of the cosmic war between light and darkness could very well be interpreted as a psychological projection, a dramatization of self at war with self. Darkness can easily symbolize a frightened and hurt corner of the mind that feels unloved and cast out. If it remains neglected, it becomes so-called evil, which tries to fill its emptiness with life stolen from others. On the other side of the coin, the blinding light becomes hardened intellect. It takes on an identity called good, which tries to establish order, as it sustains itself on the self-worth acquired by fighting evil.

They do this over and over, until the two are seen as equal and perfectly symmetrical reflections of each other. In everyday language, the essence of evil is simply the desire to be understood, while the essence of good is the capacity to understand. The two are inseparable. To the extent that we honor our personal desire to be understood, we are capable of understanding. Likewise, to the extent that we are willing to understand, we can be truly understood. When the two are fully united in the mind, the war between light and darkness tends to lose significance.

The common perception of good and evil as mutually exclusive forces is just one example of how we place opposites at war with each other, rather than allowing them to function as partners in the dance of creation. In this case, we have unwittingly torn asunder the simple human desire to be understood and the capacity to understand. Consequently, the desire to be understood goes unfulfilled, and the capacity to understand erodes into rigid dogmas doctrines.

Many techniques have been devised to tap into the blissful state of inner integration wherein every part of oneself is at peace with every other part. In truth, we cannot stop this process from happening. We can expedite its emergence by simply not rushing it. We just do what comes naturally to us. We go about our lives, touching, giving, receiving, planting the tree, smiling at the cashier, etc. Light and darkness dance harmoniously within us when we are simply being genuinely human, doing the things that humans do.

Chapter 43
Choice & Destiny

If we are inclined toward materialism, the universe is seen as chaotic. We might recognize laws of physics and chemistry that establish order, but we see those laws as operating against a background of random events and mindless chance.

If we believe that chaos does not tell the whole story, we are implying there is a fundamental order beyond the laws of physics and chemistry. If so, we are faced with a question: Who, or what, is establishing the order? In human terms, the order is attributed to choice or destiny.

Choice means we create order with our daily decisions. Destiny implies that order is established through a pre-set pattern. Like the water in a river moving in accordance with the contours of the land, our course through life is determined by invisible furrows in the field of space and time.

Choice implies that we are each independent individuals, creating our own lives as we interact with the world around us. On the other hand, destiny implies there is just one life and it has a plan which contains many smaller plans.

From a materialistic standpoint, the universe is chaotic; we are born into a certain family by chance. If we believe there is an underlying order, we might say that it was our choice or our destiny to be born into a certain family.

Shopping for Parents

One of my patients had a young daughter who was bright and precocious, and learned to talk at a very young age. At age two, she reported the following to her mother:

"Mommy, I picked you and Daddy."

"When did you do that?" asked the mother.

"When I was with God."

The mother was astonished because neither she nor her husband were religious and had no interest in metaphysics. Two years later, when the child was four years of age, her mother asked her, "Do you remember when you were little and you said you chose Daddy and me?"

255

"Yes, I remember."

"Can you tell me anything more about that?"

"Yes. I was in heaven and God was busy, so Jesus helped me. He said, "Hurry up, you have to be born soon.' So, I looked in a big book of pictures, like the police have."

"You mean mug shots"? Asked the mother, wondering how the little girl knew about such things.

"Yes," answered the child, "except that it was a book of pictures of mommies and daddies. I looked at the pictures and I saw yours and Daddy's pictures, and I said, 'I want them to be my Mommy and Daddy'. And then I was born."

The child's story, whether it is interpreted as fact, fantasy, or a combination of the two, has the element of destiny (It is time to be born) and choice (I will choose my parents).

Incidentally, the child's story is not uncommon. Another one of my patients, a four-year-old girl, said to her mother, "Last time, *I* was the mom." She did not stop there. During one angry moment, when she was being disciplined by her mother, the child said, "I *let* you be mom this time."

Managing Choice and Destiny

It is relatively easy for choice and destiny to co-exist in the mind, as long as the two concepts are viewed separately. For any given event, we give the credit to either choice or destiny. If we like the outcome, we might be inclined to call it choice. If the event does not look very nice, we might be inclined to call it destiny. Or we compromise by saying that our choices can change the flow of destiny, or vice versa.

Sometimes, however, the two concepts appear to be mutually exclusive. If we look deep enough, their dance defies logic and baffles the rational mind. Therefore, we typically do not look very deeply.

Will and Feeling Revisited

We can begin to understand the deeper mysteries of choice and destiny by considering the will and the feeling aspects of our awareness, as described in chapter 10. The will takes the initiative and makes choices. The feeling-mind yields to the flow of destiny.

When the will and feelings are not balanced, our choices seem to be in conflict with the flow of destiny. If the will and feeling-mind are *very* dissociated, choice and destiny appear to be mutually exclusive. On the other hand, to the extent that the will and feeling-mind are balanced and integrated, so are choice and destiny. The will makes choices that reflect the inner vision of destiny which emerge as feeling. If that vision could speak, it might speak of freedom, relationship, kindness, family, fairness, and justice.

Unity of Choice and Destiny

The deeper the communion between the will and feeling sides of the mind, the more deeply we sense the harmony between choice and destiny. If the will and feeling nature are integrated deeply enough, they merge into one, as do choice and destiny. When this happens, we no longer say that our choices create destiny, or that our choices are in response to the flow destiny. Instead, we would say that every choice we make is indistinguishable from the flow of destiny.

Cause & Effect

Making choice means there is cause and effect. To have cause and effect (as *we* understand them), we must live in linear time. For example, we choose to turn on the stove (cause), and the water boils several minutes later (effect).

Does this mean that choice does not exist beyond linear time? Not necessarily. It simply means that if we consider the possibility of making choices beyond linear time, things get really interesting! For example, we can no longer say that turning on the stove causes the water to boil. The two events, in one sense, simply co-exist.

(This is a good time to remember that beyond the familiar boundaries of linear time, the logic that we take for granted melts like iron in a furnace. When we speak of realms beyond linear time, our words and ideas (which are time-bound) seem to serve us best when we do not take them too seriously.

Flatland

As an analogy, if we attempt to describe a cube to someone who lives entirely in two dimensions, we would describe it as a "square." It is not entirely accurate, but a square is what a cube looks like if we squash it down into two dimensions. Likewise, if we see that same cube beyond three dimensions, it would not be a mere cube anymore. We would see its past and future, and it would take on qualities that we could not describe in terms of size, shape, texture and color.

As long as our vision is limited to three dimensions and linear time, the multidimensional qualities of the cube are invisible to us, and we see just a cube. In a similar manner, to say that we create our lives through choice or destiny is a flattened, three-dimensional explanation of a multidimensional phenomenon. From that "higher" perspective, choice and destiny are more organic and unified.

The Great Amoeba

If I am contemplating a move to the seashore, I might approach my decision in one of two ways. I might say to myself, "I choose the seashore". Or I might say, "I'm supposed to go to the seashore." The will says, "I choose the seashore." The feeling nature says, "I am drawn to the seashore; I feel destined to be there."

These two options are not paradoxical if the will and feeling-mind are well integrated. In fact, when the will and feeling-mind deeply united, we begin to see beyond linear time, therefore, we might say, "I choose the seashore because, in one sense, I'm already there."

Choice implies that we are each independent individuals, creating our lives as we freely interact with the world. Destiny implies there is just one life dancing and flowing and wiggling like a giant amoeba. When one part wiggles, all the other parts wiggle. Every movement of every particle within the great amoeba effects every other particle. We feel destined to go this way or that way in accordance with the overall movement of the giant amoeba of which we are part. And, since this great organism exists simultaneously in the past and future, every step of its dance, in one sense, has already occurred.

Prophecy

The dance of choice and destiny may be seen in precognitive events such as prophetic dreams, visions and clairvoyant seeing. Ethical psychics remind us they are looking into the probable future. They remind us that the actual events that transpire depend on the choices we make, individually and collectively.

Furthermore, the very act of looking into the probable future helps to bring that future into physical reality. Prophecy tends to be self-fulfilling. This does not invalidate the reality of precognitive seeing; we are simply looking into the detailed anatomy of destiny - which includes choice. When we receive a vision of the future, we are observing a probable future event and, simultaneously, we are helping to create it through the very act of seeing it. We are literally observing it into existence. The witness encourages the change through the act of witnessing. Therefore, if we receive images from the future and remember that it is not written in concrete, we can invoke the power of choice to change the events.

Prophecy and Sorcery

A prophet who uses the expectancy and belief of others to bring about a certain outcome is a sorcerer in disguise. The secret sorcerer simply "predicts" that such and such an event will happen as part of the natural flow of things.

The prophet-sorcerer makes sure there is an ample number of "witnesses" who believe the prediction or, at least, fear the outcome. In other words, the sorcerer, disguised as the prophet, harnesses the mental power and emotional energy of those around him like a farmer harnesses mules to plow a field.

This sort of manipulation does not have to be intentional. The prophet could very well be sincere in his intentions, which makes the prediction that much more convincing to the witnesses.

An individual with genuine clairvoyant abilities recognizes the element of sorcery within the prophecy, and is explicit about it, and is also explicit about the factor called free will or choice.

The Earthquake Prediction

A number of years ago, a psychic predicted a major earthquake in a certain area of the U.S. He published his prediction, and even insisted that the event was unalterable and would definitely occur at a specified date and time. One of my patients expressed great concern about the prediction because she had family living in the area where the earthquake was predicted. Many other individuals became anxious, fearful or excited over the prediction.

My own response was anger. Granted, the psychic may have had honorable intentions and felt he was doing a public service. He certainly had a right to publish his ideas. I was irritated, however, because he insisted that the event was immutable. I took every opportunity to voice my opinion to everyone who seemed interested in the earthquake prediction.

My reaction was so emotionally charged that I eventually felt compelled to examine it. I even involved myself in earnest prayer and meditation to speed things up a bit. This apparently unleashed even stronger emotions, including remorse about my own past irresponsible use of knowledge and power.

Anyway, the earthquake did not happen — except inside the minds of many individuals, like me, who paid attention to it.

The Final Days Are Here Again

At this juncture, we can also address the plethora of doomsday predictions and other prophecies that flood society every so often. Whether or not such predictions are valid, they tend to have an emotional impact on us and should therefore be given thoughtful consideration. When we do so, we notice several patterns:

- Historically, predictions of world-wide catastrophes and Armageddon have been more the rule than the exception. The anticipation of such events has motivated people to join various religions and mystery schools.
- The emotional impact is primarily fear. Typically, such fear has to do with loss of physical possessions, namely our bodies, houses, and lifestyles, as well as our loved ones. Therefore, the degree to which we are influenced by doomsday predictions is directly proportional to how

deeply we are identified with our bodies and other possessions. Fear diminishes as we cultivate spiritual awareness, through prayer, meditation, and personal ethics. The more we commune with our non-physical or essential self, the less vulnerable we are to fear and manipulation through doomsday predictions and other threats. In other words, the more we cultivate spiritual values, the less afraid we are of physical threats. Our spiritual values, even if we do not recognize them as such, show up as personal integrity, allowing us to face external changes with a measure of calmness and dignity. Furthermore, emotional serenity promotes mental clarity, which allows us to make sense of what is happening.

- Some prophecies have the added twist of including eternal damnation or some sort of punishment or threat on a soul level. We are warned that if we do not conform to a given doctrine or join a certain group, we will suffer in ways that go beyond the limitations of the body. This warning seems especially ridiculous when we commune with our own conscience. The more we practice honesty and personal integrity, the less likely that we can be cheated, intimidated, or deceived.

- It is interesting to note that over-concern with doomsday predictions, which implies strong identification with the body, has been the domain of religions and schools of thought that profess to hold the keys to spiritual salvation and liberation. On the other hand, many individuals who are openly materialistic tend to be less concerned about end-of-the-world prediction, even though it theoretically signals the end of their existence! This is not as paradoxical as it may seem. Individuals who cling to the idea of an afterlife often do so because they have poor contact with their essence or spirit, and, therefore, are secretly afraid of losing the body and the things of the body. On the other hand, many atheists and materialists have, by necessity, developed a deep and silent contact with their own essence, which might show as personal ethics, self-respect, and a willingness to be personally responsible for their lives.

261

A Time and A Season

Prophets sometime invoke the force of destiny by pointing to the great hypothetical cycles and seasons of life. They imply the existence of a natural order and rhythms that determine what will happen and when. Such an idea can liberate or entrap, depending on the intention. It is liberating when we use it to help ourselves relax into the flow of life, and just do our best. The same idea, however, can be used to trick people into turning over their power of choice to whoever is clever and charismatic enough to convince others that given event is part of the natural order of things. When the prophet dramatically proclaims that the time has arrived for a given event to occur, they are telling us to yield to the force of destiny.

The individual with the gift of extended perception who has a knack for reading the book of destiny, also recognizes the power of choice. Such an individual can say, "The time is now...", while also understanding that the time has *always* been now. In a thousand years, the time will *still* be now. The ethical prophet or honest sorcerer understands that personal choice, made with sincerity and calmness, *is* the force of destiny.

Alternative Prediction

One possibility is that the many predicted earth-shaking changes are metaphors of inner events. In other words, the predicted physical changes may simply be symbolic of changes in the collective consciousness of humanity.

Perhaps the predicted great conflagration symbolizes the burning of the well-established sacred cows. Perhaps the predicted two hundred m.p.h. winds will turn out to be new ideas that sweep through our lives and blow away the house-of-cards of our current political, religious, scientific and moral views. Perhaps the final battle will destroy nothing except our belief in a final battle.

Perhaps the great tidal waves will turn out to be great emotional upheavals that come crashing in from the ocean of the collective unconscious, changing the shoreline of our minds. Perhaps the melting of the polar ice caps is really a melting of long repressed feelings in the consciousness of humanity. Perhaps the worlds in collision represent a collision of conflicting beliefs.

It is also possible that the prophesized changes, whether they are inner or outer, will not significantly disrupt our lives as individuals, but rather reflect changes that occur gradually over a number of years or generations. Perhaps the outer changes that have been slated to occur in the blink of an eye, will, indeed, occur. But how long is *the blink of an eye?* Whose eye is the prophet referring to.

The blink of an eye in one frame of reference could be a thousand years in another. The supposed reduction of the world's human population might be viewed as occurring in the blink of an eye in one frame of reference, while in another frame of reference, it might be viewed as the product of many generations of intelligent living by a population of free and self-responsible people who are ruled by their own power of reason and guided by their own conscience.

Perhaps the great tailed comet that we fear will strike the earth is actually "sperm consciousness," pure single-minded determination, working methodically year after year, generation after generation, penetrating the status quo, melting the polar icecaps of frozen feelings, thus establishing a new order of justice and fairness.

The prophecies regarding physical changes to our world will either come about or they will not. Either way, the question is, *what do we believe?* Two other equally important questions are, *what are we afraid of?* And *What do we want?* These are important questions because our own beliefs, amplified by our secret fears and desires, are among the great architects of destiny. When we thus recognize these inner architects of outer reality, Sir Choice and Lady Destiny can synergistically unite in the dance of creation.

Chapter 44
Flesh & Spirit

I was so buoyant that I did not have to exert any effort to stay afloat. In the horizon, I saw the last hint of the setting sun. I swam toward the sun so that it would appear higher in the sky. Since I was aware that I was dreaming, I mentally tried to change the setting sun into a rising sun. I was also aware that the sun symbolized heaven, bliss, oneness.

However, my mental efforts to change the scene did not seem to work. Furthermore, I started encountering huge waves that were moving me in the opposite direction, toward shore. I thought the waves would pull me under, but I just bobbed up and down and drifted closer to shore as each wave passed by.

The waves kept coming. They seemed bigger and propelled me faster. I forgot about the sun as I became frightened of being smashed against the rocky shore. I also forgot that I was dreaming, perhaps because of my fear. (That is how it is with fear; it makes you forget that you are dreaming.)

The waves *did* carry me quickly to shore. However, instead of being smashed on the rocks, I found myself flying effortlessly as I gazed down upon a lush and beautiful forest. At that point, I awoke, feeling rather peaceful.

Some of the details of the dream symbolized specific events of my life during that period of time. Many of the elements, however, also had to do with life in general. The dream was yet another reminder of the subtle dance between the physical and spiritual. The message: rather than trying to escape to the realm of Spirit (the sun), I would do better to just relax and accept my own humanity and my desire to participate in Earthly life (the huge waves moving toward shore). I was being gently reminded to avoid using my mind to go against the natural flow of things (trying to change the sunset into a sunrise). I was reminded that my human emotions and desires emanate from the domain of Spirit (the waves coming from the horizon). I was reminded not to fret about being overpowered by my emotions and the hard realities of life on Earth (the huge waves dragging me under and smashing me on the rocks). I was reminded that life would not drag me under, as long as I was light and buoyant in the presence of those emotional waves. Instead of smashing me against the rocky shore of life, those same waves would carry me safely to the realization that Heaven is right here on Earth (the waves carried me to shore where I saw the beautiful forest).

The Dance of Transformation

The realm of the flesh is the realm of opposites. Spiritual awareness, sometimes called the Kingdom of Heaven, is the awareness of unity beyond opposites. Nonetheless, our human understanding of Heaven is based on comparison with the realm of flesh. Therefore, the two are, for our purpose, inseparable. They define each other. Each gives meaning to the other. Spirit animates flesh, and flesh provides a vehicle for spirit. Flesh is about complexity and diversity. Spirit is about simplicity and unity.

As with other opposites, these two are intertwined in a dance of transformation and evolution. Spirit condenses into flesh and then returns to spirit. Simplicity swells into complexity and then returns into simplicity. Unity explodes into diversity and then return to unity. When the mind goes deeply enough into stillness and silence, it can see this dance of transformation; and it can comprehend that flesh and spirit are reflections of each other.

Mirror Images

A living being that is completely physical does not ponder its existence in the universe; it simply exists. It does not contemplate its life; it simply lives. It does not ponder its separateness from other life forms; it simply interacts. To be fully physical is to give no thought to yesterday or tomorrow, for yesterday and tomorrow do not exist in the physical universe.

To be fully physical is to have little or no sense of time. Therefore, the physical being is incapable of perceiving sin, guilt, or shame, for all of these require an awareness of history.

266

To be fully physical is to be free of censorship. When a bear craps in the woods, it is not inhibited by social etiquette; it is fully engaged in the act of crapping in the woods. To be fully physical is to be totally involved with the activities of the body as it interacts with the environment. To be fully physical means we are not thinking; we are not contemplating the rightness or wrongness of our acts. We simply follow our instincts.

As we ponder *physical,* we see that it bears a striking resemblance to *spiritual.* Animal instinct is a reflection of spiritual awareness.

To be fully physical is to experience body sensations with no judgment. To be spiritual is to have awareness with no judgment. The animal nature is at home with spirit because spirit does not judge the flowerbed as being greater than the dung heap.

The two are involved in a perpetual dance of transformation. When one side ripens in fullness, it bears the pure seed of the other. The quality of that seed depends on the quality of the parent that bears it. The corruption of one corrupts the other. Clinging to one suffocates the other. Each side has an innate affinity for the other.

Then Came The Mind

As with other opposites, the dance of the flesh and spirit brings forth a third principle, in this case, the mind. The mind has the ability to perceive the physical body as separate and distinct from the rest of the universe. The mind records the adventures of the physical body as it moves through time and space. The mind draws conclusions and then plans future adventures. In one sense, the mind creates time by recording history. When the mind records and stores data, a "past" is established. In that same instant, the "future" is also created in the mind.

The ability of the mind to see the flesh as distinct and separate from spirit is truly an *ability* that is to be respected and valued. When it is regarded as a metaphysical disability that we must overcome or transcend, it does become a disability. Such a mind perceives separation and only separation. It does not comprehend the idea that the simplicity of the kitten and the majesty of spirit are the same. However, when the mind becomes still and quiet, it can contemplate a kitten and spirit; perceiving their difference and sensing their sameness. When the mind is still and quiet enough, it is free from the programming that places flesh and spirit in conflict. When the mind is still and quiet enough, we see that the needs of the flesh and the needs of the spirit are basically the same.

Rebellion of the Animal Nature

The apparent conflict between flesh and spirit has received much attention throughout history. And, rightly so, because the harmony of the two is important to our well-being as individuals and as a society.

What appears to be a battle between the flesh and spirit is actually the mind at war with itself, projecting its own inner conflict on the flesh and spirit. The conflict is between our own thoughts and emotions. Likewise, as we methodically resolve the hidden conflict in the mind, we begin to sense the natural and easy relationship between flesh and spirit.

In order to understand the inner conflict of thoughts and emotions, we must recognize that such conflict is an expression of a deeper, usually unconscious, conflict that places *all* opposites at war with one another. In other words, flesh and spirit appear to be in conflict because that is what we believe about opposites in general. We secretly believe that when opposites meet, one side must annihilate or subjugate the other. For example, historically, Christians sought the purity of spirit by rejecting and mortifying the flesh. The result was they were ruled by the flesh, simply because 'what you resist persists.' The modern version of this is seen in - conscientious metaphysicians who earnestly seek to promote unity or oneness by rejecting the notion of duality. They probably would not do so if they realized that one must be in duality in order to reject it.

This inner warfare sometimes appears as a rebellion of the animal nature. However, the animal nature becomes rebellious only when the judging mind drives a wedge between flesh and spirit. The "rebellion" is actually the animal nature continuing to faithfully express spirit, overriding the repressive mind, so it can express the freedom and spontaneity of spirit. In the presence of pure spirit, the animal nature does not rebel, for it knows that it is at home.

This is not to say that the mental realm of judgments and beliefs is less important than spiritual awareness and animal instinct. The value of the intellect is unquestioned by spiritual awareness or animal instinct. The value of the intellect becomes apparent to the intellect when it cultivates the ability to be still and listen.

Gilgamesh & Enkidu

The balancing and integration of our animal instincts and spiritual awareness is of prime importance, as suggested by the fact that it has been dramatized for us in the form of numerous myths and legends. One such myth is The Epic of Gilgamesh.

The Epic of Gilgamesh, a story from ancient Sumer, dramatizes the duality of god and animal and how the two play in the middle ground called human. Gilgamesh was a great king, a demigod with a rich heritage. He was very knowledgeable had performed mighty deeds. He did not know defeat, failure, or death.

However, Gilgamesh had no humility and no compassion for his people. "…Gilgamesh was a godlike man alone with his thoughts in idleness. (He) left his people dreaming of the past…longing for change. They had grown tired of his contradictions and his callous ways…"

In response to the people's cry of distress, the gods created Enkidu to counterbalance Gilgamesh. Enkidu was born in the wilderness. He suckled on the milk of wild animals and grew up in their midst. His body was covered with hair. He knew nothing of civilization, history, or heritage.

Enkidu lived with the animals. He ate and drank with them and set them free from the hunters' traps. "He ran with the freed gazelle, like a brother, and they drank together at a pool, like two friends sharing some common journey; not needing to speak."

Gilgamesh was part god and part human. Enkidu was part animal and part human. When they meet, each becomes fully human.

Enkidu's first encounter with humanity is with a temple prostitute who is sent to tame him. She seduces him after which the animals reject him. Then, the woman takes him to the house of a local shepherd. She shaves the hair off his body and teaches him to eat people food.

Meanwhile, Gilgamesh has two disturbing dreams that foretell of an encounter with one who is as mighty as he, which is unthinkable to him. After the dreams, Gilgamesh feels weak and melancholy and does not know why.

Meanwhile, Enkidu learns of Gilgamesh and immediately dislikes him. Enkidu finds out that the mighty king, in his arrogance and disregard for his people, forces every bride-to-be to have sex with him prior to marriage.

Finally, the newly-civilized Enkidu journeys to the city. The people are excited to see him, for he looks like Gilgamesh. Enkidu is shorter and stockier, but the two have equal strength.

When Gilgamesh goes to the house where he is to deflower a bride-to-be, he is met by Enkidu who blocks the door. Gilgamesh is enraged because the people are cheering Enkidu as loudly as they would their king. The two of them fight a furious battle, raising a big dust cloud, knocking over and breaking things until they are both exhausted. When the battle is over, Gilgamesh is the technical winner, but they both laugh and embrace like brothers.

The story goes on from there, rich in drama and symbolism, as Gilgamesh experiences the human qualities of brotherly love and humility through his friendship with Enkidu. However, things take a turn for the worse when Gilgamesh wants to do battle with the Bull of Heaven. Enkidu does not want to do this. He has a bad feeling about it. Nonetheless, on Gilgamesh's insistence, they do battle with the Bull of Heaven. And Enkidu is killed.

Thus, the god-like Gilgamesh experiences another human limitation. Even with his god-like powers, he is unable to restore life to his friend.

Enkidu dies, for he is of the flesh. Gilgamesh continues to live, for he is a demigod. However, he is stricken with a grief that also will not die.

As a mythological character, Gilgamesh represents our god-like qualities. He personifies the human mind with access to its superhuman heritage and power over the elements. Enkidu represents our animal nature. He personifies the human mind with free access to animal instincts.

The Epic of Gilgamesh teaches us that our god-like nature, separate from our animal nature, is incomplete, dissatisfied, harsh, and not quite sane. Gilgamesh finds peace only after he contacts his animal nature in the form of Enkidu. Immortal spirit is very much at home with the innocence of the animal nature.

We are also warned that if the sophisticated (god-like) human does not pay heed to the instincts and simple wisdom of his animal nature, he will lose it and come to know the sorrow and emptiness of being human. Likewise, we are reminded that if we remember to respect our innately honest animal nature, we will know the joy of being human.

The Vampire

The vampire is the personification of flesh and spirit torn asunder. Popular culture includes a macabre fascination with Count Dracula, the archetypal vampire. The fascination is a recognition. Dracula reminds us of our hidden inner tendency to relate parasitically with the life around us. Dracula reminds us what happens when we lose touch with our inner spirit and sink deeply enough into addiction.

Understanding the Ultimate Addict

We can better understand and appreciate the lesson of Count Dracula by contrasting him to another legendary-historical figure, St. Francis of Assisi.

Most people who have any knowledge of St. Francis also have a fondness for him. Our fondness of St. Francis (as with our macabre fascination with Count Dracula) is a recognition of sorts. Each one dramatizes the relationship between flesh and spirit. The image of St. Francis is the image of spirit and flesh in loving communion. Dracula is the personification of flesh and spirit torn asunder.

St. Francis Assisi & Count Dracula of Transylvania

St. Francis and Count Dracula do have some interesting parallels. For starters, both were real historical figures whose lives have been mythologized. The details of their respective lives, fact and fiction, provide insight into the relationship between flesh and spirit.

If we look at the historical data, we find that the real St. Francis of Assisi had his flaws. Likewise, the real Count Dracula was not nearly as diabolical as the character in the movies. None-the-less, the legends which have grown around St. Francis and Count Dracula are as important as the documented history.

Count Dracula

The vampire is a thief that steals on a very intimate level. The vampire steals the very life force of the individual. In everyday life, the vampire feeds on the attention and emotions of others, leaving the other person emotionally "drained." The draining can occur on a superficial level so that the other person feels fatigued. Or the vampire can reach down so deep as to seemingly take the individual's very soul.

No one wishes to be accused of being a social, emotional, or energetic vampire. The very idea of vampirism evokes so much revulsion that we do not want to consider the possibility that the tendency might exist within us. However, the very presence of such revulsion suggests that we do harbor the potential. Our fear and loathing of things in the outer world often point to similar issues on the inside.

To the extent that we harbor the hidden potential of the vampire, we tend to see vampires in the world around us, and we react emotionally to them. If that tendency has been resolved, we respond with compassion and understanding when it is encountered in the outer world.

Fear of the inner vampire compels us to keep it hidden. The more deeply we keep it hidden, the more it rules us. Hence, the issue typically persists and gathers energy in the darkness of the unconscious mind.

Not surprisingly, vampire-consciousness is poorly understood. It is difficult to understand a thing when we fear and hate it. We can begin to understand vampire-consciousness and how it is created by first understanding how we nourish ourselves.

How We Nourish Ourselves

Life is about energy. Living organisms sustain themselves by engaging in a dance of giving and receiving energy. In order for this to happen, living organisms must be in *relationship* with one another. Life nourishes itself by contacting life. For humans, this is true on the physiological level, as well as on the emotional and spiritual levels. We nourish ourselves physically by consuming other life-forms (and must therefore eventually return the favor). We nourish ourselves emotionally by contacting others. We nourish ourselves spiritually by contacting the core self or by relating to the Presence that is perceived as the source of life. Flesh is enlivened when it is touched by spirit.

In other words, we nourish ourselves emotionally and spiritually by first contacting our deep personal truth and then sharing that truth in our relationships. Contact with one's truth is energizing, whether it is the emotional truth that changes from moment to moment, or the spiritual truth that transcends time altogether. Either way, contact with truth is inherently pleasurable and enlivening.

The pleasurable quality of truth is often experienced as a sense of beauty. Even if we experience pain when we contact personal truth, the pain has a sweetness or rightness about it. Even if the truth, as we see it, is ugly, the very fact that our experience is genuine gives it a subtle and perhaps indefinable quality of beauty. When we are in touch with ourselves, we would rather endure the "ugliness" of truth than cover ourselves with a pretty lie.

When we experience truth as beautiful or precious, it nourishes us. When we share our truth, we share the nourishment. When we hold back our truth in relating to others, we block the flow of life, we withhold nourishment

273

from ourselves and others. This is how we unconsciously starve ourselves emotionally and spiritually.

We then try to compensate by feeding ourselves in other ways. For example, we might form many superficial relationships to compensate for the absence of deep intimacy, replacing quality with quantity. We might become addicted to attention and admiration. We might crave approval. We might find pleasure through watching others suffer. We might exalt ourselves by condemning or belittling others.

When we become seriously addicted to these forms of emotional feeding, we have created the inner vampire. We have created a consciousness that seeks to take without giving. Like other addictions, this one tends to emerge gradually and unconsciously, and is perpetuated by a wall of denial, fear, and self-loathing.

Not surprisingly, our fear and loathing of the vampire has spawned a cultural fascination for vampires. Vampirism has received much attention in the arts, suggesting that it has a significant place in our collective consciousness.

By examining the legend of Dracula, we can gain further insight into the inner vampire. Dracula drinks blood. Blood symbolizes emotional energy. In that sense, Dracula may be regarded as an extreme metaphor for how we emotionally feed on each other. Dracula craves the blood of others, just as we might crave the emotional energy and attention of others. We might be addicted to the admiration, adoration, fear, or envy that others project on us. There might also be a hidden part of us that feeds on the misery, pain, and perceived failure and wrongdoings of others.

Granted, it is normal and healthy to want attention and affection. It is also normal and healthy to be concerned or just curious about the problems and personal drama of others. However, when we seriously crave attention, when we are addicted to seeing others suffer or stumble, when we have to put others down so we can feel lifted up, we have created the inner vampire.

In other words, vampire-consciousness is a hunger, an emptiness that tries to fill itself with the life taken from another. Since the life is stolen life, it does not produce fulfillment and growth—it only sustains the vampire's condition so it can feed yet again.

Predator and Parasite

The vampire can function as a predator or a parasite. Predators simply overpower the victim as quickly as possible. The parasite is more subtle. It wiggles its way into the host and silently siphons off energy. If the parasite is truly efficient, it does not kill its host, or even inflict pain. In Dracula's case, when he siphons energy, the victim might actually feel pleasure. It is exceedingly difficult to fight an enemy that makes you feel good.

In other words, when Dracula is being really efficient and subtle, he does not have to overpower the body; he simply overpowers the mind. When the mind is operating according to its own inner blueprint, we feel pleasure when we do things that support health and well-being, and we feel pain when we are harmed. When the vampire takes over, it overrides nature's design. The host has no life of its own, but simply exists to sustain the parasite. To do this, the host must also become parasitic on others. One of the abilities associated with Dracula is that he can turn his victim into a vampire.

The Vampire as the Addict

Carl Jung was the first to point out that the vampire is the ultimate addict. It feeds on others but is never filled. It cannot be filled because it does not recognize the nature of its emptiness. It does not recognize that its emptiness is the result of having lost access to its inner source of sustenance.

In everyday life, contact with our inner source of nourishment shows up as the capacity to graciously receive nourishment and nurturing from the life around us — when it is freely given. Furthermore, complete fulfillment occurs only when we have given back to life more than we have taken. This is how life advances itself. The tragic condition of the vampire is a glaring reminder that we are not really nourished when we take without giving.

The Emptiness

In essence, Count Dracula symbolizes an unrecognized inner emptiness. If the emptiness were recognized, it would be filled from within, which is to say, filled with the gratitude of simply knowing the truth of oneself. That truth might cry out as the simple declaration, *"I am!"*

The radiance of that truth fills the inner emptiness and overflows to nourish others. The vampire is secretly terrified of this, fearing that it cannot contain the full knowing called, *"I am,"* and survive. Vampire-consciousness is correct in this perception. The shell that once sealed off the emptiness must give way, because *"I am"* is alive and ever expanding. The shell is being shattered.

In other words, vampire-consciousness, by its very nature, cannot tolerate the truth of its own emptiness. This is symbolized by Dracula's avoidance of daylight. The vampire, manifesting as the everyday addict, avoids the light of truth, preferring to feed secretly.

The Beast without Beauty

Dracula is often depicted as being very seductive and deceptive, and even as having hypnotic powers. To the extent that we harbor an inner vampire, we tend to be seductive and deceptive, perhaps without even realizing it. When we slip into vampire consciousness, we not only seduce others but also ourselves. We see this in the hardcore addict. For example, the addict might pretend to be the "beast" in *Beauty and the Beast.* It says, "If you will only love me, I know I can mend my ways…if you marry me, I will stop drinking, gambling, taking drugs." The victim or "enabler" is repeatedly seduced into thinking that a soft, tender kiss will do the job.

In the legend of *Beauty and the Beast,* Beauty provides the kiss that transforms the beast into a noble gentleman. The vampire, however, is incapable of receiving the healing *kiss* of Beauty – and survive. Beauty is truth. The vampire, by definition, has rejected the gentle kiss of truth. Therefore, it must be slain with the *sword* of truth.

In real life, the sword of truth is often called "tough love," which is sharp enough to cut through the lies, strong enough to stand firm in the face of seduction, and steady enough to refrain from self-serving interference. Tough love is tough enough to refuse to feed the addiction.

The sword of truth, in the form of tough love, is how we address the inner or outer vampire. The vampire is likely to return, however, until we understand how it is created in the first place.

How the Vampire is Created

We create the emotional vampire by denying the need for relationship. We create the vampire by denying the need to touch and to be touched physically and emotionally. In so doing we destroy our natural relationship with the life around us. Likewise, our broken relationship with the life around us reflects a tearing asunder of the inner relationship between flesh and spirit.

The vampire is driven by the urge to fill the inner emptiness but does not recognize that the emptiness can only be filled from within. It has lost sight of the simple yet mysterious inner dance by which spirit enlivens and becomes flesh.

Being filled from within does not mean we deny the need for relationship with others. On the contrary, when we deny the desire to reach out and touch the life around us, we shut off the flow of life from within us. We break the circuit that allows the inner current of life to flow.

In other words, the part of us that has the potential for becoming the vampire is the same part that wants to be in relationship with the rest of life. The place within us that has the potential to become addicted to harmful substances, attention, suffering, faultfinding, etc, is the same part that simply wants to experience relationship. To the extent that our sensual and emotional need for relationship is denied, we - create the inner vampire.

The End of Dracula

As the quintessential vampire, Dracula had his beginning during the latter part of the Dark Ages, when knowledge and self-expression were severely suppressed. At that time, the Christian ideal of self-denial had reached its zenith.

Granted, the monastic practice of removing ourselves from the sensual world can be a powerful tool for finding inner peace. However, we must be clear on our intent. The sincere monk removes himself from the sensual world so as to create a more harmonious and respectful relationship with the rest of life, not to tear that relationship apart. In the latter case, the ways of the flesh are rejected and condemned, thus becoming a stumbling stone on the road to spiritual freedom.

The monk who tries to find God by harshly rejecting the sensual world insidiously creates the inner vampire. Likewise, the courage to see the inner emptiness without censorship or denial, allows it to return to its primordial state: the sacred emptiness, the eternal stillness from which all life springs forth.

When we have stumbled across this truth enough times and have created enough vampires, we can then learn from experience. We learn that by quietly looking within, as the true monk does, we really do access the source of life. In so doing, we do not lose the sensual experience of relationship with the rest of life. It is reborn with a sensuality that is utterly free, for it is utterly innocent.

In other words, the vampire stops being a vampire, and is thankful for it, when we recognize the truth it is acting out – the need for relationship. The vampire returns no more when we reclaim our ability to contact each other, to savor life, to give and receive in the various ways that we are instinctively moved to do so.

Flesh and Spirit Reunited

Count Dracula dramatizes what can happen to the average human being when the relationship between flesh and spirit is severely disrupted. St. Francis of Assisi symbolizes the healing of that relationship.

St. Francis' love for animals is legendary. And apparently, the feeling was mutual. Timid animals that normally avoid humans were drawn to Francis. Predatory animals such as wolves were harmless in his presence.

St. Francis' own behavior was described as "impulsive" and "instinctual." He preferred the natural world over the sophistication and complexity of urban life. When he felt overburdened, he often sought refuge in a beautiful valley called Rieti, home to a Pagan community with whom he shared a warm friendship. At a time when devout Catholics intentionally mutilated their bodies to purge themselves of physical desires, St. Francis referred to his own body as "Brother Body."

We fear and loathe Dracula because he reminds us of our potential for living parasitically on others. Likewise, we love Francis because he reminds us of the natural harmony between flesh and spirit. When the spirit is free, the flesh is regarded with appreciation and treated with kindness. St. Francis reminds us of our own potential to connect with the natural world in a sweet and intimate way.

Somewhere deep inside, we would like to relate to the life around us as St. Francis related to animals. We would like to feel *related* to the rest of Creation in a way that is so pure and innocent that we might regard the sun as our brother and the moon as our sister.

Both Francis and Dracula were said to have great influence over animals. Dracula used animals to do his bidding, while Francis just loved them. Both were said to take part in crusades and holy wars of the time which according to their respective legends and biographies, contributed to their transformation.

Dracula could turn himself into predatory animals, mostly notably a wolf. One of the stories associated with St. Francis involves his encounter with a wolf that was terrorizing the townspeople. Francis communicated with the wolf (whom he addressed as Brother Wolf) and was thus able to bring peace between the animal and the townspeople.

Another point about Count Dracula was that he was a faithful Catholic prior to his transformation into a vampire. He believed that he was going to war in the service of Jesus Christ. He was a nobleman with political ambitions and visions of greatness. However, the events of the war compelled him to feel betrayed and abandoned by Christ, so he turned himself into the ultimate vampire.

The above experience of Dracula carries a strong warning for those who seek monastic life or "purification" as a means of achieving "nobility," so as to escape their hidden self-loathing. In contrast, Francis was not of noble birth. Prior to becoming a monk, he was a fun-loving and carefree party animal. He had no ambitions of becoming a prominent clergyman. His reason for going to war was simple: like other boys his age, he thought that wearing a suit of armor was cool and would surely attract girls. When the spirit first fell upon Francis, it fell upon a naive merchant's son.

He Failed as a Martyr

St. Francis was one of the few religious reformers of the past who was not persecuted or martyred. He did try! In his day, if you were a serious Christian, the preferred way to die was in the service of Christ. Much to Francis' frustration, however, he was not a likely candidate for martyrdom. The martyr requires the presence of an enemy. Francis simply was not very good at making enemies.

No one wanted to harm Francis, not even the Islamic Sheik, whom Francis tried to convert to Christianity during the Crusades. In the midst of the bloody fighting, Francis had the gall to walk into the Muslim camp and respectfully ask to speak with the leader. This act was considered sheer suicide.

The Christian soldiers and even Francis himself expected the Muslim soldiers to kill him. However. The Sheik was so charmed by the simplicity and unassuming humility of the little monk that he declared he would convert to Christianity if all Christians were like Francis. They parted as friends.

The True Monk

Unlike Dracula, St. Francis knows that the emptiness within him cannot be filled from without. He does not fear his emptiness, he embraces it. That is the distinction between the true monk and the vampire. The monk who contacts his inner emptiness is filled from within and shares freely with the rest of life. He becomes a brother to the rest of life. That gift of relatedness is given freely and unconditionally to all.

Chapter 45
God

"Beyond all of my ideas about God, there is God."
Islamic proverb

God the One, by definition has no opposite. Therefore, any rational understanding of God must necessarily be limited because the rational mind thinks in opposites. However, limited is not the same as useless. As long as we recognize the limitations of our human ideas about God, they have value. They guide us in our journey through life. They give us a handle on that which otherwise has no handle.

Getting a Handle on God

The way we get a rational handle on God is by comparing some of His or Her qualities with qualities that are familiar to us, such as gender. This is in fact precisely what we do when we construct our ideas about God, whether we are aware of it or not.

We perceive God as *infinite* through contrast with our own *finite* nature. We understand God as the supreme *Creator* through contrast with the *created* universe all around us. We understand that God is *timeless* through contrast with our own time-bound physical existence. We understand God as the supreme *Mother* or *Father*, by regarding ourselves as Her or His *children.* In other words, our human understanding God has value only to the extent that it is tempered by intellectual honesty and softened by humility.

Humility and Humor

Our perceptions of God are useful only as long as we are aware of their limitations. It is tempting to regard our perceptions of God as the only reality. It is easy to be seduced into acquiring such a belief, especially when we are troubled by existential fear or a lack of self-worth. Fortunately, there is a built-in barometer that tells us when we are squeezing too hard on our ideas about God. That barometer is humor. As you may recall, humor goes hand-in-hand with humility. The grace of humor helps us to loosen our grip on our ideas of God, so we do not squeeze the life out of them or have them slip through our fingers like watermelon seeds.

Actually, our concepts of God will eventually slip through our fingers anyway. However, by remembering to not take those ideas too seriously, they will tend to not slip away as fast, and when they do, we are less likely to get upset or feel disoriented. When we remember to include humor in our beliefs about God, we also invite humility. And we are guided in applying our understanding of God in ways that promote inner and outer peace.

God the Self

The concept of God-the-self declares that God is the very core of who we are. A common way of applying this idea is to make a distinction between the lower self and higher self. The lower self is the personality that laughs, cries, gets angry, does goofy things and then gets embarrassed about it. The term "higher self" refers to one's own identity beyond the body and beyond our everyday thoughts and emotions, and ultimately beyond linear time. From this perspective, the supreme God is simply the highest or deepest expression of the higher self.

When we speak of higher self and lower self, we typically assume that the higher self is better than the lower self. We try to bring the lower self in harmony with our idea of the higher self. This is entirely appropriate because it reflects the evolutionary imperative to know oneself on deeper and deeper levels. However, when we experience our own personal connection with the "higher self," we are treated to a big joke. To be in the pure experience of higher self is to make no distinction between lower self and higher self. There is just a wordless sense of wholeness or unity.

The harmonious blending of the higher self and lower self may be described as follows: *I see the lower self that I am, playing in duality, and the higher self that I am, embracing it all and loving it all.* In other words, if the higher self could speak, it might look upon every aspect of the lower self and declare, *"I AM."*

God the Other

The idea of God within, liberating though it may be, can easily become encrusted with dogma that uses the bold declaration, "I am God" as a shield to conceal a mire of confusion, guilt, and shame. The concept that *I am God* loses its potency when we deny the validity of what appears to be the opposite idea, which in its purity addresses God as would a young child looking up to its parents.

I am God has meaning only when it is experienced with the innocence of a baby. Most adults do not live in such bliss consistently. So, we have God the other to balance things out. God the Other is the supreme being who is separate and distinct from humans and far superior. None-the-less, the act of praying to an external Supreme God has meaning only when it gradually leads us to the realization that says, "I am the Divinity that I have been praying to," or "The Father and I are One." The fullness of that realization is not arrogance. In fact, it is humbling. In our human experience, we might feel this as a sense of equality or deep kinship with those who walk the earth with us.

Our ability to commune with God the other depends on our capacity to be genuine. This is why little children have no problem entering the kingdom of heaven. If we try to enter the kingdom while harboring a basement full of deception, our efforts land us in hell.

When we are benevolent, God is benevolent. When we are compassionate, God is compassionate. When we are jealous and angry, God is jealous and angry. Granted, if God is God, His will is capable of acting independently from ours, and His love is present, regardless of what we do. However, our sincerity has a profound effect on how we experience God. From a practical standpoint, God is as present with us as we are honest with ourselves.

In other words, it does not matter whether we view God as our deepest identity or the Supreme Being who created us. Either one will do, provided that the God to whom we relate is truly the God of *our* understanding, rather than the God of someone else's understanding. Either way, God seems to be a stickler for truth. Either way, sincerity is the key to Gods House.

The Principle and the Person

God can also take the form of the Principle or the Person. God the Principle is the impersonal and supreme law that governs all other laws. God the person is an intelligent being with whom we can relate.

God the Principle might work for someone who tends to be very intellectual. God the person is important for those who are more emotional and therefore feel a need to have a *relationship* with God. We cannot have a relationship with a principle. We can have a relationship only with another sentient being who is responsive to us on a personal level.

God the principle is Truth with a capital "T," transcending all opposites. As such, we can speak of it only by comparing it to our own time-bound truths. Even then, our knowledge is incomplete. We cannot fully encompass it with our words, for it is all encompassing. Infinite Truth becomes finite truth when it is spoken. This is how boundless Truth has the experience of boundaries. This is how immortality has the experience of birth and death. This is how limitless Truth gets to have the experience of human limitations.

Like the God of the ancient Hebrews, the Truth of God is nameless and faceless. A similar sentiment was expressed by Taoists of ancient China: "The Toa which can be spoken is not the eternal Toa." There is no bottle that can contain it, or book that can describe it. There is no picture that can fully reveal its beauty, no prayer or invocation that can capture it in fullness. The vessel in which we try to trap Truth eventually shatters. The string of words we use to describe Truth can become contradictory—including this very passage.

The way that our concept of infinite Truth can have some semblance of stability is when the purely intellectual concept is blended with feeling. The feeling part of human consciousness is how we get a taste of the unity beyond opposites. Through our feelings, the nameless, faceless, and impersonal presence of God becomes a person that we can relate to. Feeling gives meaning to the words; it brings the letter of the law to life. One of those feelings, humility, allows us to relax so we do not take our words so seriously that we squeeze the life out of them. This is the natural humility of a young child to whom gates of heaven are ever open.

Communing With God

Our first and most emotionally significant relationships are with our parents. Not surprisingly, when we put all pretense aside and commune with God in a way that is deeply meaningful for us, we typically relate to God in a way that resembles a young child relating to mother or father.

With regard to the gender issue, God the He and God the She are one and the same, for the simple reason that God is, by definition, One. We make a distinction between Mother God and Father God simply because we find it useful. And God doesn't seem to mind.

Mother God is the container that is big enough to contain everything else. She embraces all there is, making no distinction between the worthy and the unworthy, allowing all things to *be;* every rock, every flower, every child, every monk, every thought, every feeling. She is the presence that allows us to develop in a way that is natural for us. She endows our emotional nature with an intrinsic sense of self-worth, thus conferring on us the will to live. In so doing, she prepares us to receive the teachings of Father God.

We receive from Father God the ability to create. Mother God allows us to *be,* while Father God shows us what to *do.* When we avail ourselves of Mother God's love, we become capable of doing Father God's work. Likewise, tending to the Father's work translates into the manifestation of Mother's love in a tangible way. In truth, Mother's love and Father's work are one and the same, simply because Mother God and Father God are one and the same. At any given time, we might find value in giving greater attention to one, but the other is still invisibly present, silently supporting the one that is actively expressed.

We commune with Mother God when we feel the need for Her soothing touch. We commune with Mother God when we have a wound in the heart that seems beyond repair. We commune with Her when we feel a need for nourishment in the places where we feel incapable or unworthy of receiving nourishment. She embraces those hidden places where we feel too dirty or ashamed to be embraced. If we listen deeply, we might hear Her whispering, "I will never forsake you; I will never forget you." When we feel Her quiet presence, we relax and melt. We sense that She does not put us on a schedule. She simply nourishes and heals, and then allows us to emerge from the nest when our wings spontaneously start to flutter.

When we commune with Mother God, we cannot help but receive the teachings of Father God. We commune with Father God when we are ready to reach out to others. We commune with Father God when we feel the urge to build and to create. We commune with Father God when we seek the power and wisdom to sing our personal song, and to give the gifts that we yearn to give. We commune with Father God when we are ready to receive the understanding that allows us to relate respectfully and effectively with those around us. If we listen deeply to Father God, we might hear Him say, "Honor your Mother in all that you do, and be good to your brothers and sisters."

Be As Little Children

The Bible advises us to be as little children to enter the kingdom heaven. The mind of a child is the feeling-mind. It is a free mind. It is free of pretense. It is an open mind. It has the deep sincerity and humility to receive the nourishing and healing love of Mother God.

The inner child does not have to *do* anything to be worthy of mother's love. However, as long as we walk the Earth, such a child can exist only is the presence of a responsible adult. The mind of the adult is the will which is ever attentive to the will of Father God.

Be a Responsible Adult

The mind of the adult is ever attentive to the Laws of Father God which govern our relationship with our brethren who walk the Earth with us. These laws are simple and self-evident. They give the adult the knowledge and power to provide for the earthly needs of the inner child.

The responsible adult takes care of all of his personal needs in ways that enriches the rest of life. We see this most commonly in everyday business transactions wherein we receive money for goods and services given with thoughtfulness and care to others. Ideally, the persons receiving our goods or services pay us thankfully and joyfully because, for them, the goods or services are worth much more than the money they give.

When we conduct our business in this manner, the money we receive is the visible expression of an invisible blessing. The money we receive helps fulfill the needs of the body. The invisible blessing nourishes the soul.

Higher Power

The term *Higher Power* is, perhaps, the most generic name for God. By referring to the supreme creative presence as the Higher Power, we avoid the distinction between God the self and God the other, God the principle and God the person, God the Mother, God the Father. These distinctions are left entirely up to the individual. This way, no one has to conform to any particular image of God.

Regardless of how we experience our Higher Power, we avail ourselves of a Presence that is beyond duality and, therefore, beyond weakness and beyond conflict. Such Higher Power is available to all because it does not require knowledge of metaphysics or the schooling of any particular religion. We simply relate to it in a way that is consistent with our human understanding of it. We may speak to it, listen to it, believe in it, get angry at it, or even feel its presence within us and around us. Our sincerity alone invokes the power that can gracefully guide us in finding the courage to change whatever needs to change, the serenity to accept whatever we cannot change, and the wisdom to distinguish between the two.

Chapter 46
Religion

I was driving along a country road on a clear summer day when I passed by a church. Like other churches in that area, this one had a message board on the front lawn. The message board read, "God is love." I probably would have forgotten it completely if I had not walked into a bookstore shortly thereafter.

As I browsed among the shelves, I happened to pick up a very thick book on the principles and practice of "Agnosticism." I thumbed through it briefly and flipped to a page that stated the basic credo of Agnosticism, which was, *there is no God, except love.* I remembered the message board sign next to the church. And I smiled.

The Bridge

We turn to religion to give us a handle on that which has no handle. Religion is how consciousness, dancing through the world of opposites, attempts to connect with the realm beyond opposites. Religion is how we endeavor to experience within us the dance of mundane separateness and cosmic Unity.

The term "religion" comes from the Latin word "ligneous" which means, "to link or join" and "re" which means "again." To practice religion, in the literal sense of the word, means to be engaged in rejoining.. The purpose of religion is to provide a framework for people to come together, rejoining with each other and with God.

The general consensus by individuals who claim to have tasted the fruit of God realization or Unity, is that God is love. This realization is typically accompanied by the tendency to recognize God's signature in other religions besides your own. Thomas Merton, a Catholic monk, did a good bit of writing on this. After spending years in quiet seclusion and contemplation, he received the pleasant realization that he loved everyone. Later, while traveling through Asia, he had a conversation with a Buddhist monk. They discussed their respective schools of thought and practices. After a while, they looked at each other and chuckled when they realized that the surface differences concealed some deep similarities.

Merton's experience is not unique. Neither is it limited to those who live a monastic life. Religion is, literally, about re-joining. The more deeply and sincerely we delve into our own religious practice, the more we feel our commonality with others.

Jesus issued two commandments: to love God and to love one another. What he did not say (not explicitly, anyway) was that the two are inseparable. The same religious practice that opens our hearts to God also opens our hearts to one another.

That sense of connection with our fellow humans does not wipe out our differences, nor does it invalidate or dilute our particular religious practice. On the contrary, that sense of connection infuses our own religion with new life, allowing us to experience it in ways that are deeply meaningful to us and respectful of others.

The Trap

Every religion is potentially a bridge to realms of awareness that are beyond ordinary human understanding. Yet, that same bridge can become a trap. In order for religion to be a bridge between God and human, it must, of necessity, place itself between God and human. Therefore, in order for religion to fulfill its function, it must, at some point, step out of the way.

The use of symbols, stories or artifacts to guide us toward God must include the realization that God is not limited to those particular symbols, stories, or artifacts. The conscientious shaman or priest is aware of this. He or she sets the stage for the student to make contact with divinity, and then steps out of the way.

If the religious system and its leaders do not step out of the way, they become a replacement for God. The same principles that are designed to promote freedom, peace, and kinship are used instead to manipulate, entrap, and provoke inner and outer conflict.

How does the priest/shaman know when it is time to step out of the way? The answer is obvious if the teachings in question are used purely for spiritual communion. On the other hand, if they are used for political power or economic gain, the bridge becomes a trap, and the faithful become cattle. One of the signs which suggests that a given religion is drifting in this manner is presence of spiritual one-upmanship.

God's Favorite

Some religions claim or imply that they are special in God's eyes. They believe themselves to be closer to God than those who practice other religions. They assume themselves to be the true religion, while all others are deceived or somehow off the mark.

Such assumptions quickly break down under the light of reason. Logically, (and even mathematically!), everything and everyone in the created universe is equidistant from infinity. Technically, no matter how good you are in the human sense, you are no closer to God than anyone else, because God is Infinitely Good. This is the "good" that Jesus may have been referring to when he said, in so many words, "I'm not good; only God is good." The same idea is expressed in the Koran.

Granted, the concept that one person can be closer to God than another person might have some meaning for us because we live in the realm of opposites. It is here that time, space, and judgment can exist. However, the concept of being closer or further away from God breaks down when we actually do experience ourselves in "the Kingdom of Heaven," where all is One.

We might wonder why the perception of being God's favorite is so prevalent among the religions of the world, especially when it can obviously breed so much, divisiveness, hostility, and misunderstanding. We might wonder if the religion in question is being used as a tool for social control and political power, rather than as a means for spiritual communion.

Granted, the idea of being special in God's eyes may not be altogether fictitious. This idea might be an example of a basic truth that has violated its boundaries, thus becoming a lie, as described in chapter 18. In this case, my religion is indeed the one true religion — for me! On another level, the idea that my religious group is somehow special in Gods eyes might stem from the unconscious awareness of our true relationship with God the One. The "Eye of God" is singular and can therefore do nothing else but look upon every spark of Creation and declare, "You are my one and only, for you are all that I am." That relationship eludes us if it is merely a thought with no feeling behind it. However, it becomes very real when it is also a feeling.

Agnostic

It is the entrapping and exploitative aspect of religion that helps creates a market for agnostic philosophies. Agnostic beliefs, like any religion, may be interpreted and shaped in various ways. For example:

- The agnostic may simply question the existence of a supreme intelligence that created the universe.
- The agnostic may become the materialistic atheist who flatly denies there is any intelligence, supreme or otherwise, beyond the physical body. The atheist may assert that we are at the mercy of a mindless universe that is run by blind chance.
- The agnostic may assert there is no supreme authority; that we are individually and collectively responsible for our actions. Therefore, our decision to treat our neighbors fairly comes from our genuine sense of ethics and caring, not from fear of being punished by an overseeing God. In other words, in order for life to be worth living, the agnostic must, of necessity, be devout in exercising personal integrity.
- The agnostic may go so far as to assert that we are individually and collectively responsible for *all conditions* of our lives. Even though there is no supreme intelligence, the universe is said to be filled with creative "energy," which is ruled, not by blind chance, but by our own consciousness and our free will.
- In some belief systems, the latter philosophy is taken to extreme, in which case our only limitations on our creative

potential are those we consciously or unconsciously impose on ourselves. Therefore, each of us theoretically has the potential to tap into limitless power and create whatever we want. In other words, the agnostic philosophy, placing itself in opposition to religion, can very well evolve in such a way as to conclude that *we are* the very thing that religion promotes – which resembles some of the teachings of Jesus.

Agnosticism and Cynicism

Those who do not worship might express cynicism or contempt toward those who do. Yet, such contempt is just the buried pain of one whose spirit has been broken. The secret feeling is, "How dare they try to commune with the Beloved who is not available to me?"

On the other hand, if the individual has given up all worship simply because he or she is happy without it, there is no cynicism or contempt, just a quiet serenity—an acceptance of life as it is, and an acceptance of people as they are.

Such an attitude is not exclusive to the even-minded agnostic. It is shared by those who engage in religious worship that is internally motivated and tempered with a level of mindfulness that is capable of independent thought and self-examination. Such an attitude can exist in any religion, whether it is monotheistic or pantheistic.

Monotheism and Pantheism

Monotheism, in its purest form, recognizes the One God in all things. Pantheism, practiced in fullness, recognizes that everything is God because everything pulsates with the same life. Conflict between pantheism and monotheism arises when we look only at the surface of each. This is what we tend to do when we use any religion as a sword and shield. On the other hand, when we use either pantheism or monotheism as a means for cultivating self-knowledge and inner peace, we naturally plunge deeply and sincerely into our practice. When we look deeply enough inside one, we see the other.

Christian and Pagan

Christian and Pagan are opposites only in the sense that they embody monotheism and pantheism. Historically, the two have been at odds with one another. This may be attributed to the fact that both have been historically been used as tools for financial gain, political power, or self-glorification.

When the two systems are simply regarded as methods for the individual to commune with the creative power of the universe, there is no cause for conflict between them. In fact, they are quite compatible and complementary. As expressions of monotheism and pantheism, each side defines the other and bears the seed of the other. If we look deeply enough into one, we see the other. For example, the pantheism of the Pagan is often personified as the deity called *Pan,* which literally means *everything.* In the Bible, when Moses asks God to identify Himself, God responds, "I Am." Apparently, "I Am," is just a rough translation. A more accurate translation is, "I Am all there is."

Christians and Pagans are natural friends forced to fight. They are at odds with each other because they have both forgotten something. Each side struggles against the other; in essence, struggling against the hidden truth that brings their respective beliefs to life.

To the Christian, God often becomes a projection of the omnipotent parent who rewards good behavior and punishes bad behavior. Forgotten is the truth that God the One is, by definition, everywhere and resides in everything. To the Pagan, there are either many gods to solicit and placate, or there are no gods at all, just "energy" to be harnessed as a means of creating whatever you want. Forgotten is the truth that this "energy" is intelligent, creative, and has a life of its own.

When each perspective loses sight of the truth contained in the other, it limits its own teachings and dampens its potency. This lack of potency can only lead to the placing of great importance on the preservation of laws, doctrines, and customs, while the dignity of the individual human and the joy of spontaneous and organic communion are sacrificed.

Likewise, the pure Christian and pure Pagan both understand the same thing:

- The Energy or God that fills the universe is omnipotent, benevolent, and intelligent beyond anything we can comprehend with the rational mind.
- This Energy or God is, in a very real sense, the first cause of all creation—the Father and Mother of all that there is.
- The same infinite intelligence that created the universe resides in every corner of creation and is at the disposal of our human calling. It beckons us, *"Command Ye Me!"*
- When we call upon this Energy or God to effect a change anywhere in the physical universe, it will affect the same change in the one who makes the call, because this Energy or God makes no distinction between "self" and "other," "us" and "them," "friend" and "enemy." Whether we are casting a spell or praying, the one who makes the call is ultimately affected in the same manner as the recipient.

The Purity of Monotheism and Fullness of Pantheism

Monotheism, when practiced with purity (sincerity), tends to create earthly success. When we sincerely say, "Thy will be done," our earthly existence is infused with new life. When we really *do* seek first the Kingdom of God, all else really *is* indeed provided, and all things are made new again.

We see the same basic principle at work in the Ancient Taoist practice called, "Guarding the One," which is the intentional communion with the Unity beyond opposites, for the purpose of promoting a deeper harmony of opposites, which in turn translates into vibrant health, peace, and prosperity.

If our communion with the One is deep enough, we might feel as if we have been reborn. In practical terms, this means we experience newfound enthusiasm for earthly life. We relish our relationships and joyfully plunge into our work, whether we drive a bus, program computers, or sell real estate.

Pantheism, when practiced in fullness, culminates in an overpowering desire to seek the One God, though it may not be labeled as such. This might seem strange if we have only a

295

superficial understanding of pantheism and Paganism. Nonetheless, the inevitable result of communing deeply enough with any of the many gods is awareness of the One Unifying Presence, because they are all expressions of the One Presence.

From the energetic perspective, if we really *do* master the Pagan art of moving energy and manifesting by using rituals and the power of the mind, the result is, again, a pure desire to recognize that the creative "energy" is alive, intelligent, and omnipotent. Such a desire is not programmed from without, it emerges organically and silently from within.

On the other hand, when monotheism is *not* practiced with purity, the result is a rejection or denial of the things of the earth. In essence, we are saying "no" to God's creation. Likewise, when pantheism or any Earth-based religion is not practiced in fullness, the result is rejection or denial of the one God or Unity. In essence, we are cutting ourselves off from the source of all our power and earthly riches.

In other words, the pure practice of monotheism must give birth to the fullness and richness of earthly life, with all of its diversity, complexity, and sensuality. Likewise, when pantheism or any Earth religion is practiced in fullness, it awakens within us a pure, simple, and spontaneous remembrance of God the One; it is a simple and spontaneous desire to return home after a full and satisfying day in on this piece of real estate called Earth.

God and Real Estate

I was once in a Mexican restaurant having lunch with my friend "Allen." Allen's primary focus for most of his adult life has been the deepening of his relationship with God. Over the years, he would occasionally report to me with deep earnestness that he had experienced a new level of connection with Source.

For example, on one occasion, he came to my office looking especially happy. I mentioned this to him. I also pointed out that in recent months he had been rather joyful and carefree. When I asked him why, he just laughed and threw his arms in the air. There was no specific external blessing to which he could point. It was all coming from the inside. Shortly after that, his business started booming.

As we sat in the restaurant, sipping margaritas and munching on chips and salsa, he informed me that several months earlier he had experienced yet another new level of connection with Source. He said that in the past he would sit in meditation and eventually experience the inner door opening a bit. This time, however, the walls had come down, and they stayed down. The occasional trickle in the cosmic faucet had become an open fire hydrant gushing freely.

For Allen, sitting in prayer and meditation had become virtually irrelevant. However, he did not feel inclined to use his deep sense of inner connection to make "big changes" in his life. Neither did he feel inclined to use his newfound awareness to preach or teach.

Did Allen lose all interest in Earthly life? Did he feel inclined to retreat to the mountains and become a hermit? Not at all. In fact, his prolonged experience of God communion coincided with a newfound passion for real estate. Yes, real estate! In addition to his regular profession (which was also booming), he was putting in many hours a week negotiating deals, tracking interest rates, wrestling with tenants, hiring and firing contractors, etc.

He did not feel inclined to ask God to make his business or anything else in life smooth and easy. He simply had an enthusiasm about participating in the adventures that every new day had to offer. He seemed perfectly content not knowing what tomorrow would bring. In fact, I specifically asked Allen if he felt at all tempted to use this sense of God connection to do "magic" or get a sneak preview of the future. He replied, "No, that would be boring."

Chapter 47
Remembering Who I Am

One quiet summer afternoon, while I was home alone, I got down on the floor and started breathing deeply and rapidly, as evocative music was blasting out of my boom-box. Prolonged deep breathing (preferably under skilled supervision) can reveal troublesome issues hidden just beneath conscious awareness. On that afternoon, however, I was not burdened by any specific troublesome thoughts or emotions. I just felt a little "antsy."

After breathing deeply and rapidly for about twenty minutes, I commenced releasing deep sobs, which was interesting since I was not feeling particularly sad or troubled when I started. I was just feeling antsy.

Bringing In the Sheep

At first, I did not understand why I was sobbing. I just felt like sobbing, so I did. Eventually, however, I became aware of the various persons and situations that I was having issues with. The issues did not seem very serious. Each one was small enough that it was easy to ignore. However, I could see how the silent accumulation of these little issues might cause me to feel "antsy."

As the sobbing subsided, I became very still and eventually got the notion that "parts" of me had been scattered around, clinging onto those various persons and situations that I was having issues with. In the stillness, I felt as if those parts of me were "returning," like so many lost sheep. The feeling was one of great relief. My body relaxed and my mind became calm. For a while, I bathed in a sublime sense of wholeness.

As I lay quietly on the floor, I spontaneously started thinking about the act of remembering. I was already familiar with the idea that we are much more than we think we are. As the story goes, we are immortal heavenly beings who decided to forget who we are, so we could spend some time pretending we are weak and vulnerable humans, subject to the limitations of matter. Philosophically, I was inclined to agree with that idea, though, if pressed for an honest answer, I would have to say that I was pretty much identified with my physical form and my everyday thoughts and emotions.

That day, however, something was different. As I mentally mulled over the hypothetical cosmic remembering of the so-called higher self, I was still emotionally experiencing the "returning" of the lost parts of me that had been scattered about. At that moment, an interesting merger occurred in my mind. The word *remembering* took on a whole new meaning. Remembering became synonymous with *unifying*. In other words, the "members" of myself were coming together again. I was *re-membering* myself. At that point, my sobbing resumed and became so deep, I felt like I was going to physically explode.

In other words, this business of remembering ourselves, as I experienced it, is not merely the recalling of thoughts and images from the past, like remembering a trip to the zoo at age four. The capacity to re-member who we are depends on our capacity to feel. The feeling is one of wholeness—of bringing the pieces of oneself back together. When they return, there is no mistaking the feeling. The experience is not unlike reuniting with a long lost loved one.

In that moment of re-membering myself, I was gladly willing to give up all my worldly possessions, ambitions, and all my accumulated perceptions and beliefs about myself and others. The re-membering of myself felt more important than any of the details of my life, because such re-membering is what gives meaning to the rest of my existence.

Gathering the Honey

The next day, as I was driving to the mountains, I realized that a synonym for *remember* is *recollect* (re-collect), which literally means bringing together again pieces that were once united. As I stopped my car along a mountain road to purchase a jar of homemade honey from a roadside vendor, I realized that the hidden meaning of the words, remember and recollect is not just a quirk of the English language. In Italian, the word for "remember" is recordo, which has the same origin as the

300

word, accordo, which means together or in agreement. A similar tendency exists in a number of other languages. In other words, there seems to be a general linguistic recognition that the act of remembering is synonymous with the act of re-joining what had previously been torn asunder.

If remembering is the mental equivalent of achieving wholeness or unity, forgetting is the equivalent of separation. Since remembering of oneself involves the capacity to feel, forgetting entails suppression of the capacity to feel. Such suppression has value. To remember too much, too soon could be psychologically damaging. Therefore, the brain forgets anything we cannot safely address on a conscious level.

Forgetting things does not mean that the information is destroyed. The brain has seemingly "dispersed" the memory into many separate bits of data and prevents them from coming together into a hologram of conscious awareness. Physiologically, this simply means that the involved brain cells do not communicate.

The time of forgetting is a time of rest when we prepare ourselves for the time when the brain can allow formerly unbearable memories to surface into conscious awareness. These memories may be traumatic childhood experiences or the awareness of who we are beyond our mundane human awareness. Either one can be damaging if done carelessly or prematurely. Either one can be tremendously healing if done with care.

As mentioned earlier, the urge to know oneself is an evolutionary imperative that eventually asserts itself no matter how much we try to restrain it. We may experience this urge as the simple desire to reclaim an emotionally shattered past, or a desire to commune more deeply with the God of our understanding. The urge cannot be long denied, for it is essential for our health and well-being. If we resist this urge, it creates a condition that some would describe as "hell," a painful, burning combination of remembering and forgetting. It is the full-blown awareness of how we are inwardly torn asunder and feeling helpless to do anything about it.

Nonetheless, at some point in our personal journey through life, this hellish condition is more acceptable than the pseudo-peace of repressed inner turmoil, that familiar state of dullness or boredom, the robotic behavior that covers the low-grade anxiety and depression, or the unfulfilled desires that just will not go away.

A Time and a Season

Religion, at its best, is literally about rejoining. The cultivation of inner harmony is about remembering. The two are essentially the same.

The remembrance of oneself occurs naturally when it is neither suppressed nor forced open. Our inner wisdom knows there is a time of remembering and a time of forgetting. The time of forgetting is a time of sleep and rest when the subconscious mind gathers energy and prepares the conscious mind for a time of deeper remembering.

The time of remembering is a time of self-discovery. It is a time when the separate parts of oneself are brought together. It is a time when the "members" that had been cast out are welcomed home. It is a time when we instinctively gravitate toward truthfulness, stillness, and loving touch, for these are the three great healers, the three keys by which we unlock the door to inner wholeness. When we consistently utilize the three healers, we can more easily recognize that life is a dance of opposites, and we gradually and organically awaken to the unity beyond opposites.